Judo
Strategy

The Weak Can Overpower the Strong

Russian President Vladimir V. Putin, a black belt in judo, is floored by
a ten-year-old schoolgirl at the Kodokan Hall in Tokyo, September 2000.

Judo Strategy

Turning Your Competitors' Strength
to Your Advantage

David B. Yoffie
Mary Kwak

HARVARD BUSINESS SCHOOL PRESS
BOSTON, MASSACHUSETTS

University of
Wisconsin-Madison
Libraries

Library of Congress Cataloging-in-Publication Data

Yoffie, David B.
Judo strategy : turning your competitors' strength to your advantage /
David B. Yoffie, Mary Kwak.
p. cm.
Includes bibliographical references and index.
ISBN 1-57851-253-0 (alk. paper)
1. Strategic planning. 2. Business planning.
I. Kwak, Mary, 1966– II. Title.
HD30.28 .Y63 2001
658.4'012—dc21
2001024053

The paper used in this publication meets the requirements of the
American National Standard for Permanence of Paper for Publications
and Documents in Libraries and Archives Z39.48-1992.

To our families,
whose patience and support made this book possible

Contents

Preface

METAPHORS PLAY an important role in business. They simplify a complex world, help organize facts and intuitions, and allow you to express ideas in a lively, thought-provoking way. Moreover, metaphors can be great motivational tools because they are usually easy to understand and hard to forget. Scott McNealy, the CEO of Sun Microsystems, admits that he often finds himself "turning to metaphors and analogies, borrowing images from sports and even war to drive home my business strategy and motivate the troops."[1] McNealy believes that "the companies that succeed will be the ones that . . . employ great metaphors and analogies to define their business and tell their stories."

This book is built on two broad metaphors that we hope readers will find compelling in thinking about the strategic challenges their businesses face. Our primary metaphor comes from the sport of judo, which originated in late nineteenth-century Japan. Judo requires quickness, agility, and the ability to outmaneuver the competition. Most important, in judo, unlike many martial arts, true strength comes from turning your opponent's weight and power to your advantage.

We picked up on this idea while conducting interviews at Netscape in the summer of 1997. When we asked Netscape's head of engineering how he could ever hope to compete successfully with Microsoft, given the dominant position of Windows, he gave a very judo-like answer. "You can either look at Microsoft's operating system as an asset," he said, "or you can think of Windows as a liability that slows Microsoft down." The very fact that Microsoft was so committed to Windows, he argued, created opportunities for Netscape to use Microsoft's strength to its advantage.

As we reflected on this concept, the judo metaphor became increasingly compelling as a means for thinking about how companies could overcome stronger rivals. The same skills used by judo masters, we came to believe, could help businesses become more effective competitors. We originally wrote about these ideas in *Competing on Internet Time: Lessons from Netscape and Its Battle with Microsoft*.[2] But that project only whetted our interest in further exploring judo's potential for competitors both large and small.

Our first step was to do our homework on judo. In addition to reading up on the subject, we observed judo classes and competitions, interviewed judo masters in the United States, and traveled to Japan to speak with experts on both judo and sumo (our other principal metaphor). But we must admit that neither of us was willing to take judo (or sumo) classes. We only wanted to take the metaphor so far!

Next, we explored the management literature and learned that judo has long been used as a metaphor in business and academic circles. Many business executives were in the habit of casually describing their tactics as "judo" or "jujutsu." And the judo metaphor had already surfaced among both economists and students of strategy. Gary Hamel and C.K. Prahalad, for example, made reference to the sport in their classic *Harvard Business Review* article on strategic intent, writing "Competitive innovation is like judo: upset your rivals by using their size against them."[3] Yet no one, to our knowledge, had tried to use judo as the basis for a systematic way of thinking about strategy. Thus, our challenge became to discover if judo-like techniques were really being used by managers, and if judo delivered value as a metaphor for developing and communicating strategy.

We began by identifying examples of judo-like business behavior in both the past and the present. Between the spring of 1999 and the fall of 2000, we interviewed more than fifty executives, many of them CEOs and company directors, some multiple times. (All unattributed quotations in this book are drawn from these interviews, which are listed in the Appendix.) In several cases, we also spoke with executives at companies competing with firms in our sample. After spending a couple of days at RealNetworks, for example, we interviewed the CEO of Microsoft and key managers in Microsoft's streaming media business. Similarly, as part of our analysis of CNET, we met with the CEOs of the company's biggest rivals, IDG and ZDNet.

In one important case, we were unable to rely primarily on interviews for our analysis. What we describe as sumo strategy—making the most of your strength and power—can be a very sensitive topic for the very large companies that are most likely to profit from these techniques. Consequently, we drew heavily on public information and government documents, as well as selected interviews, in writing this section of the book. Fortunately, the Department of Justice has created an extensive online archive of documents filed as part of the case against Microsoft that began in 1998. These materials were invaluable in our research.

We were pleased that numerous managers seemed to use judo strategy, although like Molière's Monsieur Jourdan, who didn't realize he was speaking prose, they generally did so without using the term. Some of the companies we studied employed judo techniques with extremely positive results. Other companies started out looking like success stories but found it difficult to execute their strategies over time. This made it possible for us to study why judo techniques worked and why they sometimes failed. Our results largely confirmed our hypothesis that judo strategy can help many companies succeed against stronger players. But it also confirmed our suspicion that judo strategy is not a universal remedy.

We don't try to reveal any corporate secrets in this book. In accordance with Harvard Business School rules, we promised the executives we interviewed that they could review their quotes and veto the release of any proprietary information. The vast majority did not request any changes in the wording or our usage of their quotes, and in only one case were we asked to remove confidential information. A couple of companies inevitably cleaned up their CEOs' prose, but we feel comfortable that our research and message have remained intact.

We have organized the book in three distinct parts to allow readers to focus on those elements of judo strategy that interest them most. The first four chapters of the book systematically apply the judo metaphor to business strategy. We take the core principles of judo—movement, balance, and leverage—and explore specific techniques companies can use to gain an advantage over the competition. Every technique is supported with examples from real-life companies and managers, often drawn from the old economy as well as the new.

The second section of the book details how three companies have put judo strategy into action. We looked for black belts: judo masters who were the best practitioners of the art. Our choices were Jeff Hawkins and Donna Dubinsky from Palm Computing and Handspring; Rob Glaser from RealNetworks; and Halsey Minor and Shelby Bonnie from CNET Networks. Palm was part of our research design from the very first—since David Yoffie had learned about the business from Donna Dubinsky while their daughters were attending preschool together in 1995. RealNetworks was not part of our original plan, but after a couple of meetings with Rob Glaser, we were impressed with his command of judo-like techniques. Similarly, CNET was not on our original list, but after our first meeting with Halsey Minor, we realized that CNET used leverage at nearly every stage of its drive to success.

Finally, the last section of the book offers guidance to two groups of readers: those who want to know how to fight back against judo strategists, and those who want to learn more about putting judo strategy into action.

We have tried to make this discussion accessible and potentially valuable for all managers—whether you're part of the old economy or the new, an established player or the new kid in town. If you too find value in using metaphors to shape your thinking about strategy, we think you will enjoy this book.

Acknowledgments

MANY PEOPLE have contributed to the making of this book. Above all, we would like to thank the many executives who generously took the time to share their experience and their insights into competitive strategy. We are particularly grateful to Donna Dubinsky and Jeff Hawkins (Handspring), Rob Glaser (RealNetworks), Halsey Minor and Shelby Bonnie (CNET Networks), and Toby Lenk (eToys). In addition to agreeing to in-depth interviews—often more than once—they gave us extensive access to their colleagues and responded quickly and graciously to our follow-up queries by e-mail and on the phone.

We are also happy to acknowledge our debt to the experts on judo and sumo who introduced us to the subtleties and power of these forms of practice. Dale Swett and Clark Edson of the Tohoku Judo Club in Somerville, Massachusetts, patiently answered our most elementary questions and taught us more in an hour through the power of demonstration than we were able to learn in weeks of diligent reading. David Matsumoto, program director of development, USA Judo, and professor of psychology at San Francisco State University, and Naoki Murata, curator and professor at the Kodokan Judo Institute in Tokyo, helped us gain a better understanding of the philosophy behind judo. David Shapiro, editor-in-chief of *Inside Sumo*, shared his deep knowledge of sumo as well as his inspiring enthusiasm, and George Kalima and Percy Kipapa, two former *rikishi*, brought the lessons to life.

Throughout our interviews in Tokyo, we had the expert help and advice of Camille Tang Yeh, executive director of the Harvard Business School Asia Pacific Research Office, and Jeffrey McNeill, managing director of Market Makers, whose network of contacts made many of the meetings possible. In California, Chris Darwall, executive director of the Harvard Business School California Research Center, provided invaluable assistance by arranging interviews and helping to tie up the loose ends we sometimes left in our wake.

Michael Cusumano was instrumental in the early development of the ideas behind judo strategy. During our joint work on *Competing on Internet Time: Lessons from Netscape and Its Battle with Microsoft* (Free Press, 1998), we talked at length about judo strategy and how it might apply to the Microsoft–Netscape battle. Many of those ideas were incorporated into both the book and an article that appeared in the January–February 1999 issue of the *Harvard Business Review*.

Many people read the manuscript at various stages of completion and offered insightful comments that prolonged our labors but greatly improved the final results. We would like to thank Bharat Anand, Joe Badaracco, Adam Brandenburger, Pete Coughlan, Pankaj Ghemawat, Elon Kohlberg, Richard Vietor, and participants in the Competition and Strategy seminar at Harvard Business School (November 2000) for their helpful comments and reactions. In addition, we are particularly grateful to the friends and colleagues who provided us with extensive written feedback: Ben Slivka and Anthony Bay, formerly of Microsoft; Russ Siegelman, formerly of Microsoft and now with Kleiner Perkins; David Collis and Barry Nalebuff of Yale University; Eduardo Ballarin of IESE; Dennis Yao of Wharton; and Ramon Casadesus-Masanell, Giovanni Gavetti, Tarun Khanna, Jan Rivkin, and Juha Salin of Harvard Business School.

Marjorie Williams, editorial director of Harvard Business School Press, has been an enthusiastic supporter of this project from the first, and we are thankful for her encouragement when *Judo Strategy* was little more than an idea. We would also like to thank our editors, Hollis Heimbouch, Lindsay Whitman, and Amanda Gardner, who skillfully guided us through the editorial process, as well as the three peer reviewers for HBS Press for their many ideas for improvement.

We would like to acknowledge the financial support of the Harvard Business School's Division of Research and in particular of Dean

Kim Clark and Research Director Michael Yoshino. The book required extensive interviews, both on the West Coast and in Japan, which would not have been possible without the support of the school.

Finally, we need to thank Cathyjean Gustafson, David Yoffie's assistant for most of the last sixteen years, for helping with logistics, getting permissions, and keeping the project under control. Without her assistance, completing this book would have been a much more difficult task.

1

An Introduction to Judo Strategy

[Judo] depends for success upon the skill of using an opponent's own weight and strength against him, thus enabling a weak or light individual to overcome a physically superior opponent.

—*Columbia Encyclopedia*, 6th edition

IN THE SPRING of 1994, a little-known company called Mosaic Communications opened its doors in Mountain View, California. Six months later, the tiny start-up had become Netscape Communications, the hottest company in the white-hot high technology world. Netscape's flagship product, the Navigator Web browser, dominated its market from day one. Cofounder Marc Andreessen became the first of the cybercelebrities, showing up in *People* as well as *Time*. And in August 1995, a scant sixteen months after its founding, Netscape delivered the Internet's first moonshot IPO.

But Netscape's star fell nearly as quickly as it had soared. On December 7, 1995—Pearl Harbor Day, as history buffs immediately recalled—Microsoft unleashed a declaration of war, making Netscape "ground zero," in the words of John Doerr, one of Netscape's original backers and a member of its board. Under relentless attack, Navigator's market share soon began an irreversible decline, while fears about Netscape's ability to compete with Microsoft drove its share price into the ground. By the end of the decade, Microsoft was king of the browser business, and Netscape survived only as a division of AOL. Meanwhile, all across the new economy, being "Netscaped" had become a four-letter word.

Two years before Netscape was born, another company set up shop a few miles up the road in Los Altos, California. After treading water for a few years, Palm Computing shipped the Pilot, a handheld electronic organizer, in April 1996. The giants of computing and consumer electronics, including Apple, Microsoft, Hewlett-Packard, and Sharp, were already fighting for the category, and any one of them could have crushed Palm. So the company's founders, Jeff Hawkins and Donna Dubinsky, held their breath in the months following the Pilot's release.

By the end of 1996, however, it was clear that Palm had created a star. Like Netscape's Navigator, the Pilot dominated its market within a year. But unlike Netscape, Palm went from strength to strength. Despite Microsoft's repeated efforts to take over the market, Palm's share remained close to 70 percent after four years, and first-day trading valued the company at $53 billion when Palm went public in March 2000. Eight years after its birth, Palm was not only alive and kicking, to borrow from the Apple lexicon, it was "insanely great."

Why did Palm succeed where Netscape failed? What distinguishes challengers who build successful businesses from those who fall by the wayside despite an auspicious start? Which strategies hold the most promise for companies facing powerful opponents, and which are most likely to lead to defeat? These are questions that all ambitious businesses eventually face.

Stories like those of Netscape and Palm, where a tiny upstart confronts one of the largest companies in the world, throw the challenge of competing with stronger opponents into stark relief. However, even large corporations may find themselves in similar situations if they expand beyond their base. The strongest battle-hardened competitor can be at a severe disadvantage when trying to enter into a market where a powerful incumbent holds sway.

So, what strategy is most likely to succeed when size or strength is not on your side? Whether you're large or small, the answer is not to oppose strength with strength, as Netscape ultimately chose to do. Instead, study the competition carefully, avoid head-to-head battles, as Palm did, and turn your opponents' strength to your advantage. This is the lesson at the heart of judo strategy.

What Is Judo Strategy?

Judo strategy is a multilayered concept. At the most basic level, it functions as a *metaphor* that evokes powerful images about how to compete and win. Obviously all metaphors have limitations, and the parallels will sometimes be incomplete. But the judo metaphor should help you master the *mind-set* of judo strategy. If you keep the image of judo competition firmly in mind, it will be easier to visualize the moves that make it possible to beat a stronger opponent.

To help you become a judo strategist, we explore three *principles* that should inform your thinking: movement, balance, and leverage. Each principle provides a different piece of the strategy puzzle. Movement throws your competitors off balance and neutralizes their initial advantages. Balance helps you engage with the competition and survive an attack. And leverage can enable you to bring your opponents down. When used together, these three principles will help you defeat rivals of any size.

To make these principles more concrete, we provide a *toolbox* of judo tactics, illustrated with examples drawn from a broad range of companies. Some of these techniques may seem unimportant when viewed in isolation. But a small move here and a little move there can weaken your opponent and set you up for the win. Analyzing the case histories of successful companies will help you understand how the pieces of judo strategy work together and, we hope, inspire you to develop your own judo tactics.

Judo strategy is not a rigid formula to be followed step by step. In business, as in judo, competitors come in all shapes and sizes, and each challenge will require a unique combination of techniques. As a result, we can't predict exactly how judo strategy will work in your business. That part is up to you. But this book is designed to ease you into the task by providing a new mind-set, a strong grasp of judo strategy's basic principles, and a toolbox of tactics and techniques. Think of it as a field kit to carry into your next judo campaign.

JUDO STRATEGY IS:

- The *mind-set* of not opposing strength to strength
- Three *principles* of competition: movement, balance, and leverage
- A *toolbox* of tactics and techniques

Who Should Use Judo Strategy?

Judo strategy is a natural choice for smaller companies because it values skill over size and strength. By mastering movement, balance, and leverage, a judo strategist can maximize her power while preventing an opponent from taking full advantage of his strength. A *judoka*, or judo master, knows that strength only matters when it can be brought to bear—and that with the proper technique, even a child can bring a powerful competitor down.

But judo strategy is not just for the small. Large companies can become particularly dangerous competitors by uniting superior skill at judo strategy with the natural advantages of strength and size. Strength alone counts for little in judo, but in a match between two equally adept contestants, strength and size will generally prevail, as the judo establishment was forced to recognize in 1961. Traditionally, judo masters competed against all comers. Most experienced teachers believed that skill ultimately trumped power and weight. In that year, however, Antonius Geesink, a 6'6" native of the Netherlands who weighed in at 253 pounds, defeated three Japanese masters to take the world championship. Since then, judo competition has taken place in weight classes, with the exception of the All Japan Judo Championships, where competitors continue to match off regardless of size or weight.

USE JUDO STRATEGY IF:

- You're a small player facing off against stronger competitors (David versus Goliath).
- You're a large player moving into areas where powerful opponents may already be entrenched.

- You have the capabilities (speed, agility, and creativity) to out-maneuver your opponents, no matter what the balance of strength may be.

When Should You Use Judo Strategy?

In addition to downplaying the role of brute strength, judo strategy puts a premium on qualities such as speed, flexibility, and innovation. Given the prominence that these skills have assumed in the new economy, it should come as no surprise that in the pages that follow you'll encounter a wealth of high-tech and Internet names. But the value of judo strategy is not confined to periods of technological transition, as our old-economy examples show. While judo strategy has particular resonance in periods of rapid change, it can also be extremely effective in mature industries. In these sectors, the dominant players are often slow-moving giants—ideal targets for a nimble judo strategist.

Judo strategy can help you win whenever you face intense competition and a strategy of head-on attack is likely to fail. But judo strategy is not the answer for every strategic problem. It doesn't tell you, for example, how to manage customer relationships, fine-tune your supply chain, or build successful partnerships—crucial areas for every manager to consider. Instead, our focus is on defining principles for strategic competition, typically in situations where one player's loss is another player's gain.

USE JUDO STRATEGY WHEN:

- Dealing with the competition is one of your top strategic priorities.
- Competitors have the advantage of strength and size.
- You're unlikely to win by going head-to-head.

The Origins of Judo Strategy

The roots of judo strategy lie in "judo economics," a term coined by economists Judith Gelman and Steven Salop to describe a simple strategy for entering a market dominated by a large opponent.[1]

JUDO ECONOMICS: A SIMPLE EXAMPLE

The basic model makes a few important assumptions: the incumbent faces a single challenger, the challenger has no cost advantage, and the incumbent must charge all customers the same price (i.e., price discrimination is impossible). Based on these assumptions, the logic works like this: Assume that the incumbent supplies ten customers with widgets for $50. If you offer to supply the entire market at $40, the incumbent will be forced to match your price or lose all of its sales. By contrast, if you only have enough capacity to sell to one customer, the incumbent will find it more profitable to accommodate your entry by sticking to his original price and selling to the remaining nine.

Like most journal articles, their paper is strewn with assumptions, diagrams, and math. But behind the equations lies a simple idea: If you mount a full-scale attack on a stronger incumbent, your opponent will fight back—say, by slashing prices—and almost certainly win. However, you can avoid this outcome by pledging to be satisfied with a small slice of the market. In this case, self-interest will lead the incumbent to accommodate entry, rather than launch an attack that could spoil the market as a whole. Gelman and Salop called this entry strategy "judo economics" because it shows how a small company can use a larger opponent's size to its own advantage. By reducing the threat that it poses, the attacker induces the incumbent to tolerate its presence, rather than fight back.

The idea behind judo economics—turning your opponent's size into a disadvantage—has a lot of intuitive appeal. But judo economics has important limitations as well. First, it is very difficult to implement. It's one thing to say that you won't threaten bigger competitors. It's quite another to convince them that you mean what you say. Moreover, judo economics looks far less promising once the assumptions behind the original model are relaxed. If, for example, the incumbent faces not just one entrant, but a long line of potential challengers, he's much more likely to fight anyone who steps into the ring. In this way, he can establish a reputation for toughness and deter other players from taking him on. But the greatest weakness of judo economics is that it sets its sights too low.

Judo economics may allow you to survive, but only at the cost of staying small. For most managers and companies, this is not enough. You don't want to skulk around the sidelines; you want to get out there and win.

Winning, of course, can take different forms, depending on the competitive dynamics of your business. If you're in a winner-take-all industry, winning means ending up on top. If your sector can support several strong players, it means becoming one of the Big Three. In tougher environments, winning may take a more limited form: building a profitable business in a market where the vast majority of challengers fail. In this last case, judo economics may be of some help, but should your ambitions range higher it has little to say.

Judo strategy picks up where judo economics leaves off by providing a set of tools that allow you to do more than just survive—they show you how to thrive and grow. The goal of judo strategy is not just to gain a toehold in a market. It is to establish a growing and ultimately profitable position. Management sage Peter Drucker describes a concept he calls "entrepreneurial judo" in similar terms. "Entrepreneurial judo aims first at securing a beachhead, and one which the established leaders either do not defend at all or defend only halfheartedly," he writes. "Once that beachhead has been secured, that is, once the newcomers have an adequate market and an adequate revenue stream, they then move on to the rest of the 'beach' and finally to the whole 'island.'"[2]

Drucker identifies the critical problem: How can you move beyond your beachhead once competitors have been alerted to your attack? Judo strategy provides the mind-set and the techniques that make it possible to defeat larger and stronger opponents. Moving beyond judo economics, judo strategy goes back to the original source for inspiration—back to principles that judo masters have been teaching for more than a hundred years.

An Introduction to Judo

Judo's roots lie in *jujutsu*, a martial art practiced by the samurai of feudal Japan. Jujutsu was a system of hand-to-hand attack that included choking, kicking, stabbing, and slashing, as well as the spectacular throws that are synonymous with judo today. Along with archery, swordsmanship, and fighting with spears, jujutsu formed an essential part of a warrior's training. Combat could be fatal, although opponents were usually unarmed. Yet even then, despite its ferocity, jujutsu emphasized balance and flexibility more than raw strength.

From Jujutsu to Judo

Martial arts teachers began to formalize jujutsu in the early Tokugawa era (1603–1867), forming schools that specialized in different techniques. However, it was only late in the nineteenth century that judo emerged from jujutsu. The creator of judo was Jigoro Kano, an educator and civil servant who had turned to martial arts in his student days after suffering at the hands of schoolyard bullies. Kano trained in jujutsu under a number of masters before founding the first judo academy, the Kodokan, on the grounds of a Tokyo temple in May 1882.[3] As Kano told the story:

> In my youth I studied jujutsu under many eminent masters. Their vast knowledge, the fruit of years of diligent research and rich experience, was of great value to me. At that time, each man presented his art as a collection of techniques. None perceived the guiding principle behind jujutsu. When I encountered differences in the teaching of techniques, I often found myself at a loss to know which was correct. This led me to look for an underlying principle in jujutsu, one that applied when one hit an opponent as well as when one threw him. After a thorough study of the subject, I discerned an all-pervasive principle: to make the most efficient use of mental and physical energy. With this principle in mind, I again reviewed all the methods of attack and defense I had learned, retaining only those that were in accordance with the principle. . . . The resulting body of technique, which I named judo to distinguish it from its predecessor, is what is taught at the Kodokan.[4]

Soon Kano's students began to overpower opponents from rival schools in competition. Impressed by their success, the Tokyo Metropolitan Police hired Kodokan practitioners to train its forces, and the Naval Academy followed suit.

Eventually, judo's reputation began to spread outside Japan. In the early 1900s, Kano sent one of his top pupils to the United States where he trained Theodore Roosevelt in the sport. (Apparently, the honor was not without risk. According to one chronicler, Roosevelt was "very heavy and very impetuous, and it cost the poor professor many bruisings, much worry, and infinite pains . . . to avoid laming the President of the United States.")[5] Other disciples traveled around the world, bringing judo to Latin America, Europe, India, Nepal, Afghanistan, Iran, and Egypt.

The Meaning of Judo

The essence of judo is contained in its name. The first character—*ju*—means giving way; the second—*do*—means principle or way. Judo is often translated as the way of gentleness, but this can be misleading. One trip to the mat is enough to convince most people that judo is many things, but gentle it is not. Kano provided a better definition in a book published for a Western audience in 1937. Judo, he explained, means "first giving way in order ultimately to gain the victory."[6] Kano liked to illustrate this principle with a simple example:

> Let us say a man is standing before me whose strength is ten, and that my own strength is but seven. If he pushes me as hard as he can, I am sure to be pushed back or knocked down, even if I resist with all my might. But if instead of opposing him, I give way to the extent he has pushed, withdrawing my body and maintaining my balance, my opponent will lose his balance. Weakened by his awkward position, he will be unable to use all his strength. It will have fallen to three. Because I retain my balance my strength remains at seven. Now I am stronger than my opponent and can defeat him by using only half my strength.[7]

Kano makes it clear that strength has a role in judo, as in any sport. But fundamentally, a judo match is a contest of skill, not strength. A judo master seeks to *minimize* the amount of strength he needs to apply. The idea of straining every muscle in a full-out attempt to take someone down is completely contrary to the spirit of the sport. Not surprisingly, judo teachers often complain that this makes students who are naturally gifted with superior strength the hardest to train.

Judo Techniques

How, then, should you take on an opponent in the type of situation Kano describes? Pull him toward you, sweep his supporting leg from underneath with your thigh, and throw him to the ground. Slip your arm around his neck, pivot with your back against his chest, and throw him over your hip. Or as he pushes back, pull him onto his toes, drop to the ground with one foot against his abdomen, and throw him over your head. During Kano's lifetime, the Kodokan catalogued forty different throws like these. Since Kano's death, twenty-five throws have been added to the officially sanctioned list.

For spectators, at least, judo's trademark throws are the most dramatic part of the sport, and it's here that the inspiration behind the metaphor of judo strategy resides. But in addition to throws (*nage-waza*), judo also includes grappling (*katame-waza*) and striking techniques (*atemi-waza*). Grappling includes hold-downs, or pins, as well as strangleholds and joint locks that are designed to force an opponent to concede defeat. In striking, a competitor uses his hands, feet, elbows, and knees to disable his opponent by attacking vital points. These techniques, which can include the use of weapons, aim to gain victory by causing pain or even death. (Due to their dangers, these skills are practiced only in choreographed exercises that follow a predetermined script.)

How to Win at Judo

To be successful in judo, you must master three key skills. The first is using *movement* to weaken your opponent's position by destroying his balance. The second is maintaining your own *balance* as you respond to attacks. The third is exploiting *leverage* to magnify your strength. As one early judo expert wrote, "Before an opponent can be thrown there must be movement. Through movement the opponent is led into an unbalanced position. Then he is thrown either by some form of leverage or by stopping or sweeping away some part of his body or limbs."[8]

A successful *judoka* uses movement to maneuver into a position where he can apply his best techniques while preventing his opponent from achieving the same goal. Most champions rely on a small number of favorite techniques, which they use again and again. Consequently, in order to defeat a master, you have to take him out of his game. If leg throws are his specialty, get in close so he doesn't have room to move. If he's strongest at shoulder throws, keep him a safe distance away. If he's great at throws but weaker on the ground, get him on the mat as soon as you can. Always maintain the initiative and flow quickly and smoothly from one technique to the next, moving from attack to attack.

The goal of movement is to weaken your opponent's position, getting him off balance and taking away his edge. At the same time, of course, he's trying to do the same to you. How should you respond? Judo has a simple rule: Push when pulled, pull when pushed. Pushing back against an opponent is like leaning against a door. If it swings open, you'll go sprawling on the ground. But by yielding to the direction of your opponent's move, you can remain in control. Instead of pushing back, pull him around and direct his momentum in the way *you* want him to go. The same principle applies if your move fails and you lose your balance. Protect your body, but don't resist the fall. The first thing an aspiring *judoka* learns is *ukemi*, the technique of falling safely so that you can return to the attack.

Now that you've moved into position, weakening your opponent's balance while maintaining your own, how do you execute the throw? This is where leverage comes into play. Without leverage, throwing your opponent would require enormous strength. Imagine picking up a 200-pound weight and heaving it to the ground. But by turning your body into a fulcrum, you can achieve the same feat in a judo match with relative ease. If you find this hard to believe, go to any playground and watch a four-year-old on a seesaw toss her older brother into the air.

From Judo to Judo Strategy

By combining the insights of judo economics with principles from the practice of judo, we have translated these ideas into strategic tools that can help you build competitive advantage, go on the offensive against larger or stronger companies, and defend yourself against attacks. The lessons that emerge from this process are not always entirely new. Careful readers will note that judo strategy brings together elements from the work of scholars such as Michael Porter, Pankaj Ghemawat, Adam Brandenburger, Barry Nalebuff, and Clay Christensen. (We have tried to acknowledge these influences or similarities at various points without overburdening the text.) But judo strategy incorporates these ideas into a single framework, driven by the imperative of avoiding head-to-head conflict, while adding unique insights based on the metaphor of judo competition.

Principle One: Movement

Movement can put you in the best possible position for the battles that lie ahead. By making the most of your agility and speed, you can undercut a stronger opponent's ability to compete on the basis of size and strength and seize a critical edge in the early stages of a bout.

In chapter 2, we identify three techniques that embody different aspects of the principle of movement:

- Don't Invite Attack (a.k.a. "The Puppy Dog Ploy")
- Define the Competitive Space
- Follow Through Fast

The aim of the first technique is to enlarge your window of opportunity by delaying or averting a competitor's attack. Richard Fairbank and Nigel Morris, for example, used the puppy dog ploy to transform Capital One into one of the top ten credit card issuers in the United States. By escaping the notice of industry leaders, they were able to build a strong, profitable business before their competitors realized that a new powerhouse was being born. By contrast, some of the other companies we profile, such as Intuit and Juniper Networks, were less successful at avoiding attention. However, they succeeded in dominating their markets by taking their opponents "out of their game" and making the most of their advantage by following through with blistering speed.

In exploiting movement, you weaken your opponent's desire or ability to unleash a killer blow. But eventually your own success, if nothing else, will force the competition to wake up and learn to play by the new rules. Movement seeks to delay a confrontation; yet in all but the rarest cases, a day of reckoning will ultimately come. This is where balance enters the picture.

Principle Two: Balance

Balance serves both defensive and offensive goals, often at the same time. Preserving your balance is central to avoiding defeat. But in judo strategy, balance is about more than staying on your feet. In mastering the principle of balance, you also learn to rechannel your opponent's attack and stay on the offensive.

In chapter 3, we describe three techniques that can help you incorporate balance into your strategy:

- Grip Your Opponent
- Avoid Tit-for-Tat
- Push When Pulled

The common goal behind all three techniques is to engage your competitor without getting into a test of strength. In gripping your opponent, for example, you seek to maneuver him into a less threatening position before he can launch an attack. But should this effort fail or come too late, you need to resist the temptation to counter each and every one of your opponent's moves, conserving your strength instead. Under the leadership of CEO Meg Whitman, eBay used both of these techniques to consolidate its lead in the consumer-to-consumer online auction market. eBay strengthened its position by giving potential rival AOL a significant stake in its success. In addition, the company preserved its balance in the face of repeated attacks from rivals like Yahoo! and Amazon by avoiding reflexive responses to competitive challenges.

However, the heart of balance lies in learning to embrace and extend a competitor's attack. When you can neither sidestep nor withstand a coming blow, channel and redirect its force. Drypers, for example, managed to overcome Procter & Gamble's efforts to drive it out of the market for disposable diapers by mastering this technique. Unable to match P&G's promotional campaign, which blanketed Texas with coupons, Drypers just accepted its rival's coupons. The more coupons P&G distributed, the more diapers Drypers sold.

Taken together, movement and balance give you the best possible chance of diverting or surviving an attack. By avoiding a direct confrontation with superior strength, you can go on fighting against an opponent many times your size. Yet unless you are operating in a market where first mover advantages are truly decisive, these principles are unlikely to produce victory on their own. To score a long-term win, you usually need to take your opponent to the mat, and that means finding a form of leverage you can exploit.

Principle Three: Leverage

The key to leverage lies in identifying the things that your opponent holds most dear and then forcing him to choose between destroying those assets and responding to your attack. Most competitors will find the first path unthinkable, and even the most strategically flexible will consent to cannibalize themselves only after painful and costly delay. In this way, you can turn your opponent's strength against him, using his size and power to bring him down.

In chapter 4, we analyze three techniques that will help you find the points of vulnerability hidden behind your opponent's strengths:

- Leverage Your Opponent's Assets

- Leverage Your Opponent's Partners

- Leverage Your Opponent's Competitors

Each of these techniques can help you transform an opponent's strength into weakness. Freeserve, for example, became the leading Internet service provider in the United Kingdom by leveraging AOL's investments in brand, content, and customer service, as well as the revenue streams they produced. By creating a new business model that made it possible to offer Internet access for free, Freeserve forced AOL to make a painful decision: whether to match Freeserve, thereby killing its high-margin, high-cost core business, or stick to its strategy and see its market share fall.

Similarly, Charles Schwab found leverage by turning a major

opponent's competitors to its advantage. By creating a free one-stop shop for mutual funds, Schwab placed Fidelity Investments in a quandary. Matching Schwab would mean promoting competitors' funds—and selling less of its own. But if Fidelity ignored Schwab's attack, it ran the danger of losing customer accounts. In the end, Fidelity did match Schwab's move, but the underlying dynamics of its position did not change. Consequently, Schwab retained a significant degree of leverage, which translated into continued leadership in this market.

Overview of the Book

As these examples suggest, judo strategy provides many different methods for beating the competition. Consequently, we've organized this book to illustrate the widest possible variety of techniques, drawing examples from both the old economy and the new. Part I, comprising chapters 2 to 4, expands on the principles of judo strategy. In each chapter, we explore a number of cases that show how companies have used (and sometimes how they failed to use) movement, balance, and leverage to their advantage. In addition, we summarize the lessons suggested by these companies' experience in bullet points that follow the discussions of individual techniques. However, these highlights should not be taken as the final word on judo strategy's many forms. Instead, we hope that you will treat these ideas as a starting point for thinking about implementing judo strategy in your own organization.

In Part II of the book, we take a different look at judo strategy. Chapters 5, 6, and 7 present "masters" of judo strategy—managers and companies that have explicitly or implicitly embraced the ideas we describe and have built strong and growing businesses in the face of fierce competition. Chapter 5 looks at two masters of movement: Jeff Hawkins and Donna Dubinsky, the leaders of Palm Computing. Their story powerfully illustrates the potential of movement when all the pieces of the puzzle are brought into play. Palm exploited the puppy dog ploy, redefined the handheld computing space, and pushed ahead so quickly that Microsoft was still trying to catch up five years later.

Chapter 6 introduces a master of balance techniques: Rob Glaser, the hard-driving chairman and CEO of RealNetworks. Glaser was a pioneer in bringing streaming audio and video to the Internet. In five years he built a tiny start-up into a market leader with the strength to withstand repeated attacks from Microsoft, the most powerful software company in the world. As with many of the companies covered in this book, RealNetworks's ultimate fate is still undecided. That's the price of taking snapshots in a fast-moving economy. Nonetheless, chapter 6 shows how one company succeeded in using balance techniques to consolidate and power its growth.

In chapter 7, we meet two masters of leverage: Halsey Minor, the visionary founder of CNET Networks, and Shelby Bonnie, the company's cool-headed chairman and CEO. This dynamic duo took on two multibillion dollar incumbents, Ziff-Davis and IDG, and used leverage to force their competitors to choose between ceding share and cannibalizing their core business. As a result, CNET had become the unquestioned leader in online technology publishing by the end of the 1990s and put the capstone on its triumph by acquiring Ziff-Davis's online unit in July 2000.

Finally, Part III focuses on two related topics: fighting back and fighting on. In chapter 8, we explore different strategies for fighting back against a judo master, starting with more and better judo moves and ending with sumo strategy, a new metaphor for a style of competition that makes the most of a company's strength and size. Drawing on documents unearthed by the Department of Justice, we describe how Microsoft combined judo and sumo techniques to defeat Netscape. But chapter 8 ends on a cautionary note: Sumo strategists constantly face the risk of running head-on into an even bigger force—antitrust law, as it is enforced by the government and through the courts. Consequently, we use a brief case study of Intel to illustrate some of the tactics that powerful firms can use to minimize the threat of antitrust litigation and keep their destiny under their control.

Chapter 9 concludes the book with a user's guide to judo strategy, to aid readers who are interested in fighting on. We analyze some of the subtleties involved in managing judo strategy's principles and techniques. And finally, we discuss a number of best practices to help you become a judo master in your own business.

PART I

Principles of Judo Strategy

2

Movement

Don't Invite Attack, Define the Competitive Space, and Follow Through Fast

How did the British defeat the Spanish Armada? Because they had smaller, faster, more flexible ships.

—Jim Barksdale, former CEO, Netscape Communications

JUDO STRATEGY begins with *movement*. Most judo strategists will find themselves at a disadvantage in a pure contest of strength. In any given market, the balance of power rests with large, established firms that have spent years amassing customers, building partnerships with suppliers and distributors, honing competencies, and accumulating cash. But judo challengers have potential strengths as well. Lacking deep roots in a market, they enjoy the freedom that comes of having a clean slate. Skillful judo strategists can exploit this flexibility by using movement to alter the dynamics of competition to their advantage.

Movement in Judo

Movement is a critical skill in the judo ring. Top-level competitors use their quickness and agility to maneuver into a position of relative strength while simultaneously evading an opponent's grip. From the moment the referee yells *"Hajime!"* ("Begin!"), a judo master focuses on getting into position to unleash his strongest moves.

Conversely, an expert competitor avoids inviting attack when his position is relatively weak. A prudent *judoka* never initiates a struggle from an unbalanced stance when his opponent's balance remains sound.

But movement is about more than staying out of harm's way. Judo masters also use movement to define how the match will play out—or, as one Olympic medalist put it, to take an opponent "out of his game."[1] Most champions have a few favorite techniques that they rely on to bring victory. But when forced into an unfamiliar style of play, even they may be at a loss. A judo master can take advantage of this weak point by defining the competitive space in a way that requires his rival to learn new tricks on the spot. By forcing an opponent who prefers to fight from a distance to grapple at close range, for example, he can throw his rival off balance and grab a valuable edge.

Once a competitor has created an initial advantage or opening, he must remain in control of the situation by following through fast. A single technique is often not enough to win the match. Therefore, judo teachers train their students in the art of continuous attack: moving seamlessly from one charge into the next and pursuing a thrown opponent onto the mat. In judo, each move should flow into the next until the match is won. In a sport where advantage can shift in a second, faltering when it comes to the follow-through can be a fatal mistake.

Movement in Judo Strategy

In order to apply the lessons of judo to business competition, we have distilled the uses of movement into three techniques. The first is, simply, *Don't Invite Attack*. When you're relatively weak, you should avoid provoking stronger competitors into delivering a potentially fatal blow. Instead, you need to focus on reducing your rivals' temptation to attack. This technique will buy you time and space.

Second, smaller size does not have to be a disadvantage if you can move quickly to *Define the Competitive Space*. Use your freedom to maneuver to drive the competition in a direction that makes it hard for rivals to do what they do best. In this way, you can take away your opponents' most powerful weapons and give yourself a fighting chance.

Finally, once you've used the previous two techniques to establish a position in the market, *Follow Through Fast*. By defining—or redefining—the competitive space, you may secure a lead over potential rivals, but eventually they'll start to catch on. So you need to make the most of any advantage gained to establish a strong and stable position. In many cases, this means that you'll have to abandon the first technique, for as you begin to scale, it becomes harder to avoid becoming a target. In the next chapter, we'll discuss a set of techniques for responding effectively to a competitor's assault. Early in the game, however, the focus should be on using movement to get into the best possible position for the battles that lie ahead.

Don't Invite Attack

In any kind of competition, in or out of the ring, your first goal is to stay in the game. So when larger or more powerful competitors loom, avoid provoking the competition until you're strong enough to fight. Attracting too much of the wrong kind of attention too soon can be a fatal mistake. This is especially true in businesses where high fixed costs make competitors particularly sensitive to declines in sales and where the ability to target retaliation—by lowering prices in selected markets, for example—keeps the marginal cost of fighting challengers low. As the judo economics model shows, your opponent may hesitate to strike back if he's likely to damage his entire business as a result. But if he can pick and choose his targets, then watch out or, better yet, lie low.

This advice goes against the grain for many ambitious executives. It's often said that in a crowded marketplace, you have to shout to be heard; to win customers and build value, you have to be aggressive, and often that means attacking giants head-on. There's a kernel of truth in this argument. In order to make a dent in the market, you *do* have to attract attention and win credibility among customers and partners, and sometimes the media as well. This is particularly true in business-to-business markets and in industries where network effects are strong.[2] But in most cases, this goal can be accomplished without initiating or inviting a full frontal attack.

Instead, judo strategy counsels smaller challengers to appear as inoffensive as possible so that stronger players will either fail to notice them or choose to leave them alone. In order to emphasize the importance of looking unthreatening, we have borrowed the term "puppy dog ploy" from economists Drew Fudenberg and Jean Tirole to describe this technique.[3] While this image may lack gravitas, posing as a puppy dog can win you the time you need to build up your strength, as the three following examples show.

Transmeta: Going Undercover

If you want to avoid becoming the focus of hostile attention, the simplest tactic may to be to follow the example set by Transmeta and go undercover. Following its founding in 1995, the secretive chip design company kept its number unlisted and a terse message—"This Web site doesn't exist yet"—greeted visitors to its site. In an industry known for its high ratio of noise to signal, Transmeta stood out by refusing to answer even the simplest questions about its plans.

Ironically, Transmeta's obsession with secrecy had Silicon Valley buzzing about the company for years. The more Transmeta tried to keep to itself, the more outsiders wanted in—especially when they learned that Linus Torvalds, the creator of the Linux operating system, had joined the team. By not saying anything, Transmeta became one of the most widely hyped start-ups of its cohort, making it onto 1998's *Red Herring 100*, even though the editors admitted that they knew "precious little" about its business.

Finally, in January 2000, Transmeta revealed that the company had developed a line of microprocessors that ran both Windows and Linux applications using a fraction of the power required by the contemporary generation of Intel chips. This meant that Transmeta's Crusoe chips were ideally designed to power laptops and other portable devices—a market that was expected to explode. It also explained the need for the silence that had enveloped the company for four and a half years. "We're up against the mother of all competitors, Intel," observed Frank Priscaro, Transmeta's director of brand development.[4] If Transmeta had made a premature play for the limelight, Intel could have torpedoed the start-up's prospects by launching a competing product or, at the very least, an aggressive public relations campaign. So the company kept its strategy under wraps until its management believed it was strong enough to fight.

To a large degree, the tactic worked. While Intel knew about some of the technologies Transmeta was exploring, "we did not know what they were doing," said Paul Otellini, the head of Intel's microprocessor business. "It really was a dark secret until just before they announced."[5] But when Transmeta did emerge from obscurity, it was with a splash. Analysts and journalists from all over the country were invited to a rented villa in Northern California for an all-day briefing on the Crusoe line of chips. And in the months that followed, Transmeta received wide play in the media with a series of front-page deals. Gateway and AOL, which had invested in the company, agreed to use Crusoe chips for a new line of Internet devices, and several major computer manufacturers, including Sony and IBM, announced plans to release Crusoe-based laptops by the end of the year.

Transmeta might have done even better if it had maintained its cover a little longer or kept its unveiling more low-key. While Crusoe's high-profile debut led to some important contracts, it also forced Intel to respond. Within months, the giant chip maker moved to offer a competitive product, and a few of Crusoe's original backers, including IBM, put their Transmeta plans on hold. Nonetheless, Transmeta's momentum drove it to a successful initial public offering in November 2000, giving the company a market capitalization of nearly $6 billion shortly after its debut.

Capital One: Flying under the Radar

The puppy dog ploy is particularly critical in a company's youth, as the Transmeta story suggests. However, more established players can also use this technique to keep valuable markets to themselves. One company that successfully adopted this strategy is Capital One, the seventh largest credit card issuer in the United States. Led by former consultants Richard Fairbank and Nigel Morris, Capital One was founded in 1989 as the credit card division of Richmond, Virginia–based Signet Bank. Five years later, Signet spun the unit off.

Fairbank and Morris began the business with a simple idea: using information technology to revolutionize the business of pricing and issuing credit. Capital One collected detailed information on its customers and then tested hundreds, even thousands of offerings on consumers who fit various profiles. Through massive testing and rigorous analysis, Fairbank and Morris sought to identify new customer segments and customize new offerings in a way that minimized Capital One's risk.

The success of this strategy depended on the company's ability to keep industry giants, such as Citibank, from matching its moves. Once other players began to imitate its products and compete directly for customers, Capital One's returns would rapidly decline. So Fairbank and Morris became dedicated practitioners of the puppy dog ploy. As a former executive with the company explained, "Capital One is extremely confidential and very, very hush-hush about everything. When we roll out a new product, we never, never announce it to the world or do a big PR campaign. We never even celebrate our successes publicly; we celebrate in-house. We wouldn't even tell MasterCard or Visa what we were doing."

Rather than stir industry interest with eye-catching advertising campaigns, Capital One's marketing efforts relied on telephone solicitation and direct mail. Competitors might come across its mailings, but "they never understood the strategy underlying the products," said the former executive. "Citibank, for example, would never know whether we were doing a test cell or rolling out a product, and they wouldn't know what customers we were targeting, unless we told them. As a result, we have largely been able to stay under the radar screen," the same executive explained.

It was not until 2000 that Capital One finally abandoned the puppy dog ploy in favor of traditional, high-profile consumer marketing. Yet while the company's products remained secret for most of Capital One's early history, its edge was clear.[6] By exploiting information technology to the fullest while refusing to give away its game, Capital One became one of the biggest and most profitable credit card issuers in the United States in less than ten years.

Frontier Airlines: Positioning Alongside Competitors

As the previous examples suggest, the puppy dog ploy is relatively easy to apply in industries where trade secrets play an important role. But what if you compete in a business such as the airline industry, where critical details—such as where you fly, when you fly, and for how much—are available to all? Keeping your competitors in the dark may be impossible, but that doesn't mean you can't use the puppy dog ploy. Instead, take a lesson from Sam Addoms, the soft-spoken CEO of Frontier Airlines, and learn to position alongside your competitors. By making it clear that you don't plan to compete head-on, you make it that much easier for opponents to ignore your attack.[7]

The original Frontier Airlines operated for more than thirty years before being absorbed into Continental along with People Express in 1989. The new Frontier took wing out of Denver in 1994. Six years later, it had become the second largest carrier at Denver International Airport. With 7 percent of the market, Frontier posed no immediate threat to United Airlines, which carried nearly nine times as many passengers. Nonetheless, it emerged from the vicious competition of the 1990s as the only start-up competing successfully with a major carrier at a hub.

Frontier's strategy was carefully calibrated to avoid triggering United's wrath. The airline's choices in critical areas such as scheduling and pricing positioned it as a limited threat. Addoms favored a policy that he called "skimming": operating a restricted number of flights on United's major routes.[8] Frontier also planned its schedule around United's to avoid the impression that it was targeting traffic feeding into long-haul flights.[9] And Frontier kept a close eye on fares, seeking to offer customers better value without setting off a price war it couldn't win. By contrast, another Denver-based start-up, Western Pacific, used price as its primary weapon against United in 1997. When the larger carrier struck back, Western Pacific was forced into bankruptcy, while Frontier, which had also been drawn into the struggle, just survived.

Addoms points out that no company can avoid detection completely in this industry. "There is no 'under the radar screen,'" he maintains. "Everything we do and everything every airline does is completely visible to every competitor and of tremendous importance to every competitor. To suggest that there's some behavior pattern that cause you to be invisible is wrong. It's a myth."[10] But despite these constraints, Addoms has clearly mastered the essence of the puppy dog ploy. As he says, "You have to know what sets the other guy off."[11] The capacity to identify and avoid these triggers has been the key to Frontier's ability to operate successfully in United's unfriendly skies.

Two Cautionary Tales

Many start-up airlines have exited the business after missing or ignoring these cues. A notable example is People Express, which inaugurated low-cost, no-frills service in the busy Northeast in 1981. Operating out of Newark International Airport, People Express began with flights to smaller cities such as Columbus, Buffalo, and Norfolk, Virginia.[12] But the ambitious start-up soon challenged the majors with rock-bottom fares on their most popular routes: $19 to Boston, $59 to Chicago, $99 coast-to-coast. At the same time, People Express mounted an aggressive marketing blitz. As Donald Burr, the airline's founder, recalled, "We went around telling everybody that we're going to be great, do great, and conquer the world."[13]

The major airlines' reaction was predictable and swift. When People Express introduced service to Chicago in 1984, United and American matched its fares (with some restrictions) while continuing to offer free checked baggage, assigned seats, meals, and magazines—all the amenities that People Express lacked. The People Express challenge also prompted rival airlines to lower their own costs, allowing them to prolong a series of fare wars that bled the upstart dry. Several years later, the People Express story came to an end when it was acquired by Continental, and what had once been the fastest-growing airline in history disappeared without a trace.

Rather than play the puppy dog, People Express chose to "moon the giant," a phrase one Netscape executive memorably used to describe his own company's behavior toward arch-rival Microsoft.[14] Like People Express, Netscape painted itself as a giant-killer from day one. Despite the company's vulnerability, cofounders Jim Clark and Marc Andreessen seized upon every opportunity to attack Microsoft head-on. In the spring of 1995, Clark took the stage at an industry event and labeled Microsoft the "Death Star," depicting Netscape as the rebel alliance that would liberate the galaxy. Meanwhile, Andreessen, then a brash twenty-four-year-old, was busy telling interviewers that the rise of the Web would make Microsoft Windows obsolete, or nothing more than "a mundane collection of not entirely debugged device drivers," in his oft quoted words.[15]

This aggressive positioning helped the start-up in the battle for publicity, and for a while Netscape's fortunes soared. But by going out of their way to taunt Microsoft, Clark and Andreessen helped push the Internet to the top of Gates's list of priorities and secured Netscape's position as enemy number one.

DON'T INVITE ATTACK ("THE PUPPY DOG PLOY")

- Keep a low profile and avoid giving away your game.
- Position alongside competitors instead of attacking head-on.
- Don't moon the giant—unless you want to lose.

Define the Competitive Space

While the puppy dog ploy is basically about defense, with this next technique offense comes into play. The goal is no longer just to stay alive; now you want to seize the advantage by defining the rules, parameters, and boundaries of competition. "Success comes from playing the right game," as Adam Brandenburger and Barry Nalebuff have observed.[16]

Jim Barksdale, the former CEO of Netscape Communications, vividly captured the same insight. "In the fight between the bear and the alligator," he said, "the outcome is determined by the terrain."[17] Each animal presents a fearsome figure on its own turf. But the bear will flounder in a swamp, while the alligator surrenders many of its advantages when forced to fight on dry land. Consequently, in a battle where the two are evenly matched, the victory will go to the combatant fighting on home terrain.

The moral for challengers is clear: Move the battle away from your competitors' home territory. Force them to compete by new rules. Impose new standards, target new customers, distribute through new channels, and bring new partners into the game. Define a competitive space that you can dominate, and do it before stronger rivals move in. Most champions rise to the top by learning to do a few key things better than anybody else. Trying to compete with a powerful player at what she does best invariably turns out to be a losing game. But every champion has areas where he's weak, often precisely because he's invested so heavily in his core strengths. Take advantage of these weaknesses to define a game that you can win.

Skillfully applied, this technique delivers a one-two punch. By moving to new terrain, you can catch your competitors off guard. In this sense, *Define the Competitive Space* shares the spirit of the puppy dog ploy. Rather than attack the heart of the enemy empire, you move in along the periphery, choosing a line of approach that your target may initially ignore. But once the enemy has been roused, the critical difference between the two techniques becomes clear. A powerful rival who has the advantage of fighting on his home turf can send a puppy dog flying with a single well-placed blow. In unfamiliar territory, however, the same opponent may struggle to respond.[18]

In the long run, able opponents will adjust and learn to compete on new terms. In the short term, however, the challenge of mastering new tactics can sap their strength and slow them down, as the following examples suggest.

Intuit: Changing the Paradigm

Depending on the opponent and opportunity you face, *Define the Competitive Space* can take a variety of forms. Intuit, for example, vaulted to leadership by redefining the standards for its category. By the time Intuit entered the market for personal finance software in the 1980s, there was already a well-established pattern of competition: the longest list of features always won. Andy Tobias's Managing Your Money, which held 70 percent of the market, had more features than Dollars and Sense, the contender it had displaced, and Dollars and Sense had more features than the incumbent it had sent out of the ring.

Intuit didn't have a chance under these rules. Scott Cook, a former Bain consultant, had started the company on his own nickel and hired a college student, Tom Proulx, to write the code. With a total of seven employees and $151,000 in financing from family and friends, there was no way Intuit could out-feature Managing Your Money or even Dollars and Sense. So Cook didn't even try to build a "better" product; he built the right product instead. "Quicken was the absolute opposite of the then-existing software paradigm, which was, 'More features' is always better," Cook explained. "We had a very short features list and we didn't do most of what the other products did. But what we did do happened to be the things that people actually did all the time, like write checks, keep a check register, occasionally reconcile it to the bank. And we did that stuff very fast and very intuitively." On the press tour for Quicken's launch, Cook lugged his Compaq to reporters' offices in city after city and challenged them to print a check. In forty tries, not one person succeeded with Dollars and Sense. With Quicken, a check popped out, Cook said, "generally within four minutes, some as quick as within two."

Cook's secret weapon lay in his background. Prior to joining Bain, he had worked for four years at Procter & Gamble as a newly minted Harvard M.B.A., and he took to Intuit what he had learned at P&G: understanding consumers through research, driving research and development to produce a product that consumers actually want, and then investing heavily in usability testing. "We didn't use that term at the time—it hadn't been invented," Cook explained:

> But we were the first people to do actual consumer testing of software where we brought in people who hadn't seen the software and had them attempt to use it. And then whatever they found confusing, you fixed. No one else had ever done that.
>
> The software industry basically came out of an industrial paradigm where you built stuff for companies where people got paid to use the stuff, so usability wasn't very important. We brought a consumer paradigm, the Procter & Gamble paradigm, to the industry.

By changing the rules, Intuit made it extremely difficult for its established rivals to compete. Neither of the previous market leaders grasped the true nature of Intuit's challenge. Managing Your Money tried to compete by introducing a new, lower-priced offering (Quicken had started at $99 to Managing Your Money's $199) and failed. At Dollars and Sense, the story was the same. "I talked later to the guy who ran Dollars and Sense," Cook recalled, "and he said, 'All we thought you were doing was inexpensive software. We just didn't get that there was something there.' Even when we had 70 percent share of the market and they were tiny, they still didn't get it. And that's the power of the paradigm. If you're locked in one, it's really hard to see the world through any other eyes."

Several years later, Intuit used the same technique to defeat Microsoft, which beat Intuit to the market for Windows-based small business accounting software by nine months to a year. Accounting software had always been modeled on the paper methods used by accountants, but Cook decided to do something different in creating QuickBooks. "The vast majority of small businesses don't have accountants on staff," Cook explained, "and they don't understand accounting, and they don't want to learn. They need to keep books, but they hate accounting. So we built the first accounting software with no accounting." There were no debits or credits, journals or ledgers in QuickBooks. Intuit designed the product to work "like a human as opposed to working like an accountant," noted Cook. And neither Microsoft nor Intuit's other accounting competitors copied QuickBooks's approach for another five years. "By shifting the paradigm," Cook maintained, "we were able to drive Quick-Books to market leadership basically within a month."

Relative to Microsoft, Intuit may have been both small and late, but as Cook recounted, "When we launched QuickBooks for Windows, we crushed them so badly they exited the market and never came back." Indeed, Bill Gates may have paid Cook the ultimate compliment. Rather than continue to compete, he tried to buy Intuit in 1994—only to see the Department of Justice veto the deal.

Juniper Networks: Segmenting to Success

Juniper Networks also rose to the top by defining the competitive space. But the young networking company, which faced a much larger market, took a slightly different approach. Rather than set new standards for the market as a whole, Juniper sliced off the high end, where its principal competitor, Cisco Systems, was relatively weak. Like many large companies, Cisco was stuck in the position of trying to be all things for all customers all of the time—a task that almost no one can carry out well. By making focus the key to success, Juniper built an extremely high-performance product that was hard for Cisco to match. As a result, Juniper Networks became the first company ever to take significant share from Cisco in the market for routers.

Routers are the traffic cops of the Internet. At the edge of every network, a router sorts through the incoming and outgoing data packets and decides where each one should go. Routers operate in all types of networks, ranging from local area networks inside companies to the Internet. When Cisco built its first router in the mid-1980s, the company's goal was to help customers link together different types of computers—Apples, IBMs, DECs—typically using a variety of transport protocols. However, it was not until the explosion of the Internet in the 1990s that the router, and Cisco along with it, came into its own.

When Cisco went public in 1990, its sales amounted to around $70 million a year. By 1996, the company's revenues had grown more than fiftyfold, and its share price had soared 10,000 percent.[19] Led by CEO John Chambers, Cisco had begun to diversify into related product areas through an aggressive acquisition campaign. But routers remained Cisco's core product. Several companies, including 3Com and Wellfleet Communications, tried to attack Cisco in the router market. But none made much of a dent until Juniper arrived on the scene in the fall of 1998.

Juniper CEO Scott Kriens deftly diagnosed earlier competitors' mistakes. "They were trying to sell the same application to the same customers—multiprotocol routers to enterprise customers," he observed. "And that's a tough undertaking no matter what your ability to execute." Kriens, who had sold his previous company, StrataCom, to Cisco, knew better than to strike directly at the segment that Cisco valued most. So Juniper chose another line of attack, Kriens explained:

> We were targeted toward entering at the very top of the market. Our entry strategy was to win the largest backbone networks in the Internet. We had watched several companies try to enter at a lower point and then try to climb to higher ground against superior force, which was fundamentally flawed strategically. And so we felt we had one chance, which was to enter at the top with no legacy and no baggage and obligations to support lower positions. And then if successful, to build the business from there down.

The backbone market was not the high end of the enterprise market, the company decided. It was a market on its own. And Juniper planned to dominate it by building routers that were optimized for the needs of backbone operators—giant carriers and Internet service providers like UUNET and AT&T. "One hundred percent of what Juniper does is focused on Internet applications and Internet back-bones," Kriens explained. "We are not trying to compete with Cisco by doing what Cisco does. We are interested in competing for the same customers, but we do something that is architecturally very, very different."

"Cisco's products," he continued, "were designed to solve the problem of making different computers communicate among a couple of hundred thousand employees. That is totally unrelated to connect-ing a billion people together on the Internet with only one format or protocol called IP." Moreover, in order to handle the enormous load created by hundreds of millions of people going online, Juniper took a different approach. While Cisco relied on software to make its routers work, Juniper focused on adding intelligence to the underlying chips. "Software and silicon are diametrically opposite cultures," Kriens explained, pointing to a fundamental disconnect that made it even harder for Cisco to compete in the space Juniper had defined.

Cisco did fight back, of course. But despite Cisco's attack, Juniper remained focused on its market, and by mid-2000, the company's strategy had paid off. Two years after launching its first product—the M40 router, which could process 40 million packets per second, ten times as many as Cisco's then top-of-the-line machine—Juniper held 30 percent of the high-end router market, and its routers were embedded in nine of the top ten Internet backbones (see figure 2–1).[20] "This is Juniper's ballpark," proclaimed company founder Pradeep Sindhu, and while it was early innings yet, Juniper Networks was clearly coming on strong.[21]

Inktomi: Pioneering the Market

Juniper and Intuit were both second movers (or later, in Intuit's case) that succeeded by redefining the competitive space. Inktomi, by contrast, essentially created the Internet caching market and used its first-mover advantage to build a healthy lead in the face of formidable competition.

Berkeley computer scientists Eric Brewer and Paul Gauthier founded Inktomi in February 1996. Five months later, David Peter-schmidt, an Air Force veteran who had helped take Sybase public,

Figure 2-1: Jumping Juniper!

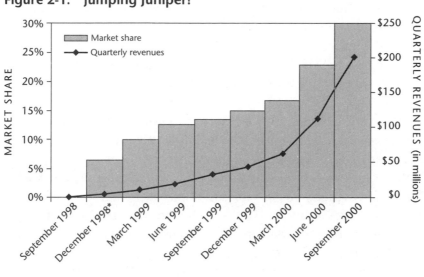

*The figure for December 1998 represents revenues for the preceding twelve months.

Source: Dell'Oro Group, company reports, and authors' estimates.

became the company's CEO. Brewer and Gauthier had developed a parallel computing platform that harnessed multiple workstations to deliver supercomputing power. The first application they developed to run on top of this platform was a search engine, which debuted as HotBot in May 1996. The search engine was a nice business (Inktomi later licensed it to companies like Microsoft and Yahoo!), but Peterschmidt was looking for more. Shortly after joining the team, he organized a three-day off-site meeting for the entire company—all twelve employees—where Inktomi's mission was redefined as building products to help the Internet scale.

The company's first area of focus was Internet caching. A cache server stores Web pages that users have viewed and uses these files to satisfy subsequent requests, reducing network congestion and shortening the infamous World Wide Wait. While Microsoft and Netscape already sold cache servers for company networks, Internet caching was a market waiting to be invented in 1996. "We knew from our search engine experience that about 60 percent of the content traffic on the backbone was redundant transmission, and we thought, if you could take the redundant traffic off the backbone, you were going to save a lot of bandwidth usage and charges," Peter-schmidt recalled. "It didn't take a rocket scientist to figure out that if you built this product and were successful in getting it deployed, the benefits would be enormous," added Richard Pierce, Inktomi's COO.

Inktomi believed that software, specifically its Inktomi Traffic Server, offered the best solution to the Internet caching problem. But powerful competitors had other ideas. Cisco, the company soon learned, was working on a caching appliance—a black box that ISPs could slot into their networks. "We had met with Cisco around the summer of '97," Peterschmidt recounted, "and when we started talking about what we were doing, you could almost see the shields go up. It was pretty obvious to us that they were very uncomfortable in that discussion, and our only conclusion was that they were obvi-ously seeing the same demand in the market and were probably try-ing to come in with some type of competing product."

In some ways, Cisco's approach seemed like the natural solu-tion. "The marketplace was used to buying black boxes. They *liked* black boxes," Pierce recalled. But Inktomi had no chance of winning if it chose to play Cisco's game. The company's only shot at victory lay in getting established in the market ahead of Cisco and pre-emptively defining the space.

Few observers at the time would have picked Inktomi to win. When Inktomi and Cisco both hit the market in the fall of 1997, Peterschmidt recalled, "I can remember people coming up to me saying, 'You guys are dead. Cisco just announced they're coming into your marketplace.'" But to just about everyone's surprise, Ink-tomi quickly captured the lead, signing up big-name customers beginning with AOL. Inktomi clearly benefited from the competi-tion's stumbles: Cisco's Cache Engine was widely panned. But the company's strategy was also critical to its success.

Inktomi had designed Inktomi Traffic Server as a platform for applications. This allowed other companies to build services on top of Inktomi's software, such as filtering technology, which prevents material like pornography from reaching users' screens. By defining the competitive space in terms of a *platform* rather than an *appliance*, Traffic Server had the potential to deliver much greater functional-ity than Cisco's black box. "This is a tremendous differentiator over the appliance guys," Peterschmidt explained. Moreover, by enabling third parties to create complementary products, Inktomi was able to add value to its platforms by leveraging the resources of other companies. This was particularly important in a situation where "we were clearly the David and Cisco was clearly the Goliath," as Pierce recalled.

Two and a half years later, the network caching market remained highly dynamic, as new challengers like Akamai, which entered the arena in Inktomi's wake, tried to redefine the rules yet again. But within the core market it pioneered, Inktomi remained the company to beat, with more than half of the market by mid-2000.[22]

DEFINE THE COMPETITIVE SPACE

- Change the paradigm by redefining standards for the market.
- Segment the market and make focus the key to success.
- Use first-mover advantage to build a market where you choose the rules.

Follow Through Fast

By combining the first two movement techniques, you buy time and space. To use this window of opportunity to the fullest, you must build your lead through continuous attack. One day soon—and these days, that's sooner than ever—competitors will wake up to the threat that you pose. Initially they may stumble, but some will eventually adapt to the new terrain. And once they find their footing, they'll bring the advantages of superior size and strength into play. Before that happens, you want to build the strongest position possible.

Speed is clearly central to this process, particularly in industries where network effects are strong, and scale, scope, and learning economies play an important role. In such cases, where the first mover can reap rich rewards, the crucial question concerning speed is not "Why?" but "How?" How do you make the most effective use of your resources to follow through fast? How quickly can you build internal resources? And how can you find creative ways to draw on resources beyond your direct control? Inktomi, for example, pursued a strategy that allowed third parties to add value to its platform, harnessing their capabilities to reinforce its lead. And as we discuss below, Ariba used similar tactics to help narrow the gap between its competitors' resources and its own.

But speed should never become an obsession to the point where it excludes other critical concerns, such as product quality, customer satisfaction, and long-run profitability. For judo strategists, speed is a means not an end. Following through fast means moving quickly without becoming overextended or losing your balance. If you outstrip your resources, your weakened position will increase your vulnerability to attack—as many humbled new-economy firms have learned.

Ariba: Speeding to Scale

Ariba, one of the initial leaders in the business-to-business (B2B) e-commerce software market, showed early on several characteristics common to masters of speed and control. Less than four years after its founding in 1996, the company had pulled ahead of competitors such as database powerhouse Oracle and fellow start-up Commerce One by focusing on two priorities: getting out in front fast and building an organization that could scale.

In order to move fast, Ariba chose to focus initially on a relatively narrow slice of the market, rather than run the risk of spreading its resources too thin. The company rejected what Bobby Lent, a cofounder and senior vice president for strategy, called the "boil the ocean" solution: delivering a complete e-commerce marketplace from the very beginning. Instead, Ariba adopted a carefully phased approach, "sequencing our way toward the vision."

Ariba's first target was the strategic high ground of buyer procurement systems. "All historical commerce effects started with the buyer," Lent explained. "We call it the golden rule of commerce: he who has the gold makes the rules. Buyers are like gravity wells for suppliers; suppliers can't help but be attracted to them and do whatever it takes to get attached to them." Once Ariba had converted a large number of buyers, Lent said, it could move toward building connectivity to suppliers and ultimately toward building marketplaces and commerce networks. By working through this sequence, the company could rapidly build a position in the market without putting its performance and credibility at risk.

At the same time, Ariba's top management focused on creating an organization that would be able to meet the challenges of rapid growth. At an off-site meeting the day after the company's creation, the founding team created a playbook that encapsulated the company's vision, mission, values, team rules, long-term goals, and strategy. CEO Keith Krach and his colleagues realized that the first years would be the easiest, in the sense that they could keep an eye on everything that was going on as long as the company remained small. But once Ariba took off, it would be an enormous challenge to keep everyone aligned.

To head off this problem, for the first year and a half Krach personally took every new employee through the playbook. As the company grew, all-hands meetings and leadership training workshops replaced the one-on-one approach. Yet despite the company's growth—from 280 to 1,500 employees in one year— Ariba's management remained determined to evangelize the playbook to all employees. "We're talking to every single person in the company," Lent maintained, "even the operators on our phones."

Ariba took a similarly thorough approach to the task of integrating acquired firms. Despite its growth path, the company could not compete with rivals like Oracle on the basis of homegrown resources alone. Without infusions of critical complementary technology and skills, Ariba would be left behind. Yet the acquisitions process is one that has tripped up many a fast-moving firm. The task of integrating different cultures, processes, and workforces can easily slow an acquirer down.

Taking a page from the book of successful acquirers like Cisco and GE, Ariba tried to minimize these pitfalls by systematically applying a three-stage process. The first task was to identify the right targets for acquisition. In addition to fitting into Ariba's product and technology plans, these companies had to meet two criteria. "We feel that culturally, there's got to be an immediate fit," Lent maintained. "And we also look at whether they are adding A-plus people to us. Each acquisition should increase the average IQ of our company."

Once a likely target had been identified, Ariba required a senior executive to take responsibility for the acquisition. "We will not take an acquisition to the board and get their approval to pursue it—in essence get the license to kill," Lent said, "until we can demonstrate that we have a business owner lined up inside the company who is ready to take on the task of integration." And finally, once that hurdle had been passed, Ariba turned back to the playbook to apply a "bear hug" to each acquired company's employees. "When we first sit down with a company that we have acquired, we take them through the history of Ariba," Lent explained. "We explain to them that when we founded the company, we decided that every Aribian would be like a founder. We emphasize that they have the same status and are as much founders as anybody else in this company."

"Bear-hugging" acquisitions made it easier for Ariba to expand its internal capabilities at high speed. Even so, the company couldn't do everything in-house. "Consequently," Lent said, "we began building partnerability into everything we were doing from a very early stage." "Building partnerability" meant creating tools, methodologies, and training systems that enabled other companies to implement Ariba systems without having an army of Ariba developers on site to hold their hands. By mid-2000, Ariba was training around 1,500 people per month from companies like IBM, which had committed to have 5,000 people trained on Ariba by the end of the year. This approach was commonplace in the enterprise software market, where most developers relied on resellers to help sell and implement the systems they built. But Ariba went to unusual lengths to make the process smooth. "As a result," Lent explained, "on a typical engagement installing our software today, we have generally one, maybe two, Aribians and anywhere from seven to a maximum of fifteen people from one of our partners involved. By contrast, our competitors typically involve fifty people from their own company, and as many as 200 people from their partners." This difference was reflected in Ariba's ability to win customers. In the first nine months of 2000, Ariba announced more than 160 buyer-side e-procurement deals, compared to thirty for Oracle and forty for Commerce One.

By late 2000, Ariba was facing new competitors and challenges as demand fell off across the B2B e-commerce sector as a whole. Only time would show whether or not the foundation laid by the company's founders would meet Ariba's future needs. Nonetheless,

Lent and his colleagues could take pride in one clear accomplishment: Through focus, sequencing, and investments in culture and partnerability, they had succeeded in building one of the fastest-growing software companies of all time.

Netscape Communications: The Speed Trap

Like Ariba, Netscape Communications started out fast. The start-up beat Microsoft to the Web browser market by eight months, launching Navigator in December 1994. CEO Jim Barksdale, who had previously served as COO of Federal Express, believed strongly that speed and flexibility were crucial to competing effectively with large players such as Microsoft and UPS. "How did FedEx compete with the Airbornes and UPSs when they got started?" he liked to ask. "How did the British defeat the Spanish Armada? Because they had smaller, faster, more flexible ships."[23] Under Barksdale's leadership, Netscape implemented a number of innovative policies that aggressively pushed forward its lead. But Netscape's story also illustrates another important lesson: If you move too fast, it can be hard to stay in control.

Three moves played a critical role in driving Netscape's growth. The first was the internally controversial decision to make Navigator "free but not free." In other words, while nonacademic customers were expected to fork over a licensing fee of $39 after a free trial of ninety days, Netscape had no mechanisms in place for forcing individual consumers to pay. The browser was free, in effect, and as a result, adoption rates soared. More than 10 million people were using Navigator by the summer of 1995, six months after its official release.[24] One year later, Navigator's installed base reached 38 million, making it the most popular personal computer application in the world, ahead of Microsoft Office and Lotus 1-2-3.

But in order to reach this milestone, Netscape had to do more than make Navigator eminently affordable. The company also had to make it easy to obtain. Rather than focus on winning retail and OEM distribution, Netscape turned to the Web.[25] By allowing anyone to download Navigator, Netscape put its software within reach of millions of consumers overnight. In addition, this strategy had two other benefits related to the drive for speed. Web-based distribution supported the policy of "free but not free" by eliminating the cost of burning, shrink-wrapping, and sending out CDs. It also allowed Netscape to speed up another critical process: testing software before it was released.

Testing had traditionally been a highly labor-intensive process requiring battalions of professional quality assurance engineers and tens, if not hundreds, of thousands of beta testers at carefully chosen companies. Microsoft, for example, had drafted 400,000 people to test Windows 95. Netscape lacked the time and resources to organize a similar process from scratch. But once again the company found help online. In October 1994, Netscape posted a beta version of Navigator to the Web. Company engineers had finished most of the design work on the product, but there were still a lot of quirks to iron out. By downloading the beta, trying it out, and filing their complaints, customers served, sometimes unwittingly, as Netscape's virtual quality assurance team. One month later, 1.5 million users had given Navigator a trial run. "We can release a beta and get immediate feedback," Lou Montulli, one of Netscape's first developers, crowed. "Our beta cycles are a couple of weeks long. That's unheard of. We get amazing amounts of feedback from millions of people and shake out all these bugs very quickly and turn it around."[26]

These techniques helped Netscape dramatically shorten its product cycles to around nine months, compared to the two to three years that a company like Lotus might have previously spent updating a single release. But there was a downside to Netscape's emphasis on speed. Rushed development resulted in poorly architected software or "spaghetti code," as it was often called inside the company. One Netscape developer voiced the frustration of many when he said in 1997, "We wrote this code three years ago, and its major purpose in life was to get us in business as fast as possible. We should have stopped shipping this code a year ago. It's dead. This code should have been taken out back and shot."[27]

In addition, as Netscape shot skyward, its management resources were often overtaxed. CEO James Barksdale's decision to enter a wide variety of markets, sacrificing focus for growth through breadth, increased the strain on the management team. At the same time, the company failed to plan adequately for its growth. This failure was particularly visible in Netscape's relationships with potential or actual partners. Like Inktomi, Netscape relied heavily on independent software developers to add value to its platform and boost its momentum. But the company quickly became notorious for its arrogance and its lack of support—both sins that could be traced, in large measure, to Netscape's remarkably rapid rise.

FOLLOW THROUGH FAST

- Stay focused and sequence growth to avoid becoming overextended.
- Make maintaining internal alignment an early priority—before the challenges of growth emerge.
- Use partnerships to leverage resources beyond your immediate control.

3

Balance

Grip Your Opponent, Avoid Tit-for-Tat, and Push When Pulled

An oak that hung over a river was uprooted by a violent storm of wind and carried down the stream. As it floated along it noticed some reeds growing by the bank, and cried out to them, "Why, how do such slight, frail things as yourselves manage to stand safely in a storm that can tear me up by the roots?" "It was easy enough," answered the reeds. "Instead of standing stubbornly and stiffly against it as you did, we yielded and bowed before every wind that blew, and so it went over us and left us unhurt." The moral of the story is: "It is better to bend than to break."

—Aesop's Fables

MOVEMENT CAN HELP YOU avoid head-to-head battles with bigger, stronger opponents, as we discussed in chapter 2. Eventually, however, you'll have to meet the competition. In judo strategy, just as in judo, you have to learn to come to grips with your opponents if you want to win.

Ideally, your first encounter will take place on your schedule and your terms. Realistically, however, you should always be prepared to meet an attack. By using the puppy dog ploy, defining the competitive space, and following through fast, you're buying time to build a foothold and to start to grow. But the faster you grow and the larger you become, the harder it is to stay out of your competitors' sights—and the more likely you are to face a powerful assault.

43

Balance is the skill you have to master in order to engage an opponent and survive. As illustrated by the fable of the oak and the reeds, balance and flexibility are your allies in the face of superior strength. When you're weaker than your opponent, giving way to preserve your balance is often the wisest response to overwhelming force. But giving way shouldn't be confused with surrendering the initiative or giving up. If you give way, it's with a purpose: to respond more effectively when returning to the fight.

Balance in Judo

One of the first things new students learn in judo is *shizentai*, a naturally stable standing position. In *shizentai*, the body is relaxed but ready for combat. "The body keeps stability and does not fall," as one judo master explained, and "as the limbs are kept soft they can shift to any action at any moment."[1]

By preserving his balance, a *judoka* remains in the ideal position for both initiating and countering an attack. But exhibiting perfect posture isn't enough to win a match. In order to achieve victory, you need to destroy your opponent's balance as well. Positive action becomes all but impossible for a competitor whose balance is askew. By throwing your opponent off balance, you can destroy his power to take the initiative and set him up for a fall.

Gripping your opponent is the first step toward weakening his position. In addition to limiting your opponent's ability to maneuver, gripping makes it easier to sense what he's going to do. Consequently, at the beginning of a match, each player battles to seize hold of the other's collar or sleeve. Once one of the competitors secures a grip, he tries to push or pull the other into a weak or unbalanced stance.

The recipient of this treatment must follow a simple but counterintuitive rule. Rather than resist, he should give way to his opponent's momentum, pushing when pulled and pulling when pushed. Judo masters reject the tactic of opposing strength to strength, which we characterize later as a tit-for-tat approach. Meeting force with force exhausts a competitor's energy without advancing the match. Moreover, by shoving back in response to a push, a *judoka* opens himself to defeat. By channeling all his power in a single direction, he loses his flexibility and puts himself at the mercy of an opponent who remains able to move freely as the situation demands.

Judo practitioners are taught instead to conserve their strength and maintain their balance by giving way. But "giving way" is a far from passive act. A *judoka* does not simply stand, unresisting, and let himself be pushed around. He remains alert and active, meeting and extending his opponent's charge. By capturing his opponent's momentum, a skillful competitor can throw a stronger player off balance and move one step closer to mastery of the game.

Balance in Judo Strategy

Applying the metaphor of balance to strategy leads us to three general techniques. The first is *Grip Your Opponent*. In the course of most contests, there comes a time when movement loses its power to avert a direct attack. Success brings visibility, and eventually even the slowest competitors will figure out that you're a threat. That's when you need to seize the initiative and decide how you're going to engage the competition. By working with opponents (and with potential rivals), you can strengthen your position and limit their room to maneuver while postponing, diverting, or even preempting efforts to attack you head-on. But as you get in close, make sure that you protect your options and set your own terms. The primary goal, after all, is to grip your opponent, not to let him get a grip on you.

Even if you succeed in gripping your opponent, at some point you may still find yourself under attack. In this situation, your first priority should be to *Avoid Tit-for-Tat*. When competing with stronger players, meeting force with force is a quick route to defeat. Resisting every move will wear you down, put you on the defensive, and recast the competition as a trial of strength—the game that you're least likely to win. So rather than get dragged into a war of attrition, stay on the offensive and respond to attackers on your own terms.

Finally, and perhaps most important, learn to *Push When Pulled*. When facing a powerful, head-on attack, remember the fate of the oak in Aesop's fable and resist the temptation to stand "stubbornly and stiffly against the wind." If you're up against an irresistible force, first give way—and then harness that force to your own ends.

Look for ways to capture your opponent's momentum and ride it where you want to go. Build on your competitors' products, services, or technology, if you have the opportunity, and embrace their moves. This means more than just avoiding tit-for-tat. With *Push When Pulled*, you're moving close to leverage (the subject of the next chapter) by using your opponent's strength to advance your position.

Taken together, these balance techniques can help you conserve and make the most of your force. Gripping reduces your vulnerability to attack, avoiding tit-for-tat minimizes the impact of an attack, and pushing when pulled lets you rechannel the force of an attack to your advantage. All three techniques can be used separately or, more powerfully, in combination.

Grip Your Opponent

Engaging competitors is always a challenge, and doubly so when your opponents' resources are greater than those you command. But if you have to meet the competition, it's far better to do so on your terms. Decide what you want from other players and then secure your grip—ideally, long before they figure out how they want to deal with you.

Gripping can serve a variety of goals. By gripping early, you may succeed in preempting competition, securing victory, in essence, by making it unnecessary to fight. Alternatively, you can build relationships with current or future rivals that limit their room to maneuver or allow you to benefit at their expense. Microsoft, for example, got an early grip on its rival Apple Computer by cooperating with Apple to write applications for the Macintosh in the mid-1980s. Over time, Microsoft became Apple's most important software supplier—a position that ultimately gave Bill Gates enormous bargaining power.[2] (This is a point that we will return to in chapter 8.)

There are many ways to grip another player. If you want to avoid future combat, give potential competitors a stake in your success through partnerships, joint ventures, or equity deals. Priceline.com, for example, sold Delta Airlines an equity interest in the company to deter the airline from offering its own competing service.[3] Alternatively, if you want to limit your rivals' options and reduce their incentive to develop their own capabilities, offer them the use of your services or products instead. Several Japanese consumer electronics companies took this route in the 1960s and 1970s, gripping their larger American competitors by producing low-end products that were sold under their rivals' brands. In many cases, these tactics will involve what modern strategy jargon calls "co-opetition": competing and cooperating with a company at the same time.[4] But keep in mind that the true goal of gripping isn't to benefit all sides; it's to defend and strengthen your competitive position.

Amazon.com: Co-opting Competitors I

Amazon.com, the world's largest e-tailer, implemented gripping by going into business with the competition. A little more than a year after first testing the waters of the toy market on its own, the company responded to feelers from Toys "R" Us by agreeing to partner on a cobranded site. While not the first movers in this case, Amazon.com executives made the most of their opportunity to grip a powerful competitor, simultaneously strengthening the company's hand for the future and removing an important rival from the scene.

Amazon.com took its first steps into Toys "R" Us territory in late 1998, when it began selling a small selection of toys, mostly board games, through its gift center (which was later closed). Following the success of this venture, Amazon.com started planning a full-blown toy store in February 1999. While the toy industry differed from the book business in important ways, Amazon.com executives believed that the new category was a good fit. Toys were "very difficult to shop for in the physical world," explained Harrison Miller, general manager of the toy store. And Amazon.com already counted a lot of families—and moms in particular—among its customers.

The online toy market was quickly filling up. Start-up eToys had come out of the previous holiday season as the leading Internet toy seller, with $23 million in sales in the last quarter of 1998. In addition, a number of high-profile players, including KB Toys, Disney (through its controlling interest in Toysmart), and Toys "R" Us, the number two toy seller in the country (behind Wal-Mart), were also moving online. Yet despite the stiff competition, Amazon.com became the second-largest online toy retailer, second only to eToys, by the end of 1999. The company sold $95 million worth of children's products, including toys, books, music, and videos, in the last three months of the year. In addition, Miller maintained, "Amazon.com really distanced itself from the field in terms of reliability, taking orders up until the 23rd of December and delivering over 99 percent of those items in time for Christmas." But the end of the holiday season brought less welcome news as well. In early 2000, Amazon.com wrote off $39 million in inventory, the bulk of which was toys. Due to the company's inexperience and lack of historical data on customer purchases, the toy category was clearly not going to be a romp.

Then in early February 2000, Amazon.com got a call from John Barbour, the CEO of Toysrus.com, suggesting that the two competitors combine their strengths. The Amazon.com response was cautious at first. "I think the natural bias, especially when you're moving at Internet speed, is to say, 'We have a plan. We're going for it. It's going to be great,'" Miller recalled. However, as Miller and his colleagues mulled over Barbour's proposal, the idea began to make more and more sense. Toysrus.com brought tremendous assets to the table, including enormous buying power and one of the country's best-known brands. For its part, Amazon.com contributed its expertise in e-commerce site development, marketing, fulfillment, and customer service. In summing up the economics of the partnership, Miller explained, "these guys have cost leverage for purchasing products that is pretty much unique. And we have unique leverage in fulfillment, customer service, and technology for e-commerce because of our scale."

The ten-year agreement announced in August 2000 established a division of labor in which each company specialized in what it did best. Toysrus.com bought and owned the inventory (aside from low-volume specialty items, which Amazon.com handled on its own). Amazon.com ran the cobranded Web site and managed customer service and fulfillment out of its distribution centers. Toysrus.com booked the revenue and paid Amazon.com a fixed yearly payment, a variable per unit charge, and a single-digit share of total revenues. In addition, Amazon.com, which owned the traffic, had the opportunity to cross-sell products to customers who came in search of toys. This strengthened Amazon.com's position against even stronger competitors, such as Wal-Mart, that sold a wide range of products online.

Questions about the workings of the partnership remained. Would the logistics of the toy business prove too costly for Amazon.com? Would Toys "R" Us be willing to allocate hot products to the online venture rather than sell them through its stores? On balance, however, observers applauded Amazon.com's move. By one estimate, the partnership turned a business that lost $32 million in the last quarter of 1999 into a $12 million gain for the same period in 2000.[5] Equally important, by allowing Amazon.com to grip—and be gripped by—Toys "R" Us, the deal took a potentially dangerous competitor out of the game for the foreseeable future. "Five years ago, Amazon.com was literally in Jeff [Bezos]'s garage. So to us, ten years is an eternity," Miller observed.

eBay: Co-opting Competitors II

Meg Whitman, the president and CEO of eBay, has also proven to be an accomplished practitioner of gripping techniques. Whitman is a smart, highly intuitive, and deeply hands-on manager who worked at Bain & Company, Walt Disney, Stride Rite, and FTD before landing at Hasbro, where she was managing Playskool and Mr. Potato Head when eBay came calling in early 1998.

One of Whitman's most challenging tasks upon joining eBay was dealing with potential rivals. eBay's management had always been watchful of the competition. From the very beginning, founder Pierre Omidyar worried that a Web portal or one of the existing auction companies would crush his start-up. In order to minimize this danger, eBay tried to stay off the radar screen of potential competitors, intuitively implementing the puppy dog ploy. As Whitman explained, "We decided that the best thing to do was to get critical mass in the marketplace before people really understood what was going on."

Whitman kept a close eye on numerous companies, starting with OnSale, a business-to-consumer auction pioneer. Vertical marketplaces also drew her attention, as did "anyone who had large amounts of traffic," Whitman said. But the biggest players—"the gorillas of the Internet"—were Yahoo!, Amazon.com, and above all, AOL. AOL wasn't just the leader in eyeballs and traffic. It had a much deeper relationship with its customers than a garden-variety portal; it understood communities, like the one eBay was trying to build; and it was very good at driving traffic into targeted areas. All this made the company a powerful threat. "If they had done an AOL Auctions button," Whitman admitted, "it might have been very bad for us."

eBay tried to prevent this outcome by building a close relationship with AOL. Between the fall of 1997 and the summer of 1999, senior executives at eBay negotiated three successive deals, each of which allowed them to grip their potential opponent a bit more tightly. eBay brought the same goals to each round of talks—to increase its distribution and to keep AOL out of the market. But the dynamics of the relationship changed throughout this period as eBay's strength grew.

eBay and AOL: Round One. The first agreement was negotiated by Steve Westly, vice president of marketing and business development, and his deputy, Tom Adams. In initiating the talks, Westly had both offense and defense on his mind. AOL could give eBay a tremendous boost, but it also had the ability to do it enormous harm. "If AOL's on the other side, you have a problem," as Westly explained.[6] So in addition to using AOL to extend eBay's reach, Westly hoped to stop AOL from helping—or becoming—the competition.

Unfortunately, eBay had just $750,000 to spend. ("AOL saw $750,000 as an ad buy," Westly later recalled. "On our side, people said, $750,000 is so large—it's half our budget, have you gone mad?")[7] In return for that sum, eBay got links on the AOL network for twelve months. Exclusivity, however, was not to be had at such a meager price. AOL granted eBay the right to be the sole person-to-person auction service in just two small areas and then for only ninety days.

Nonetheless, the first deal was a winner. The mass-market demographics of the two companies were a dead-on match. Moreover, eBay's executives soon learned how to fine-tune the relationship, identifying the specific screens where they wanted their links. As a result, AOL helped eBay acquire customers at bargain-basement rates.

eBay and AOL: Round Two. Hoping to build on this success, eBay went back to the table in March 1998. This time the company wanted to negotiate an arrangement that would give it greater exclusivity within a larger area of AOL. The second deal took six months to finalize. This time eBay guaranteed $12 million in payments to AOL over three years. In exchange, AOL added eBay to its keyword list—making it possible for AOL subscribers to type in "eBay" and go directly to the company's site. In addition, eBay received exclusive placement in a greater number of categories for a minimum of one year. However, Whitman noted, eBay's exclusivity had to be taken with a grain of salt, since AOL could still enter the business on its own or partner with someone else.

When eBay asked AOL for a noncompete clause in the second round of negotiations, the bid was turned down. This signaled, somewhat ominously, that AOL was pondering the possibility of entering the auction space on its own. But despite this setback, Whitman believed that the deal would help eBay achieve its goals. "It would give us more of a runway," she explained. "We knew that getting big fast was going to be important. So we said, okay, even if they enter our space, it will take them six or eight months and we'll be six or eight months ahead."

eBay and AOL: Round Three. With the first two deals, eBay got a tentative grip on its most powerful potential rival. The third deal allowed eBay to consolidate its hold. In March 1999, eBay and AOL signed an agreement that required eBay to pay AOL approximately $18 million a year for four years. In return, AOL agreed to make eBay the exclusive auction provider on all AOL properties around the world, to cobrand eBay's auctions under the eBay@AOL name, and to sell ads for the cobranded site over those four years. In addition, AOL agreed not to enter the auction market for two years. eBay had established a firm grasp on a partner that was left with little incentive to enter eBay's space.

From Whitman's perspective, aggressive, low-cost customer acquisition was still eBay's primary goal. However, she also admitted to interest in preempting an AOL attack. As she explained, "Seventy-five percent of the rationale behind the deal was the quality of the traffic, and 25 percent was to delay their entrance in this space. If we're good partners, and we provide their users the functionality, then it's a win-win." Whitman recognized that AOL could still decide to launch its own auctions. "You never can say never with AOL," she pointed out. But through its latest deal—which gave AOL margins of almost 98 percent, according to Whitman—eBay was doing its utmost to ensure that AOL would remain on the sidelines of the game.

GRIP YOUR OPPONENT

- Design joint ventures and equity deals to co-opt or deflect the competition.
- Sell your services to opponents in order to stop them from developing competing capabilities on their own.
- Partner with (potential) opponents to strengthen your position in future competition while taking current or future rivals out of the game.

Avoid Tit-for-Tat

Once a competitor starts to attack, keeping your balance is a challenge. Your gut tells you to match each and every move as you try to stop your opponent from gaining the upper hand. But as a judo strategist, the last thing you want is to get locked into a tit-for-tat struggle or a war of attrition, as tit-for-tat often becomes.[8]

Tit-for-tat is the defensive strategy your opponent wants you to adopt because it lets him set the rules of the game. The key to winning with judo strategy, by contrast, is to take the initiative. Scott Cook, the founder of Intuit, captured this insight when he described how Intuit surmounted repeated attacks by Microsoft for over a decade. Going head-to-head with Microsoft was a "low percentage game," he pointed out. "So we did end runs, we did paradigm shifts, we went after customers with tactics that our competitor didn't even know existed, rather than just copy what Microsoft did and try to blunder our way through."

Avoiding tit-for-tat involves sidestepping losing battles, but it doesn't mean failing to respond. Instead, you need to study your opponent carefully before deciding which attacks to counter, and how. "Go to school on your competitors," as Cook likes to say. Figure out what works and what's just a marketing flash in the pan. Separate the truly compelling propositions from the chaff you should ignore. Figure out the moves you can match without getting dragged out of your depth, and craft counterattacks that play to your strength when you can't afford to respond in kind.

Matching an opponent's move makes sense in certain situations—when you can match without provoking an escalatory response, for example, or in cases where you can easily neutralize your opponent's advantage and recapture the lead (often a sign that the enemy has strayed onto your home turf). But if matching means getting dragged into a war of attrition, or a pure trial of strength, then resist the temptation to fight tit-for-tat and strike back on your own terms instead.

Novell: A Cautionary Tale

In the early 1990s, Novell, the king of network operating systems, nearly wrote its obituary by embracing a strategy of tit-for-tat. Ray Noorda, Novell's CEO, was an able manager who coined the term co-opetition. Noorda liked to say that competitors were partners in growing the market as well natural combatants against complacency within the organization. But it was on Noorda's watch that a Greek tragedy, driven by the classical flaw of hubris, began to unfold.

Several companies, including Banyan and Microsoft, had targeted Novell's business by the early 1990s. A highly focused competitor, Novell had managed to stay ahead of its rivals by emphasizing technology, features, and service rather than price. Even as Microsoft slashed prices on networking products, Novell, with revenues only one-fourth of Microsoft's, held its own. As late as 1992, Novell still owned two-thirds of the market.

But then Noorda made a nearly fatal mistake. Microsoft had attacked Novell's core business, so Noorda decided to retaliate in kind, taking the battle to Microsoft's home turf. After trying unsuccessfully to merge with Lotus Development Corp., the company that created the market-leading spreadsheet program 1-2-3, Noorda went on an acquisition spree. Between 1992 and 1994, Novell bought AT&T's UNIX, WordPerfect, and Borland's QuattroPro. The goal was simple, if breathtaking: to storm the markets for operating systems and office productivity suites, attacking Microsoft head-to-head.

By late 1995, the company was in shambles. Unable to compete with Microsoft across the board, Novell lost focus, even in its core business. Forced into retreat, Novell shed the UNIX business and sold WordPerfect and QuattroPro for $116 million—two years after paying $1.4 billion for WordPerfect alone. In 1997, Novell recorded its first loss in fourteen years. It took a new CEO and a radical new strategy in the late 1990s to bring Novell back to life.

eBay: Knowing When—and How—to Fight Back

eBay's Meg Whitman avoided Noorda's mistakes. In the face of repeated attacks, Whitman kept her balance and waged an intelligent war that avoided tit-for-tat while keeping the combat on her terms. While eBay had dodged a big bullet by gripping AOL, the company couldn't preempt all of the competition. Not that Whitman didn't try: In 1998 and 1999, eBay executives met with a long list of companies, including Amazon.com, Yahoo!, and Microsoft. In none of these cases, however, were they able to replicate their success with AOL.

Yahoo! Attacks. Consequently, eBay faced its biggest scare yet in the fall of 1998. On September 24—not coincidentally the date of eBay's initial public offering—Yahoo!, the world's leading Web portal, announced plans to enter the person-to-person auction business. To make things worse, Yahoo! wasn't just attacking eBay's business; it had eBay's entire business model in its sights. While eBay charged sellers for listings and took a commission on completed sales, Yahoo!Auctions would be entirely free. "Good God, it's the best-known Internet brand in the world or second to AOL," was the reaction at eBay, Steve Westly recalled. "They have more traffic then you can imagine, and they are going to provide the service for free. It sounds pretty scary."[9]

Whitman's first move was to create a SWAT team that met every Monday, Wednesday, and Friday from 5:00 to 7:00 p.m. The team's mission was to take apart Yahoo!'s offering, examine every aspect of its business, and carefully track whether Yahoo! was gaining traction and taking share. "We crawled through their product," Whitman recalled. "We had ten people using that product, buying and selling on it every single day for months, and they issued a report every single week on what they thought was better, what they thought was not as good, and how we could potentially leapfrog them."

The first decision Whitman had to make was whether or not eBay should respond tit-for-tat by matching Yahoo! on price. "Free is usually a pretty good proposition," Whitman dryly observed. And nowhere was this truer than on the Web, where hundreds and thousands of companies, with Yahoo! in the lead, had trained consumers to expect it all—news, sports, e-mail, and chat—for free. However, as the SWAT team studied Yahoo!, it became clear that free auctions were not nearly as compelling a proposition as they had initially feared. In fact, Whitman believed, eBay's continued success was due in part to its decision to charge fees to sellers. "We felt that charging was good for the health of the marketplace," she explained, "because people wouldn't put their junk up for auction if they had to pay even twenty-five cents." At a minimum, the small charge on eBay led many sellers to rewrite item descriptions, use different pictures, and in some cases, withdraw products that didn't sell. This kept the overall quality of listings high.[10]

Consequently, Whitman and her team decided to stand firm on price. But in other areas, eBay chose to respond in kind. The reality of competition had exposed some weaknesses in eBay's service, which the company needed to fix. Yahoo!, for example, made more extensive use of pictures and organized auction categories in a more effective way. In addition, Yahoo! simplified the registration process and offered a bidding tutorial for newcomers to the auction world. eBay quickly matched these innovations.

These were simple defensive moves. In the important area of marketing, however, eBay went back on the offensive, responding aggressively to Yahoo! while choosing its own means of attack. Yahoo! was driving traffic to its auctions by advertising heavily elsewhere on its site. For eBay, trying to get equal exposure on the Web would have been an expensive and pointless exercise in tit-for-tat. Instead, Whitman did an end run around Yahoo!, choosing to intensify eBay's grassroots marketing campaign. Despite the size of the collectibles market—over $100 billion in annual sales—category-specific trade shows, focusing on anything from dolls to vintage cars, remained a major venue for buyers and sellers to meet. While trade shows were already part of eBay's outreach program, once Yahoo!Auctions launched, eBay redoubled its efforts, covering around 150 shows. "We figured Yahoo! would never do that," Whitman explained. "There was no way that they were going to have the manpower or even the interest in doing grassroots."

"Yahoo! could have been an eBay killer," Whitman said in retrospect. "They are a great company with a huge brand and enormous traffic. They execute really well, and they had a terrific product." But by avoiding tit-for-tat, eBay succeeded in staving off the Yahoo! threat.

Amazon.com Attacks. By the spring of 1999, the sense of urgency created by the Yahoo! emergency had faded, and the thrice-weekly meetings had been scaled back to once a week. But an even more serious threat was emerging. At the end of March, Jeff Bezos, the founder and CEO of Amazon.com, e-mailed the company's 8.3 million customers to announce that Amazon.com's own person-to-person auction service was now online. Nine months earlier, eBay had approached Amazon.com about working together. "It made so much sense for us not to compete directly, but to complement each other," Tom Adams believed. Bezos, however, clearly had other ideas.

In some ways, Amazon.com was a much more dangerous threat than Yahoo! According to industry pundit Stewart Alsop, Amazon.com's entry into auctions meant eBay was "dead meat."[11] Amazon.com understood e-commerce like no one else, and the company had made its auctions, in Whitman's words, "incredibly streamlined and easy to use." In addition, when it came to marketing, the giant e-tailer was prepared to go head-to-head. "Amazon was willing to throw money around to buy market share from us by negotiating expensive deals with partner sites," Jeffrey Skoll, eBay's first president, remembered thinking at the time. "If Amazon is willing to come in and spend twice what we're spending to have those guys affiliated with them, we're going to have a tough time competing against that if we want to stay a profitable Internet company."[12] To make matters worse, Amazon.com seemed to understand eBay's grassroots strategy as well. When Amazon.com started showing up at trade shows, "this could be trouble," Whitman thought.

Whitman immediately reinstated the SWAT team's thrice-weekly meetings, but after poring over Amazon.com's auctions, it returned with encouraging news. eBay had made so many recent improvements to its service that despite Amazon.com's e-commerce expertise, in most areas eBay remained even or ahead. Bezos had made security a big selling point for Amazon.com by offering free insurance, paid out on an honor system, for all sales under $250. But eBay had already introduced insurance about a month earlier. Amazon.com's listing fees were lower than eBay's (ten cents to twenty-five cents), but in the wake of eBay's experience with Yahoo!, price was no longer a major concern. Perhaps most important, eBay's Amazon.com watchers found that the new challenger had "no community whatsoever on the site," as Whitman explained. "There was not even a chat board. It was very sterile, and we knew that that was potentially a problem [for them]."

Based on the early returns, Whitman concluded that eBay did not need to make any radical changes. There was just one area where Whitman felt compelled to match Amazon.com's attack. Since most of Amazon.com's auction sellers were larger merchants, virtually all of them accepted credit cards in payment. By contrast, most of eBay's smaller sellers could accept only checks or money orders. Whitman initially planned to fill this gap by developing escrow and payment services in partnership with Accept.com. But when Bezos got wind of eBay's plans, he swooped in and snatched up the company. At that point, Whitman decided that eBay needed to have its own payment system in-house. Thirty days later, eBay acquired Billpoint, a Redwood City, California–based start-up that facilitated person-to-person credit card payments.

FairMarketPlace Attacks. By the summer of 1999, eBay had surmounted attacks by Yahoo! and Amazon.com, two of the most powerful forces in the new economy. But the company was still not out of the woods. That September, another powerful contender, the FairMarketPlace alliance, entered the ring. eBay now faced a consortium of more than 100 companies—including three of the leading Web portals—which planned to merge the auction listings on their sites. "We were nervous," Whitman admitted. "The minute that Microsoft, Lycos, and Excite decide to gang up on you, you have to be pretty concerned."

The SWAT team sprang into action once again, but within two weeks, Whitman realized that the would-be eBay killer was a dud.

The combined sites had some 70,000 items for sale—two percent of eBay's listings. Moreover, the product was weak, said Whitman, eschewing diplomacy for once. "We kept our eye on them," she conceded, "but predictably they got zero traction."

No Contest. As the decade drew to a close, eBay had done far more than survive. It had consolidated its role as the dominant player in online consumer-to-consumer auctions and strengthened its product offering in response to competitors' attacks. By one analyst's estimates, the average eBay listing generated close to three bids, while over at Yahoo!, the average item had less than a 30 percent chance of getting a single bid. Yahoo! and Amazon.com closed less than 15 percent of their auctions, compared to eBay's success rate of 65 percent. And with more than $11 million in gross merchandise sales on an average day, eBay was doing more than 25 times as much business as Yahoo!, while Amazon.com wasn't even in the contest (see figure 3–1).[13]

Whitman could easily have lost her footing in the battles that buffeted eBay in her first two years with the company. Other employees were constantly proposing ambitious and costly competitive plans. "Many people inside eBay came up with great ideas about how to compete against Yahoo! and Amazon.com that involved losing lots of money," Whitman recalled, "but I said, 'We're not thinking about doing that.'" While she always took the competition seriously, Whitman never became obsessed with countering every attack. Instead, eBay focused on its core strengths and remained centered on its strategy, avoiding battles it couldn't win while selectively responding to its opponents' best moves. By avoiding a downward competitive spiral, eBay's measured response kept it at the top of its game.

AVOID TIT-FOR-TAT

- Avoid escalatory moves that can drag you into a war of attrition or a multifront war.

- Study competitors carefully and copy only their most compelling ideas.

Figure 3-1: No Contest: eBay Trounces Yahoo! and Amazon.com, December 1999

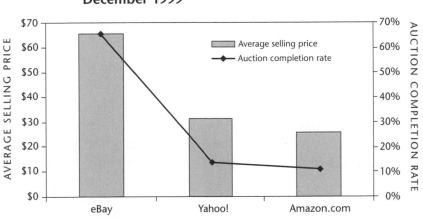

Source: Research by Prudential Securities, cited in Eliot Walsh, "eBay: Crushing the Competition," <http://www.investorlinks.com/commentaries/sectorwatch/00-01/000124-iionline-indus.html> (accessed 24 January 2001).

- Remain on the offensive, even when responding to attack, by using tactics that play to your strengths.

Push When Pulled

The two previous techniques will help you keep your balance and minimize the prospect or impact of a competitor's attack. But *Push When Pulled* goes one step further. With this technique you move to weaken your opponent's position by using his momentum to your advantage. By incorporating a competitor's products, services, or technology into your attack, you can throw her off balance and confront her with a painful choice: whether to abandon her initial strategy or to watch it fail.

Drypers and Wal-Mart: Turning Competitors into Advertisers

Many companies, in the old economy as in the new, have mastered the technique of push when pulled. A classic example comes from the diaper business, which saw an upstart named Drypers emerge in the 1980s. Drypers challenged market leader Procter & Gamble by offering a branded product at a lower price, giving consumers a choice between no-frills store brands and premium-priced Pampers. When Drypers entered the market in Texas, P&G responded with unusual vigor, bombarding the state with coupons for $2—more than twice the usual seventy-five cents. Dave Pitassi, Drypers's CEO, realized that if he did nothing, the company would suffer a "quick and ugly death."[14] But Drypers could not afford to print and distribute coupons all across the state.

Pitassi, who had just finished reading a book on judo, came up with a creative response. Rather than try to match P&G's offensive, Drypers used the bigger company's momentum to its advantage by turning its competitor's coupons into its own. The company launched a statewide advertising campaign to tell consumers that P&G coupons could be used on Drypers, and sales shot up. In a matter of weeks, Drypers had added as much as fifteen points to its market share in some stores. Within two months, the company was running at full capacity, and was cash positive for the first time. Thanks to Pitassi's inspired use of judo strategy, P&G's attack had backfired. By harnessing his competitor's momentum, Pitassi had used P&G to underwrite Drypers's promotional campaign.

While Drypers fits the classic start-up profile—scrappy and small—large companies can also push when pulled to powerful effect. Wal-Mart, for example, used this technique against Kmart in the 1980s as it battled to seize the discount retailing crown.[15] At the time, Wal-Mart's average prices were slightly lower than Kmart's, but Kmart aggressively advertised weekly specials in order to pull customers into its stores. Once there, they often bought other products as well. Wal-Mart was reluctant to match Kmart's advertising and promotional strategy because its business model relied on low costs and "Everyday Low Prices." Matching Kmart would undermine Wal-Mart's core advantage. So managers in several stores used judo strategy instead. They posted Kmart's weekly circular at the front of their stores and promised that Wal-Mart would match or beat any of the advertised deals. Since consumers knew that Wal-Mart also had better prices on most other merchandise, this created a real dilemma for Kmart. The more it advertised, the more it drove customers to its competitor.

Microsoft: Learning to "Embrace and Extend"

In the technology industry, *Push When Pulled* has come to be known, thanks to Microsoft, as "embrace and extend." While the context differs, the central intuition is the same: when facing attack, ride your competitor's momentum instead of seeking to withstand an irresistible force.

In perhaps the most famous example of this technique at work, Bill Gates announced in December 1995 that Microsoft planned to "embrace and extend" Internet technologies in order to defeat Netscape in the Web browser war. Rather than stick to homegrown technologies that would be wholly under its control, Microsoft was prepared to build on most of the Web-based technologies that Netscape had helped develop and pioneer. "We will embrace all the popular Internet protocols," Gates declared. "Anything that a significant number of publishers are using and taking advantage of, we will support. We will do some extensions to those things. This is exactly what Netscape does."[16]

At the same time, Microsoft licensed Java, the self-proclaimed "write once, run everywhere" programming language developed at Sun Microsystems. Sun had positioned Java as a direct threat to Microsoft's hegemony in PC operating systems. The idea was that a Java program, once written, could run on a wide variety of computers and computing devices, no matter what operating system was being used. At a stroke, this could cut through one of Microsoft's principal competitive advantages: the vast amounts of software that only ran on—or ran best on—Windows or Windows NT.

Microsoft had initially tried to oppose Java's spread. But as the buzz around Java increased, the company switched gears and decided to embrace it instead. By developing extensions that made Java run faster on Windows, Microsoft tried to redirect Sun's momentum to its advantage and succeeded in significantly weakening the Java threat. Sun eventually sued, and after several years of costly litigation, the two companies reached a settlement in January 2001, without any admission of wrongdoing on Microsoft's part.

Finally, as part of its commitment to "embrace and extend" the Internet, Microsoft walked away from the nearly $1 billion it had invested in a proprietary online service called Microsoft Network (MSN) and recast it as a free Web-based service. After spending years to build a proprietary dial-up network that girdled the globe, Microsoft wrote off most of its investment and refocused on channeling the Internet's momentum to its advantage.[17] In the process, the company transformed what had been a no-win proposition into one of the Internet's most visited sites.

Mastering Ukemi

Microsoft's decision to kill the original MSN illustrates a particular aspect of *Push When Pulled* that we call business *ukemi*. In judo, *ukemi* refers to the technique involved in falling safely and with minimal loss of advantage in order to return more effectively to the fight. *Ukemi* is the first thing that new students of judo learn, and it is a critical discipline in judo strategy as well. No matter how skilled you are as a strategist, you are unlikely to win every skirmish. But losing a battle need not lead to losing the war. By beating a strategic retreat, you can conserve your resources and regroup in better position for the confrontations ahead. This is particularly important when a competitor strikes with such force that no amount of tweaking or adjusting will get you back in the game. (In this sense, *ukemi* might also be considered as a special case of our dictum to avoid tit-for-tat.)

Charles Schwab. America's largest discount broker, Charles Schwab, absorbed this lesson in the late 1990s when it decided to integrate eSchwab, its original entry in the Internet brokerage market, into its core business. While Schwab had moved quickly to embrace the Internet, the company's initial strategy had been to keep Internet trading and its higher-priced core discount brokerage business apart. Customers who used eSchwab were required to open a separate account, and in order to have access to Schwab branches or phone representatives, they had to pay additional fees.

By 1997, this approach was under heavy attack from competitors, such as E*TRADE, that offered similar services at lower prices, forcing Schwab executives to face a difficult choice. They could allow Internet customers full access to Schwab's services, sacrificing

$125 million in revenues as a result, or they could do nothing and watch Schwab's share of the online trading market erode. The Schwab team opted for the first alternative, and the pain was deep. As co-CEO David Pottruck recalled, "We had huge unit growth, but the compression on prices, revenues, and profits hammered our stock, which went down by 25 percent at a time when everybody in the industry's stocks were up by 25 percent. In the first six months of 1998, this did not look like a brilliant strategy." But the decision paid off in the long run. In the second half of the year, "our asset growth kicked in," Pottruck said with a smile. "And we started seeing elasticity of trading beyond our wildest expectations. Our stock started to climb, and in January of 1999 we reached a new milestone, passing Merrill Lynch on market capitalization."

Ukemi can be a difficult skill to learn. The decision to fold a position often meets with resistance from those within the company who have the most to lose. But careful preparation can minimize the pain associated with taking a fall. "We're nuts about communicating strategy all around the company," said Dan Leemon, Schwab's chief strategy officer, in explaining how Schwab managed to accomplish its transition without widespread discontent or losing any of its senior staff.[18]

Ryanair. Larger companies, of course, have both the organizational resources and the deep pockets that are often necessary to absorb a temporary loss. But while harder to implement, *ukemi* can be even more critical for smaller firms facing determined opponents, as the history of Dublin-based Ryanair shows. Cathal and Declan Ryan started Ryanair with a single forty-four-seat turboprop plane in 1986. The brothers' strategy was to build a beachhead by offering better service and simplified pricing on the London–Dublin route. But this plan soon came to an end when British Airways and Aer Lingus launched a full-scale price war, dropping fares by 20 percent.[19] By 1991, facing mounting losses, Ryanair was on the verge of bankruptcy.

That's when the company's founders decided they had to give up the struggle and find another strategy. They dropped the effort to match British Airways and Aer Lingus on service and made price the focus of their offering. In a Herculean effort, all unnecessary expenses were eliminated, including in-flight food (not even peanuts were served) and pens for headquarters staff (employees were asked to bring in their own).[20] With its new cost and fare structure, Ryanair returned to profitability in 1992 and remained there throughout the 1990s. The Ryan brothers had learned the same lesson as David Pottruck and Bill Gates: Rather than continue to fight a losing battle, it is better to fall of your own accord and rebuild momentum.

PUSH WHEN PULLED

- Find ways that allow you to use your competitor's moves to your advantage.

- Take the force out of your competitor's attack by building on his products, services, and technology, if you can.

- Don't fight losing battles: conserve your energies, fold your position, and return to the fight.

4

Leverage

Leverage Your Opponent's Assets, Partners, and Competitors

Give me a lever long enough and a place to stand, and I will move the earth.

—Archimedes

DEPLOYED SKILLFULLY in concert, movement and balance allow you to face-off against stronger rivals and gain a lead. By mastering movement, you can build a strong initial position and get ahead of competitors before they respond. The techniques of balance, in turn, allow you to engage bigger or stronger rivals without getting knocked down. Your aim, in the process, is to weaken your opponents' position while strengthening your own.

In some cases, movement and balance will be enough to build and consolidate an insurmountable lead. In most cases, however, you will need leverage to score a win. As an old judo master said, "That one does not fall in a bout means that one is not beaten."[1] It doesn't mean that you've won. By avoiding a fall, you've hung on for another round or another day—or another few seconds in an actual match. But in order to win, you need to take your opponent to the mat. And that's where leverage comes into play.

Leverage in Judo

Leverage follows closely upon balance—or more precisely, the loss of balance—in the practice of judo. Upsetting your opponent's balance

65

is not a goal in itself; it's a preliminary to the throw. In judo, each technique has three stages: *kuzushi*, breaking a competitor's balance; *tsukuri*, getting into position; and *kake*, the actual attack. Gripping and learning to push when pulled are the techniques that will get you through stages one and two. Finding leverage, or a pivot around which you can maneuver your opponent, is what *kake* is all about.

Jigoro Kano, the founder of judo, liked to use dramatic examples to show how the relationship between balance and leverage works. "Suppose a man is standing in front of me," these verbal demonstrations usually began:

> If at the moment he leans forward, I apply my arm to his back and quickly slip my hip in front of his, my hip becomes a fulcrum. Then I can throw him flat on the ground by a slight twist of my hip, or a pull of his arm...even if he is two or three times as heavy as I.
>
> Or suppose that my opponent leans forward a bit and pushes me with one hand. This puts him off balance. If I grab him by the upper sleeve of his outstretched arm, pivot so that my back is close to his chest, clamp my free hand on his shoulder and suddenly bend over, he will go flying over my head.[2]

With these examples, Kano was illustrating the principle that Archimedes articulated more than 2,000 years before: Given the right lever and fulcrum, anyone or anything—no matter how large—can be moved. Leverage, of course, is not the only possible method of attack. Using brute strength alone, a naturally powerful competitor may be able to force an opponent down. But judo rejects sheer power as an unreliable and inefficient tool. A competitor who relies only on his strength will be helpless the first time he confronts an opponent who tops him in size. In addition, he is easily outmaneuvered by an opponent who has mastered the concepts of push when pulled and leveraged attack.

Leverage embodies the fundamental principle behind judo: maximum efficiency with minimum effort—or as Kano put it, "the highest or most efficient use of mental as well as physical energy, directed to the accomplishment of a certain definite purpose or aim."[3] This makes it a highly effective technique, particularly for the relatively weak, but also for the strong.

Leverage in Judo Strategy

In moving from judo to judo strategy, we focus on three different ways that you can apply leverage. In each case, the object is the same: to use a competitor's strength to your advantage. In judo, your opponent's body becomes a lever in your hands. In judo strategy, a competitor's assets, partners, and rivals can all play a similar role.

By *Leveraging Your Opponent's Assets*, you can convert a competitor's strength into weakness. The idea is simple: Launch an assault that transforms a competitor's assets into hostages or handicaps that make it difficult for him to respond. By exercising leverage, you can make it painful—sometimes nearly impossible—for even a stronger opponent to counter your attack.

Similarly, by *Leveraging Your Opponent's Partners*, you can convert an opponent's allies into brakes on his ability to react. Many powerful competitors have built up networks of suppliers, distributors, and complementors who are a significant source of strength. But by exploiting differences among them, you can turn a rival's partners into false friends. Using the tactic of divide and conquer, sow dissension within the opposing camp. Set old allies at odds by creating situations where their interests are no longer aligned. You may have to look carefully, but on close inspection, even the most solid looking bloc is likely to have a fissure you can exploit.

Finally, in addition to assets and partners, most highly successful companies have accumulated plenty of competitors as well. And here's where the third potential source of leverage lies. By turning the ability to work with your opponent's competitors into a source of strategic advantage, you can make it doubly difficult for a rival to respond to your moves. Even if your opponent has enough flexibility to try to follow your lead, convincing his competitors to cooperate will be an uphill climb. This makes *Leveraging Your Opponent's Competitors* a particularly potent threat.

A single principle lies behind all of these techniques: By creating a conflict for your opponent, you can prevent him from countering your attack—not because competitors are foolish or blind, but because leverage is designed to put them in a very real bind.

While the underlying inspiration is always the same, leverage can take an almost infinitely varied number of forms. In the stories below, we provide only the beginning of a list that we hope will start you thinking creatively about the forms of leverage that lie within your grasp.

Finding leverage is not a mechanical exercise. Becoming a master of leverage demands the ability to think outside the box. In other words, as a judo strategist, you need to ferret out potential weaknesses where others see strength. And where others see threats, you need to identify opportunities.

Leverage Your Opponent's Assets

It may sound trite, but a company's greatest assets can often become its greatest liabilities. Whether intangible, like brand names and intellectual property, or tangible, like property and plant, "assets collect risks around them in one form or another," as Michael Dell, Dell Computer's visionary chairman and CEO, once said.[4] Anything that represents a significant investment can become a barrier to change. And exploiting these barriers will help you find the leverage you need to win. In accumulating assets, a company ties its success to a certain way of doing business. It chooses not only what it will, but also what it will not, do. And that's fine—until the rules of competition change. Then the asset of years past may turn out to be less of a blessing than a curse.[5]

As a judo strategist, your task is to find moves that transfer your opponents' assets to the other side of the ledger, creating sources of weakness out of their strengths. This can mean attacking long-established revenue streams, challenging your competitors to destroy valuable assets, or creating new business models that turn their assets into strategic liabilities. Take, for example, an opponent's economies of scope. Investments in complementary businesses can create important synergies. But a judo strategist sees their downside, too. Coke had greater leverage selling to McDonald's when Pepsi owned Kentucky Fried Chicken and Taco Bell. In the same spirit, Nortel had an advantage in selling to telephone companies when its competitor Lucent was still part of AT&T.[6]

Depending on the market and the opponent you face, your leverage may take a different form, but your basic goal should remain the same: to use the existence of your opponents' assets to make it painful or even impossible for them to counter your attack.

Turning Assets into Hostages

Turning a competitor's assets into hostages can be a win-win situation—for the attacker, that is. By carefully crafting your attack, you can force your opponent to choose between two options: destroying his own assets or failing to respond. In essence, the assets that you target become dependent on your opponent's good behavior. Once he decides to match your attack, they disappear.

Charles Schwab. One variation on this technique uses a larger opponent's customer base to cut him down to size. Owning a large share of the market is, of course, one of the ultimate measures of success. Yet by the same token, the market leader also has a great deal to lose. Fidelity Investments learned this lesson the hard way in the early 1990s, when Charles Schwab saw an opportunity for leverage in the market for individual retirement accounts (IRAs).

The IRA market was one Fidelity clearly dominated. In early 1992, the Boston-based powerhouse was opening new IRAs at a rate of 400,000 per year, and by Schwab estimates, generating around $45 million in annual fees.[7] "They were at least five times our size," said David Pottruck, who later became Schwab's co-CEO. But where others might have seen weakness, the Schwab team saw an opportunity to turn Fidelity's strength to its advantage. A senior Schwab executive, Jeff Lyons, came to Pottruck one day with a radical idea: to waive all fees on IRAs with more than $10,000 in assets. (At the time, customers were charged $22 per year.) "Fidelity and Merrill Lynch and most of the other firms that are much bigger than us have much bigger IRA programs than we do," Lyons argued. "So they will all find it very difficult to cut their fees. If we move our IRA fee to zero, we can get huge incremental assets. And as an added bonus, by removing the fee, we also create a halo over the entire Schwab brand and offerings."[8]

This proposal set off a lively internal debate. Cutting IRA fees would be an expensive decision, eliminating $9 million from the bottom line at a time when Schwab's annual income was around $80 million. But the team calculated that Schwab could break even on the move if it gathered an additional $2 billion in assets. (More assets meant more trades and more commissions, which would make up for the loss of annual fees.) "Anything above that would be gravy," Pottruck explained. Equally important, the team believed that this was a move that Fidelity, with its much larger customer base, would be reluctant to match. "And if they did," Pottruck recalled thinking, "it would cost them a lot of money, which also would be good for us. So, the least pain for us, the most pain for them."

Schwab eliminated its fees for IRAs above $10,000 in April 1992, and the company picked up the extra $2 billion in assets it needed within a year. "Free is the magic number in the consumer business," Pottruck observed:

> People hate fees. It's sort of irrational. I remember going to a cock-tail party and a client said to me, "I just brought my mother's IRA to Schwab, and it's $88,000 and the reason I did it was because you got rid of that fee." I said, "Let me understand. You mean to tell me that $22, more or less, was a reason to have her IRA here or not have her IRA here?" And he said, "Yeah." It's not about economics. It's about emotion.

Fidelity was struggling with another emotion as it watched Schwab surge ahead: envy, mixed with fear. Whatever it did, in the short term at least, Fidelity was bound to lose. If it matched Schwab's move, the company would wipe out $45 million in revenue in one stroke. But if Fidelity failed to respond, Schwab could soon take the lead. After nearly eight months, Fidelity finally followed Schwab's example, eliminating fees on IRAs with at least $5,000. But by then Schwab had already achieved its goals. By leveraging Fidelity's lead, Schwab had gained market share, built a profitable business, and slashed its competitor's profitability, all in one move.

Sega. In entering the U.S. video game market, Sega used a similar form of leverage to power itself to the top. At the end of the 1980s, Nintendo dominated the market, with 80 percent share.[9] Twenty million households—one in five—owned Nintendo systems, and Nintendo had sold more than 101 million copies of its chart-topping games.[10] Sega held about 7 percent of the market, and with $680 million in worldwide revenues in 1990, it remained roughly one-third Nintendo's size.[11] Yet three years later, Sega had brought the giant down to earth. The two companies were in a dead heat in the U.S. home video game market, which had grown to $6 billion by 1993.[12]

In part, Sega owed its success to the fact that it was first to market with faster, sixteen-bit machines. As other analysts have pointed out, this move used leverage to freeze Nintendo in place.[13] Nintendo, which dominated the market for eight-bit video game systems, was reluctant to cannibalize its existing revenue base. As a result, it took two years to match Sega's move. But Sega was not just about hardware. Its strategy for software was a second and equally important part of its attack. Hot games, after all, were what made consumers buy machines.

Nintendo had built its reputation by providing wholesome family entertainment, targeting kids not yet in their teens. The Nintendo brand had a high comfort factor for parents, who typically supervised purchases for the under-thirteen group. "In a world full of dangers, you can trust us" was Nintendo's implicit promise.

When Sega entered the market, it decided to change the rules of the game. Rather than follow Nintendo and cultivate a family-friendly image, it targeted an older, hipper audience. In the process, it challenged Nintendo to follow suit and destroy its brand equity— or to do nothing and lose. While Sega's most famous character was Sonic, a hyperactive hedgehog, the company also licensed titles that contained generous doses of sex and violence, such as Mortal Kombat, which invited players to rip out their opponents' hearts.

Nintendo's initial response was to stick to its base. When the company licensed its own version of Mortal Kombat, which was based on a popular arcade game, it required the developers to clean up much of the gore. (In one example, a character transformed his enemy into ice cubes rather than tear out his spine.) Nintendo's stand may have given the company the moral high ground, but customers used their dollars to vote for Sega. In its first full year on the market, Sega's version of Mortal Kombat outsold Nintendo's two-to-one.[14] (See figure 4–1.)

Nintendo reversed course in 1994, issuing its own unsanitized Mortal Kombat and unveiling an edgy new advertising campaign. By then, however, it was too late to undo much of the damage that Sega had done. Even senior executives at Nintendo admitted that the days of 80 percent market share would never return.[15]

Figure 4-1:   Mortal Combat: Sega versus Nintendo

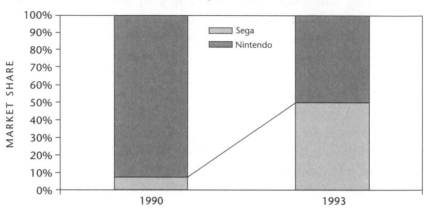

Source: Data from Nikhil Hutheesing, "Games Companies Play," *Forbes,* 25 October 1993.

Turning Assets into Handicaps

In the preceding examples, Schwab and Sega forced their rivals to cannibalize their assets in order to compete. Once their opponents took that step—and in both cases, it took a while—the playing field was more or less level. But in other cases, leverage can do more than impose a one-time hit. It can also make it difficult for an opponent to compete effectively even after he's made the decision to match an attack.

Southwest Airlines. Herb Kelleher, the cofounder and CEO of Southwest Airlines, has spun this lesson into gold over the past thirty years. Since its inaugural flight in 1971, Southwest has grown from a three-jet upstart into the fourth largest carrier in the United States. But nothing could have seemed more improbable when Southwest got its start. The airline business is one of the most capital-intensive industries in the country, an environment that makes it difficult for challengers to do well. Moreover, the major carriers had already snapped up a critical set of assets: large banks of landing slots at big-city airports coast-to-coast.

Southwest's competitors, such as American Airlines, used these landing rights as the basis of hub-and-spoke systems that allowed them to maximize their reach. Hundreds of smaller aircraft converged on a hub like Dallas every day, feeding traffic into high-margin, long-haul flights. This system could be expensive to operate, as it required extensive coordination, large terminals for transferring passengers, and often a highly heterogeneous fleet, ranging from tiny puddle-jumpers to Boeing 747's. But the hub system paid off by allowing each of the major carriers to dominate traffic within a region and exercise significant control over fares. In addition, it protected the incumbents' position by ensuring that barriers to entry remained relatively high.

Nonetheless, early in its history, Southwest found a way to turn its opponents assets' to its advantage. Southwest's strategy focused on offering high-frequency, short-haul, point-to-point flights at the lowest prices around. Virtually everything the company did was aimed at promoting efficiency and cutting costs. To reduce airport fees, Southwest operated out of secondary airports like Love Field and Midway, leaving rivals to fight it out at Dallas/Fort Worth and Chicago's O'Hare. Southwest flew an all-737 fleet to save on training and parts. There was no wait for connecting flights or for passengers to find their assigned seats (it was first-come, first-serve) or for meals to be loaded (only peanuts were served). As a result, Southwest typically turned a plane around in twenty minutes—half the industry average—and maximized the time that planes spent in the air generating revenue. This made it possible for Southwest to keep fares extremely low—50 percent to 60 percent below competitors' rates, on average, for unrestricted fares—and still become the country's most profitable airline.

The major carriers might try to match Southwest's rates on selected routes, but only at the cost of cannibalizing their own sales. Moreover, Southwest's strategy ensured that even if the major carriers were willing to make this sacrifice, they would be at a permanent disadvantage when competing head-to-head. If Southwest and its larger competitors charged the same fares, the majors could never match Southwest's profitability due to the cost of maintaining the assets—the terminals, the complex reservation systems, and the mixed fleets—that had originally underwritten their strength.

Some of Southwest's opponents did take up the challenge of trying to outdo the master at his game. As Herb Kelleher often groused, "I say to people: 'Hey, they don't just launch low prices against us;

they launch whole business divisions.' What do you think United Shuttle, MetroJet, and Delta Express are all about?"[16] But Southwest's leverage ensured that any counterattack would be difficult, costly, time-consuming, and in the end, unlikely to succeed.

Freeserve. While the Southwest story has become familiar, fewer people have heard of Freeserve, a once-unknown challenger that took a similar path to replace AOL Europe as the leading Internet service provider (ISP) in the United Kingdom. By the fall of 1998, AOL Europe, a joint venture between America Online and German media group Bertelsmann, was solidly established as the country's largest ISP.[17] Including customers of its CompuServe subsidiary, which ran second to AOL UK, AOL Europe had signed up roughly 800,000 subscribers. After that, the competition quickly trailed off. Just as it had in the United States, AOL seemed to have locked up the British market.

Yet three months after launching service in September 1998, Freeserve knocked AOL UK from its perch. By January 1999, Freeserve had 1 million customers, and 8,000 new subscribers were signing up every day. Five months later, with 1.3 million accounts, Freeserve was more than twice the size of AOL UK. (See figure 4–2.) The reason behind Freeserve's success was hardly secret. While most AOL UK subscribers paid around $29 a month for unlimited Internet access, Freeserve offered the same service for free. The company had partnered with Energis, a British telecommunications carrier, to split the fee that Energis received from British Telecom each time it terminated a call. By encouraging increased Internet use, Freeserve would drive up Energis's revenues, and both partners would win.

The simplicity of the model led to a flood of copycat services, launched by sponsors ranging from Tesco, Barclays, and Virgin to Arsenal, a popular soccer team. British Telecom even introduced a free service in February 1999. But not AOL UK. For nearly ten months, the company seemed paralyzed as Freeserve took the market by storm.

In public, at least, AOL tried to shrug off the competition. "It's like Tiffany's saying it's worried about Wal-Mart," AOL president Bob Pittman said of free services in the United States.[18] But behind the bluster, AOL UK found itself in a bind. The company was losing

Figure 4-2:   Freeserve Blows by AOL UK

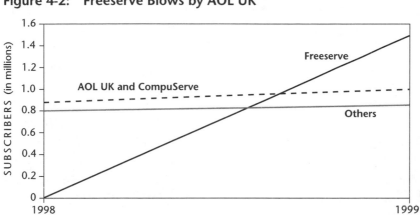

Source: Authors' estimates; Neal Boudette and Stephanie Gruner, "AOL Launches a Fresh Campaign in Europe," *Wall Street Journal*, 1 October 1999.

market share to Freeserve at an unprecedented rate. But Freeserve's leverage made it doubly difficult for AOL UK to respond with a free service of its own. As the market leader, AOL UK had a great deal to lose. Taking monthly fees down to zero could mean sacrificing more than $150 million in revenue per year. And in the short term, at least, call-based revenues were unlikely to make up this loss. Freeserve, after all, got only 10 percent of the cost of each telephone call, or around $0.17 for each hour spent online.

But this wasn't the full extent of the problem. With the Freeserve challenge, AOL UK faced not only the loss of revenue, it faced the loss of its competitive advantages as well. AOL UK owed much of its success to investments made in the past—in its marketing machine, in customer service, and in its identification as a price-competitive but premium brand. If it chose to match Freeserve, all of these assets would dimish, rather than enhance, its ability to compete. When it came to marketing, for example, AOL UK was clearly at a disadvantage compared to Freeserve, which was a unit of Dixons, the largest retailer of consumer electronics in the U.K. Every customer who bought a computer at Dixons received a free Freeserve CD. With Dixons accounting for 60 percent of the country's sales of PCs, Freeserve could reach an enormous audience at negligible cost. Since

Freeserve's other costs were also low and it planned to make money from advertising and e-commerce, Freeserve could credibly claim to be on the path to breakeven. AOL UK, by contrast, had to advertise heavily and pay partners to distribute its CDs. This made it even harder to contemplate giving up subscriber fees, which made up the lion's share of AOL's sales in Europe.

After months of debate, AOL UK met Freeserve halfway by cutting monthly fees by 45 percent in May 1999. Three months later, it finally launched a free service under a fighting brand, a strategy that we discuss in chapter 8. But by then, a great deal of damage had already been done. Freeserve went public with a market value of $2.4 billion in July 1999. Eighteen months later, despite AOL's counterattack, Freeserve remained the United Kingdom's number one ISP.

eToys: A Cautionary Tale

While leverage can be an extremely powerful tool, it's important to remember that success is never guaranteed. In laying out the principles of judo strategy, we've focused on the concepts that drive various techniques. But identifying the right move is only half the battle. When it comes to competing with stronger opponents, execution remains key. Despite the best-laid plans, any number of tactical errors can trip up a skilled judo strategist.

The fate of eToys, the onetime leader in the online toy market, illustrates this lesson. eToys's strategy deftly leveraged the business models of brick-and-mortar giants, such as industry leaders Wal-Mart and Toys "R" Us. In addition, eToys identified and exploited leverage against fellow e-tailer Amazon.com, although to a lesser extent. Ultimately, however, critical errors in execution helped bring the company down.

In founding eToys, Toby Lenk began with the classic mind-set of judo strategy. "When I conceived this business plan four and a half years ago at home at 2 a.m.," he recalled in late 2000, "I said, 'Rule No. 1: Don't go head-to-head with Wal-Mart.'"[19] Wal-Mart and Toys "R" Us had grown to dominate the category by focusing on moving the largest possible number of toys at the lowest possible price. As a result, their inventory was heavily weighted toward high-volume, mass-market toys, and operating costs were cut to the bone. These had proven to be important advantages within the constraints of the brick-and-mortar world. But Lenk's strategy turned them into liabilities on the Web. Rather than compete on price, eToys made selection and service its key selling points. The company appealed to parents by carrying a wide range of specialty toys from smaller manufacturers as well as big-name products like Barbie. In addition, it sought to take the pain out of the toy buying process by providing customers with a wealth of product information while eliminating a trip to the store.

Established competitors such as Toys "R" Us found it difficult to counter these moves. In the brick-and-mortar world, shelf space was limited, leaving little room for specialty toys. Hiring and training employees to handle specialty products, which typically required more hand-selling, was also much more expensive and time-consuming than providing the same services on the Web. Moreover, Toys "R" Us, which had more than $4 billion tied up in stores nationwide, faced a common but no less painful dilemma when it came to operating online. As it moved onto the Internet, the company faced the risk of cannibalizing in-store sales—a particularly costly move since, by one estimate, each store visit typically resulted in $38 in unplanned purchases.[20]

By contrast, Internet-only competitors, such as Amazon.com, were free of these constraints. Moreover, Amazon.com and eToys benefited from the same long-run economics: By Lenk's calculations, a virtual retailer could support $750 million in sales by spending $50 million to $80 million on logistics and distribution, while a land-based retailer required at least $500 million in real estate, distribution centers, and working capital to generate the same volume of sales. However, eToys's management believed that they had at least one significant source of leverage against Amazon.com: the larger company's strategy of offering Earth's Biggest Selection™. By focusing on children's products, eToys planned to align itself with its customers' interests in ways that Amazon.com, with its emphasis on scale and scope economies, would find hard to match.

Some of eToys's advantages were relatively short-lived: Amazon.com ultimately patched its software after learning that searching for "toys" on its site turned up references to "sex toys." But eToys's focus on a single market also had more durable benefits for parents. eToys, for example, chose not to offer shortcuts, such as one-click ordering, to cut down on unauthorized ordering by children. The company took its name off its boxes—a potentially important platform for building brand awareness—in order to help keep gifts a surprise. Even the packaging eToys used was kid-friendly: Made of corn starch, it was harmless when ingested.

This ability to focus gave eToys the opportunity to build a solid business despite competition from both online and brick-and-mortar giants. And the company performed strongly in its first three years. In the 1999 holiday season, eToys outsold Toysrus.com by more than two-to-one and stayed ahead of Amazon.com to remain the biggest seller of children's products online. In addition, when it came to service and delivery, eToys outperformed much of the competition, including Toysrus.com, which later paid a $350,000 fine to settle charges related to shipping delays brought by the Federal Trade Commission.

But eToys had troubles, too. In order to expand quickly, the company outsourced around half of its fulfillment operations in the fall of 1999, only to see its partner's logistics systems melt down in the face of unanticipated demand. In the month leading up to Christmas, eToys had to send 200 people to its outsourcer's fulfillment center to clean up the mess, a mishap that proved disastrous for the cash-constrained start-up. eToys lost credibility with customers, and its revenue growth fell sharply over the following year. Equally important, the company lost credibility with Wall Street. The logistics problems dramatically raised eToys's expenses just as investors were starting to look for profits.

To avoid future delivery problems, eToys invested heavily in building its own automated distribution center. Yet unlike Amazon, which had raised billions of dollars at the height of the market to pursue a similar strategy, eToys had failed to raise additional capital when its market capitalization topped $8 billion in the fall of 1999. As a result, the company found itself scrambling for money in the wake of a market downturn. By the end of 2000, eToys shares, which had once climbed as high as $86, were trading at around $0.20, and the company was down to its last three months' worth of cash. In February 2001, eToys filed for bankruptcy and announced that it would shut down its site. Lenk's venture had begun with a well-crafted strategy and a first-class product. But in the end, eToys's stumbles in a critical holiday season, combined with the failure to raise enough funding for the race to break even, had made it impossible for the company to succeed.

LEVERAGE YOUR OPPONENT'S ASSETS

- Turn assets into hostages by forcing your opponents to cannibalize their own strengths in order to respond to your attack.

- Turn assets into handicaps that make it difficult for your opponents to compete, even after cannibalization has taken place.

- Execute, execute, execute—leverage is necessary but not sufficient to win.

Leverage Your Opponent's Partners

A strong network of partnerships is often critical to a competitor's success. In years past, many a company sought to control its environment by bringing a vast array of activities in-house. Since the late 1980s, however, the importance of focusing on your core competence has become a common refrain. This makes partners more important than ever in the struggle to build and maintain competitive advantage.

Partners today fill a wide range of roles. Suppliers sell you components, contract manufacturers provide your factories, distributors extend the reach of your sales force, and marketing partners burnish your brand. But direct relationships like these are not the end of the story. Arm's-length partners can also have an impact on a company's prospects. Complementors, for example, provide goods and services that increase the value of your products—like software for computers—and drive up demand. You may not deal directly with your complementors, but odds are that you rely on their existence just the same.[21]

Partners clearly bring many benefits to the table. They can help save money, management attention, and time, enabling companies to scale much faster and further than their own resources would allow. But like all legacies, partnerships can also become confining, reinforcing established strategies and blocking change. As a judo strategist, your job is to identify relationships that can be turned to a competitor's disadvantage. Your competitor's partners may initially look like your enemies, but they can become your allies as well. With the right strategy, you can use them to limit your opponent's ability to compete.

Sony: Out-Partnering Competitors

In the second half of the 1990s, Sony took this route to race ahead of both Nintendo and Sega in the home video game market. The two market leaders kept partners on a tight leash, charging steep royalties and allowing only a limited number of independent developers to produce games for their machines. In addition to allowing Nintendo and Sega to control game quality, this approach ensured that they would be able to keep a healthy share of the games market for themselves. Hit games did more than drive sales of consoles; they were a gold mine in their own right. In twelve years, Nintendo sold 1 billion games, while Sega sold 4.5 million copies of a single title—Sonic the Hedgehog—in one year alone.[22]

When introducing PlayStation, Sony leveraged this strategy by holding the market leaders hostage to their own success. Rather than try to dominate game developers, Sony's approach was to give them free rein. The company made PlayStation development tools widely available and cut licensing fees in order to encourage potential partners to sign up. As a result, by the spring of 1996, 250 PlayStation games had been released, and Sony had captured 40 percent of the market, selling 5 million consoles in the first eighteen months.[23] Three years later, consumers could choose from nearly 3,000 PlayStation titles—more than ten times the number available for Nintendo 64—and Sony had sold more than 50 million PlayStations, generating over $1 billion in profit in a single year.[24]

Pepsi-Cola: Finding the Weak Link

While Sony found leverage in its competitors' domination of their partners, Charles Guth leveraged his opponent's dependence on its partners. By adopting this strategy, Guth succeeded in transforming Pepsi-Cola from "a mere shell of a corporation" into a household name.[25] Pepsi-Cola got its start in the 1890s, around the same time as Coca-Cola. Forty years later, however, when Guth bought Pepsi, the companies' paths had sharply diverged. Coke was considered a national monopoly, while Pepsi had recently emerged from bankruptcy for the second time. According to business historian Richard Tedlow, Pepsi-Cola "simply was not in the traffic" following World War I. Rivals like Canada Dry posed a much stronger challenge to Coke, and Pepsi's situation was so bleak that Guth tried unsuccessfully to sell the company to Coca-Cola in 1933.

Upon being rebuffed, Guth came up with the strategy that catapulted Pepsi to success. At the time, Coke cost five cents for a six-and-one-half-ounce bottle. Guth decided to match Coke's price—but offer consumers twice as much. In the words of the once-ubiquitous jingle:

Pepsi-Cola hits the spot.
Twelve full ounces, that's a lot.
Twice as much for a nickel too.
Pepsi-Cola is the drink for you.

Depression-era consumers responded quickly to Pepsi's message, returning the company to profitability within three years. By the end of the decade, Pepsi had grabbed the number two position in the U.S. soft drink market, and the twelve-ounce bottle accounted for a quarter of all carbonated beverage sales, nearly four times its share in 1935.[26]

Despite this evidence, it took Coke *twenty-two years* to launch a larger bottle. In large part, this delay was the work of Robert Woodruff, Coke's autocratic CEO, who had a stubborn attachment to the hobble-skirted bottle that had become an international icon. But sentiment was not the only obstacle in Coca-Cola's way. A key set of partners—the company's bottlers—also factored into the company's resistance to change. Coke's network of bottlers was one of its greatest assets. By the 1930s, well over 1,000 plants were bottling Coke, thanks to an army of franchised bottlers who devoted their entrepreneurial energy—not to mention their capital—to making Coke the most widely available soft drink in the country. However, once Pepsi launched its assault, it became clear that the bottlers could be a significant handicap as well.

Coke's bottlers had invested millions of dollars in six-and-one-half-ounce bottles and associated equipment. Matching Pepsi's strategy would have meant writing off much of that investment.[27] In addition, the flexibility of Coke's bottler network turned out to be a disadvantage when it came to meeting an attack. Coordinating the roll-out of a new bottle to hundreds of independent businesses would have been a gargantuan task. Moreover, the quality of the bottlers was uneven. Some were reaping fortunes, while others were treading water. Coca-Cola wanted to keep all of its partners afloat, making it even more difficult to respond to Pepsi's thrust. It was not until 1955 that the company introduced the ten-ounce "King Size" and the twenty-six-ounce "Family Size" bottles. And by then, Pepsi was solidly established nationwide.

Dell Computer: Learning to Divide and Conquer

A half-century later, Michael Dell used a variant of this strategy to beat the leaders of the personal computer industry: a mighty line-up that included Compaq, Hewlett-Packard, and IBM. A gifted strategist, Dell intuitively thinks in judo strategy terms, as his description of his philosophy of competition reveals:

> Understanding the profit pool of your industry—where your competitors really make money—can open your eyes to new opportunities. Think of a competitor that has high market share and is very profitable in a specific part of the market. Then think about how compelling it would be to exploit that strength as a weakness. Your competitor will most likely not be able to respond to an aggressive attack without significantly reducing its profit. *We call that playing judo with the competition.*[28]

"Direct from Dell," the company's biggest innovation, was judo strategy at its best. Dell took one of the biggest strengths of rivals such as Compaq—their powerful distribution networks—and used it to bring the competition down. Compaq relied on an enormous number of wholesalers, retailers, and value-added resellers to make its products available around the world. These partners essentially acted as Compaq's sales force, supplementing its resources and extending its reach.

But Dell understood that Compaq's distribution network could be a burden, too. It added cost and time to the selling process and, perhaps even more important, relied on highly imperfect information. Compaq had to guess what customers would want and build computers in advance of sales. Then it moved inventory to its channel partners and hoped that its products would be sold before they became obsolete. In an industry where the prices of materials and finished goods dropped roughly 1 percent each week, guessing wrong carried a high cost.

Dell did things differently. The company sold each PC before it was built. That meant no guessing, very little inventory, and much lower cost of goods. As Dell explained, "Let's say that Dell has eight days of inventory. Compare that to an indirect competitor who has twenty-five days of inventory with another thirty in their distribution channel. That's a difference of forty-seven days, and in forty-seven days, the cost of materials will decline about 6 percent."[29]

Moreover, Dell was able to upsell many customers on features by building to order and giving people the chance to customize their PCs. While Dell was often pigeonholed as a low-cost, low-price player, its average selling price was higher than that of many of its competitors. As a result, Dell took share from its competitors throughout the 1990s while boasting higher profitability at the same time. By the end of the decade, the company was the number one seller of personal computers in the United States, and Michael Dell had become one of the richest individuals in the world.

So why didn't Compaq follow where Dell had led? Faced with a better business model, shouldn't the industry leader be able to replicate its challenger's success? In this case, thanks to Dell's leverage, the answer was no. Compaq had three choices, and in the short term, at least, all of them were bad. First, the company could stick to what it was doing—which clearly wasn't going to work. Second, it could copy Dell, but that would mean completely reconfiguring its engineering, manufacturing, sales, and marketing organization. And third, it could try to do both at once, selling directly to customers and through distributors at the same time. But this alternative involved a double risk. Distributors who felt betrayed were likely to put less effort into selling for Compaq, while the costs of maintaining two different models would weigh the direct sales operation down.

Compaq opted for the third course and discovered, not surprisingly, that it is hard to make a hybrid strategy work. After introducing its "Optimized Distribution Model" in 1997, Compaq found that 59 percent of its resellers had begun to favor its competitor Hewlett-Packard.[30] In the meantime, Compaq still couldn't match Dell on cost.

Michael Dell had already learned this lesson in the early 1990s, when he briefly tried a hybrid strategy before bailing out of retail distribution in 1994. He discovered that his product people were supporting both the indirect and the direct channels, but they were "doing half a job on each." [31] In addition, the manufacturing staff was torn between building a facility that supplied the retail channel or a plant for the direct model, which demanded very different specifications. Even the sales and support representatives were torn by serving two masters. As Dell recalled, "Exiting retail . . . forced all of our people to focus 100 percent on the direct model. That single-mindedness was a powerful unifying force."[32]

By focusing exclusively on the direct channel, Dell had turned his competitors' partners into liabilities. Using a divide-and-conquer strategy, he had forced Compaq into a situation where its partners' interests were directly opposed to its own. By sticking with its distributors, Compaq would be committing itself to compete on the basis of less flexibility and higher costs. But in moving to match Dell's strategy, Compaq could find itself abandoned by its partners just when it needed them most.

LEVERAGE YOUR OPPONENT'S PARTNERS

- Out-partner your opponents by showing other companies that they can do better by working with you.

- Play on your opponents' partners' weaknesses in order to make it difficult for competitors to respond.

- Divide and conquer: force your opponents into unpleasant choices by pitting them against their partners.

Leverage Your Opponent's Competitors

Compared to the first two leverage techniques, this one sounds like child's play. What could be easier and more natural than allowing your opponent's competitors to wear him down? We all know the old adage, "the enemy of my enemy is my friend." But judo strategists are not content to sit back and let someone else do their job. Staying on the offensive means actively crafting a strategy that uses your opponent's competitors to hold him back.

There are at least three different ways to leverage your opponent's competitors. First, you can add value on top of his competitors' products. Second, you can build coalitions with his competitors. Third, you can serve as a distributor for his competitors. In each case, you create leverage by making it difficult for your competitor to match your moves.

Netscape: Adding Value to an Opponent's Competition

Despite its other travails, Netscape successfully exploited this technique to build momentum in its battle with Microsoft. While Microsoft was determined to win the browser war, defending and promoting its position in the operating system market remained its top priority at all times. And that meant doing whatever it took to kill UNIX, the chief competitor of Microsoft's industrial-strength Windows NT. Throughout the 1990s, UNIX remained the preferred solution for high-speed, high-volume networks, and most corporate customers maintained heterogeneous computing environments mixing UNIX and Windows NT.

The operating system rivalry provided Microsoft's competitors with a valuable source of leverage. By developing applications that added value to UNIX platforms, they could strengthen their position in a way that Microsoft would never match. As Paul Maritz, the head of product development at Microsoft, explained, "We have no desire to sell anything on UNIX."[33] By limiting development to its own platforms, Microsoft hoped to force companies in search of the latest and greatest technology to convert to Windows NT.

Netscape took advantage of this opportunity by pushing the cross-platform message at every turn. "It doesn't matter what the operating system is," Netscape cofounder Marc Andreessen liked to say. "The operating system should be a plug-in that fits beneath Navigator."[34] In addition to supporting Windows, Windows NT, and Apple's Macintosh, Netscape tuned its software to run on more than sixteen versions of UNIX, ranging from HP UNIX to Solaris, which was developed by Microsoft rival Sun Microsystems. This allowed companies to deploy Web-based technologies across their existing networks. And it opened a market that Netscape could own. By the time AOL acquired Netscape for $10 billion in 1999, the cross-platform server business accounted for more than 80 percent of Netscape's $600 million in revenues. And this remained an arena in which Microsoft never chose to compete.

JVC: Building Coalitions with an Opponent's Competitors

The first technique works when your opponent's competitors already have products in the marketplace. A second variation relies on building a coalition that draws your opponent's competitors into the ring. This tactic can be particularly potent in markets where standards play an important role and where the key to success lies in being the first to achieve critical mass.

The early market for videocassette recorders (VCRs) provides the setting for a classic example of this tactic at work.[35] JVC was the challenger in this case, taking on Sony, a much stronger company. Sony was first to market with its VCR, launching the Betamax format in Japan in 1975. At the time, JVC was developing its own standard, VHS, which had the advantage of making it possible to record for two hours instead of one. But the company lacked the strength in manufacturing, distribution, and marketing to compete with Sony on its own.

So JVC went on an aggressive campaign to license the VHS format to other manufacturers, as well as offering to produce VCRs for other companies to rebrand. A long list of Sony's competitors, including Matsushita, Hitachi, Mitsubishi, Sharp, Sanyo, and Toshiba, signed up. One year later, Sony came around to the idea of building its own coalition, but by then it was too late. All the best partners were gone.

The resulting competition between the Sony and VHS camps is well documented. Over the next twelve years, the two sides battled it out, but in the end—largely by virtue of having built a big coalition early in the game—JVC won the standards war. By the mid-1980s, Sony's share had dwindled to under 3 percent, and it abandoned the Betamax format in 1988.

Charles Schwab: Distributing an Opponent's Competitors

Charles Schwab demonstrated its mastery of a similar technique in the early 1990s when the discount brokerage decided to move aggressively into the mutual fund business. Schwab had already established a beachhead in the sector by setting up a mutual fund supermarket that allowed investors to purchase funds from a variety of families for a small charge. By 1989, mutual fund commissions contributed $10 to $12 million to Schwab's coffers annually.[36] But this remained a drop in the bucket next to Fidelity Investments, the country's largest mutual fund company, which managed $48 billion for its investors and collected close to half a billion dollars in fees each year.[37]

David Pottruck, then the head of Schwab's brokerage arm, set the scene.

> Chuck Schwab had a vision—he knew that we needed to become a mutual fund player. So our choices were to go up against the Fidelities, the T. Rowe Prices, the Scudders, and the Vanguards with our own family of funds. They all had a huge lead, and they had infrastructure. They had research departments. They had fund managers. They had stuff we didn't have.

Schwab did not have the discretionary capital or management resources to build these capabilities. Moreover, Pottruck emphasized, "All these companies at that time were much bigger than we were."

The odds were not promising. But Pottruck intuitively grasped the power of leverage as a competitive tool. "Success comes from trying to reinvent the rules of competition in a way where the competition really finds it hard to follow you," he explained. Determined to become a major mutual fund player, Schwab executives came up with a radical plan: allow consumers to buy mutual funds through Schwab's supermarket for free. Instead of charging customers, Schwab would get the fund families to pay them for distributing their funds. This was a much more significant change than simply eliminating its own fees. And as Pottruck explained:

> If you think about the proposition, we had to go out to mutual fund companies and say to them, "We have been handling your mutual funds for eight years on a third-party basis for nothing, no cost to you. We would now like you to pay, and by the way, if you don't pay, we'll still handle your funds." It doesn't get people to jump out of their chairs and say, "I can't wait to pay you." So getting mutual funds to sign up for that proposition wasn't easy.

But Schwab had an ace up its sleeve. The management team was convinced that eliminating fees would cause fund sales to rise. In order to prove their case, Schwab launched a trial in early 1992, waiving fees in a couple of its branch offices and absorbing the loss. "Lo and behold," Pottruck recalled, "it was a no-brainer—the funds with no fees sold more."

Evidence in hand, Schwab began to woo mutual fund companies, asking them to pay an annual fee of 25 basis points for assets that Schwab's OneSource program sent their way. But even then, OneSource was a difficult sell. "We did a lot of begging. Tom Seip (one of our former key executives), John McGonigle, and I wore out the knees on several suits," Pottruck recalled. Of the twenty fund companies initially approached, only eight took the bait.

OneSource launched in July 1992, offering consumers eighty-two no-load funds. In the year that followed, OneSource collected $4 billion in assets, and fund managers clamored to take part in the program, even as Schwab raised the fees it charged the funds.[38] Within two years, the no-fee supermarket had passed its breakeven point of $10 billion in assets and transformed Schwab into the third largest distributor of mutual funds in the United States.[39]

Schwab initially expected to have this market to itself. Fidelity had no economic incentive to sell competitors' funds. Pottruck and his team reasoned: "For a Fidelity, if they sell their own fund, it's 100 basis points. If they sell a third-party fund, it's 25 basis points. It's relatively unprofitable for them to be selling other people's funds." Consequently, Pottruck believed that other fund families would be unwilling to join forces with Fidelity: "Our thought was the mutual funds are never going to let Merrill Lynch and Fidelity sell their funds and pay them because they're going to be afraid that these other firms will just use it as window dressing to really sell their own funds." Schwab's position, by contrast, was doubly strong. "Schwab doesn't have actively managed mutual funds of its own," Pottruck explained, "which is a proposition for the consumer of unbiased choice and an opportunity to say to the fund companies: 'We're really going to really help you sell your funds and we're not going to use your funds to bait and switch to our funds.'"

Confounding Schwab's expectations, Fidelity soon matched its move. In July 1993, Fidelity, which had been operating its own multifamily FundsNetwork since mid-1989, dropped transaction fees on 195 no-load funds from ten different families. One year later, Fidelity offered 25 percent more no-fee funds than Schwab: 350 to 282.[40] Yet despite Fidelity's entry into the no-fee market, Schwab's leverage kept it in the lead. By the end of the decade, the company held more than $284 billion in assets in mutual funds. Third party-funds distributed through OneSource accounted for 36 percent of the total, Schwab's money market and index funds held 37 percent, and third-party funds carrying a transaction fee accounted for the rest. Altogether, mutual fund service fees generated more than $750 million in revenue in 1999.

Throughout this period, Fidelity's third-party fund distribution remained a fraction of Schwab's in size. Many fund companies were slow to join, remaining suspicious of Fidelity's true goals. As a senior executive at Invesco told the *New York Times* in 1994, "We don't sell our funds through Fidelity. It goes to a competitive issue. Their interest is in selling customers Fidelity funds. They say they are happy to sell anything, but they've mostly sold their own."[41] (Invesco later rethought its position and signed on.) In addition, competitors were unhappy about Fidelity's ability to monopolize communications with customers and soak up assets flowing into money market funds (something that Schwab also did).

But the biggest brakes on the growth of Fidelity's supermarket came from within Fidelity itself. While managers close to the retail brokerage believed that the company would win in the long run by offering customers a broader range of options, many of Fidelity's highfliers disagreed. Fidelity had risen to prominence by managing money, not by distributing other companies' funds. And executives were keenly aware that every dollar taken in by another fund family was, to some extent, at their expense. "You have a very large fund-manufacturing factory there that clearly has a vested interest in continuing to manufacture proprietary products," one senior executive explained. Consequently, many at Fidelity tended to view other fund companies primarily as rivals, not customers (as at Schwab), and in the ensuing battles over strategy, initially at least, FundsNetwork often lost out.

By the end of the decade, Fidelity had overcome some of its internal resistance. In fact, for a few fund families, Fidelity was outselling Schwab's OneSource. Yet from Schwab's perspective, this was a win-win situation. As long as Fidelity held back, Schwab could count on the lead. But if Fidelity focused on third-party distribution, Schwab would still gain. "If we force Fidelity to offer third-party mutual funds at 25 basis points instead of 100 basis points," Pottruck pointed out, "they have fewer bullets in their cannon to aim our way."

LEVERAGE YOUR OPPONENT'S COMPETITORS

- Add value to your opponents' competitors' products.
- Create critical mass by building coalitions with your opponents' competitors.
- Provide a distribution channel for your opponents' competitors' products and services.

PART II

Masters of Judo Strategy

5

Jeff Hawkins and
Donna Dubinsky

Mastering Movement at Palm Computing

"How can a gorilla learn to fly? Only by abandoning the
essence of the gorilla."

—The Zen of Palm

DEEP IN THE HEART of Silicon Valley, Los Altos is a quiet resi-
dential community that prides itself on its village atmosphere and
tree-lined streets. It is also the unlikely birthplace of a revolution,
launched by Jeff Hawkins and Donna Dubinsky from a small office
on El Camino Real. In six years at the helm of Palm Computing,
Hawkins and Dubinsky took the dog-eared dream of handheld computing and produced a runaway hit. In the process, they jump-
started an entire sector with more than $3 billion in annual sales.

Jeff Hawkins founded Palm in January 1992 with somewhat
more modest dreams. His goal was to build the leading developer
of handheld computing applications, or "the Lotus of handheld
computing." Hawkins was convinced that handheld computing
was the wave of the future. "Everybody's going to have a little handheld computer," he remembered thinking at the time. And every
one of those little handheld computers, he planned, would run
applications developed by Palm.

By the late 1990s, however, this vision had been left far behind.
Palm Computing was not the Lotus of the palmtop category; it was

its IBM, its Microsoft, and its Compaq—all rolled into one. Despite the presence of formidable rivals with a collective investment in the category of nearly $1 billion, Palm's Pilot owned the handheld space within a year of its launch. At the end of 1996, Palm held 51 percent of the market for handheld computing devices. One year later, the company accounted for two-thirds of handheld sales; by the end of 1998, Palm's market share had grown to 79 percent.[1]

Throughout this period, Palm's operating system, the Palm OS, consistently outclassed and outsold its main competitor, Microsoft's Windows CE. Microsoft marshaled masses of money, manpower, and marketing muscle behind Windows CE, but year after year, Palm managed to stay ahead. Capitalizing on this success, 3Com, which had acquired the company in 1997, spun off the Palm division in March 2000. Palm, like the Pilot, had a spectacular debut, garnering a market capitalization of $53 billion by the close of trading on its first day.

How did Palm beat out Microsoft to grab the brass ring? Why did it succeed where so many others failed? In large part, credit must go to the company's intuitive grasp of judo strategy techniques. Dubinsky and Hawkins proved to be masters of the puppy dog ploy, steadily building momentum while avoiding provocative moves that might invite a fatal attack. They also moved deftly to define the competitive space, staying well away from their opponent's favored terrain. And finally, they followed through fast, capitalizing on their initial advantage with a well-executed plan of continuous attack.

From the Zoomer to the Pilot: 1992–1994

Jeff Hawkins, a gifted engineer with a passion for the brain, and Donna Dubinsky, a voluble, high-energy Harvard M.B.A, joined forces in mid-1992. A Cornell-trained electrical engineer, Hawkins had worked at Intel before moving to GRiD Systems, a Fremont-based manufacturer of desktop and portable personal computers (PCs), and then going on to found Palm Computing. Dubinsky had earned her stripes at Apple Computer, joining the company shortly after it went public in 1980. While different in many ways, Dubinsky and Hawkins formed a natural team. Hawkins was the visionary and innovator who gave Palm its soul, Dubinsky the tough-minded executive who made the company work.

Palm initially planned to develop applications for pen-based handheld computers, a new generation of machines that would be small, cheap, and portable enough for anyone to use. Hawkins had first been drawn to this field in the mid-1980s, when he left GRiD to pursue his fascination with the workings of the brain. "My wife thought I was crazy," said Hawkins, recalling his decision to enroll in Berkeley's Ph.D. program in biophysics. But it turned out to be a fateful choice. "Once there, I discovered people using neural networks to do pattern recognition, like handwriting recognition," Hawkins explained. "When I saw a company trying to sell a pattern recognizer for a million dollars, I said, 'This is crazy. I can do this better.'"

Hawkins developed and patented a pattern-recognition algorithm and left academia after two years. Back at GRiD, he used this technology to develop the GRiDPad, a clipboard-sized tablet that "read" block printing. Based on the GRiDPad's success among field workers, such as sales representatives and route-delivery drivers, Hawkins became convinced there was a market for a consumer handheld device. Tandy, GRiD's parent company, tried to persuade him to pursue his ideas in-house. But Hawkins preferred to strike out on his own. After obtaining $300,000 from Tandy in return for 10 percent of his new company and some technology and distribution rights, Hawkins collected $1 million in venture capital, and Palm Computing opened its doors.

The Dreaded Newton Effect

Palm was entering a crowded field just as the original "insanely great" company joined the fray. In January 1992, while Hawkins was busy starting Palm, Apple CEO John Sculley dropped a bombshell in Las Vegas at the Consumer Electronics Show. In a speech that made headlines across the industry, Sculley announced that computing and consumer electronics were about to converge, creating a $3.5 trillion market for a new generation of devices he dubbed personal digital assistants, or PDAs.[2] In dramatic tones, Sculley painted a future in which simple handheld devices would allow people to access and use information instantaneously, no matter where they were. And he concluded by announcing that Apple planned to bring out the first of its PDAs, later named the Newton, in 1993.

Palm planned to go head-to-head with Apple—and a long and varied list of competitors, including Psion, Microsoft, IBM, Hewlett-Packard, Texas Instruments, AT&T, and NCR. But the tiny start-up didn't intend to do battle on its own. Palm's first product, the Zoomer, was the product of a coalition: Casio made the hardware, GeoWorks developed the operating system, Palm wrote the basic applications, and Tandy handled distribution.

The Zoomer launched in October 1993, two months after Apple's Newton, which it roughly matched in size (under one pound) and price ($700). While many critics praised the Zoomer's applications, the device was big, slow, and expensive, and as Hawkins admitted, the handwriting recognition was "just no good." But even if the Zoomer had been a better product, it would have had difficulty escaping what one analyst dubbed the "dreaded Newton effect."[3] Apple had overpromised and underdelivered, especially when it came to handwriting recognition, a weakness that the comic strip *Doonesbury* mercilessly lampooned. "The Newton really was an enormous setback for the whole business," Dubinsky observed. "It was such a public failure that it cast a cloud over the whole space."

Odds and Ends

Hawkins went back to the drawing board and came up with a second-generation design that fixed many of the Zoomer's flaws. But the Newton effect struck again. "Casio refused to do it," Dubinsky recalled. "Tandy refused to do it. Everybody was saying, 'I'm not investing any more in this category—it's a dog.' We had real trouble getting support for a second product, so instead we were doing all sorts of odds and ends of handheld software." One of these projects was a piece of software that synchronized data between Hewlett-Packard–made handheld devices and desktop computers. The majority of Zoomer buyers had bought a similar application, driving home an important lesson about what a handheld device should be: "These are not independent little machines," Dubinsky concluded. "They are accessories to PCs."

Doonesbury BY GARRY TRUDEAU

A second project was one that everyone said would fail: a revolutionary approach to handwriting recognition that forced people, not computers, to adapt. Hawkins's Graffiti used a simplified, single-stroke alphabet—the A had no crossbar, for example—that was much easier for computers to "read." "We said to people, 'It's not going to learn the way you write—you're going to learn the way it wants you to write.' This was a radical concept," Hawkins recalled. "Everybody said, there's no way people are going to change the way they write. Well," he smiled, "people did, just like they learned to type."

"You Know What To Do"

Despite these signs of progress, Palm was losing steam. "We only had trickles of revenue," Dubinsky recounted. "We were tied to products that were not being successful—Graffiti for the Newton was just not a big revenue item." The company had managed to close a round of funding before the failure of the Zoomer, so it had money in the bank. "But we didn't have prospects. We didn't have a future," she recalled.

Dubinsky and Hawkins were stuck in a rut until the day in early 1994 when one of their investors showed them the way out. Bruce Dunlevie, one of the venture capitalists backing Palm, looked at the downcast partners and issued a challenge: "I'm sick of you guys complaining. You know what to do—why don't you go do it?"

"I had never thought about starting from scratch," Hawkins

explained. "But the next day I knew. I said 'Okay, it has to include connectivity; it has to be small enough to fit in your shirt pocket; it has to cost $299; it has to have Graffiti; it has to have one-button synchronization with a cradle; and it has to be faster and easier than using paper.'"

Starting Over: 1994–1996

Starting with a little block of wood that closely approximated the dimensions of the finished Pilot, Hawkins set about creating his dream device. He began with a simple question: What does the customer really need?

Hawkins had already identified his highest priorities in response to Dunlevie's prod: one-button synchronization and Graffiti in a package that was small, fast, and cheap. But listening to the industry's conventional wisdom threatened to complicate his task. "I can't tell you the number of meetings," Dubinsky complained, "where people said, 'You can't do a product unless it's got embedded wireless communications; no one is going to want it. You can't do a product without a spreadsheet. You can't do a product that doesn't have a PC card slot.'"

Early organizers and PDAs sought to be feature-rich. Everyone believed that success in the category required packing more and more features and applications into a tiny device—a strategy that Microsoft CEO Steve Ballmer described as "making a bathroom with a lot of pipes and no toilet seats: It could be very uncomfortable, even if it was fully functional." Pleading guilty to having followed the same approach, Ballmer admitted, "We had lots of plumbing in our handheld strategy and not a lot of cosmetics."

Palm Computing chose a different path. "We looked at this list of things [people in the industry] told us we had to have, and we said, 'Most of the products available today have all those things, and they're failing,'" Hawkins recalled. So the Pilot, in many ways, was designed as the un-PDA. Palm's first device did not do many things. But it did a few important things simply, quickly, and very well. The Pilot was "extremely high performance from a user perspective," in Dubinsky's words. There was no boot-up delay and no hourglass or wait cursor of any sort. Moreover, the Pilot hewed to the telecom industry standard of "five nines": In other words, it worked 99.999 percent of the time. By contrast, personal computer programs often crashed several times a day.

In redefining the category's goals, Palm did more than build a better product. Hawkins and Dubinsky laid the groundwork for a style of competition that strongly favored Palm. If Palm had set out to create the digital equivalent of a Swiss army knife, jam-packed with specialized tools, the contest would have been their competitors' to lose. Competing on the basis of features lists was a large company's game. But simplicity, usability, and elegance were standards that competitors like Microsoft had never been able to meet. This gave tiny Palm Computing an important edge.

The Zen of Palm

Rob Haitani, one of Palm's senior product designers, later developed a tongue-in-cheek presentation that encapsulated Palm's strategy and helped communicate the vision to other employees. Under the title "The Zen of Palm," Haitani used three riddles to lay out "the path to enlightenment." In order to succeed, he said, Palm had to solve three conundrums: "How can a gorilla learn to fly? How do you put a mountain in a teacup? And how do you keep a lizard from crawling off a cliff?"[4]

How *can* a gorilla learn to fly? "Only by abandoning the essence of the gorilla," Haitani said. By embracing simplicity, Palm would force Microsoft to abandon its favorite tactic—adding more features—in order to compete. Odds were that the software giant would be unable to perform this unnatural act. Consequently, "Microsoft won't crush us," the Zen of Palm maintained, as long as Palm remained faithful to its own approach.

Palm's strategy was to "put a mountain in a teacup" by figuring out what really mattered to users. "Dig for a diamond and put it in the teacup," the Zen of Palm counseled. "Do you really need the dirt and rocks?" No, was the answer. Palm left that pointless task to Microsoft and its allies instead.

Finally, in order to "keep a lizard from crawling off a cliff"—or avoid losing its lead—Palm "moved the cliff" by continuing to rewrite the rules of competition. Innovation was not a one-shot game. In order to stay ahead, Hawkins and Dubinsky needed to ensure that Palm continued to set the pace by defining both the technologies and the business models that dominated the handheld space.

Creating Out-of-Box Delight

One of Palm's most important innovations lay in the company's decision to adopt a business model that broke with prevailing practice by tightly integrating software and hardware design under a single roof. Dubinsky and Hawkins believed strongly that a single concept had to drive both software and hardware design because space on the palmtop was so tight. The Zoomer had failed, in part, Dubinsky maintained, because it had emerged from a process of design-by-committee. "There was no overriding vision. There was nobody in charge," she recalled.

The Pilot, by contrast, was shaped by a single vision, ensuring that its hardware (the buttons, stylus, and screen) and software (the operating system and applications) formed a cohesive whole. This model lay outside the experience of most of the players in the organizer and computing worlds. (Apple was an exception, but in the wake of the Newton, the company was still licking its wounds.) Japanese giants like Casio and Sharp were skilled at building small devices, but software was foreign terrain. Consequently, Dubinsky and Hawkins felt that they could write them off. "We knew how they thought; we knew how they worked," Dubinsky explained. "They could not innovate, they could not do software, and they knew nothing about platforms, so basically we didn't think they could touch us."

Microsoft, clearly, was a much more formidable competitor, but it was equally ill-equipped to compete by Palm's new rules. Microsoft typically licensed its software to a wide range of partners that embedded it in different hardware designs. Or as Dubinsky put it, Microsoft would "do this sort of reference design and throw it over the fence to their partners"—hardware manufacturers like Compaq, Dell, and IBM. Microsoft had reaped rich rewards from this strategy in the personal computer market, but Palm executives were confident that it would fail in handheld computing. "Microsoft's business model was just really the wrong model for this space," Ed Colligan, Palm's vice president of marketing, explained.

"There were all these people in the food chain: the operating system provider, the application provider, the tools developer, and the hardware developer. And we just felt, no, this is different. There needs to be an out-of-the-box turnkey experience that is delightful for the consumer."

MOVEMENT AT PALM:
DEFINE THE COMPETITIVE SPACE

The Challenge: You're up against powerful opponents who have spent many years developing successful strategies and techniques.

The Solution: Define the competitive space in a way that gives you the advantage by making it difficult for your competitors to compete.

- Redefine product standards to make success depend less on resources and more on skill.

- Create new business models that run counter to your competitors' established style of play.

Going to Market: 1996

While Hawkins focused on creating the Pilot, Dubinsky set about raising additional funds. It was an uphill battle. "I couldn't get anybody to invest $1 million," Dubinsky lamented. "We were in the wrong place at the wrong time." The Internet was just taking off; the industry was at the dawn of a new era, and Palm was in a blackballed category. "A billion dollars had been lost in this space," Dubinsky recalled. "It was littered with corpses, all launched by big, reputable companies: the Simon phone by BellSouth and IBM, the Envoy by Motorola, the Newton, the Zoomer. The list was just nonstop."

Moreover, the prospect of competing with Microsoft, which was developing its own operating system for pocket-sized devices, frightened off potential investors. Prospective partners such as Compaq and Toshiba "weren't going to do something that pissed Microsoft off," Dubinsky explained. Around Palm, the Microsoft factor became known as "the Bill call," as in, "What are you going to do when you get the Bill call? Are you going to back off of this deal?"

In talks with potential investors, Dubinsky recalled, the issue constantly arose: "How could you possibly compete with Microsoft? Who would possibly fund that? Nobody!"

Finally, U.S. Robotics (USR), a $1 billion company that specialized in manufacturing modems, decided to take the plunge. Assuring Dubinsky and Hawkins that they could continue to run Palm as an independent subsidiary, USR acquired the company in September 1995. Two years later, Palm became a unit of 3Com, a $5 billion manufacturer of networking products, when 3Com acquired USR.

50,000 Rich Male Nerds

With USR's financial backing in place, Palm unveiled the Pilot at Demo, an exclusive industry conclave, in January 1996. The venue, which had been chosen over USR's protests, reflected a deliberate strategic choice. Senior executives at Palm's new parent strongly favored introducing the Pilot at the Consumer Electronics Show in Las Vegas the same month. In Las Vegas, Palm would have had an audience more than a hundred times Demo's size. "But we felt that the Pilot would get lost in Las Vegas," Dubinsky recalled. Even as part of USR, Palm lacked the resources to take the mass market by storm. "Our only chance of success would be if the early adopters liked it," Dubinsky said.

Demo's 600 industry leaders gave the Pilot an enthusiastic welcome. But even then Dubinsky and Hawkins hardly knew what to expect once the product hit retailers' shelves in the spring of 1996. "Our first year's projection was 100,000 units," Dubinsky recalled, "and all we knew was that it was wrong. We didn't know if it was high or low. So we sort of held our breath."

For the first five months, sales were flat at around 10,000 units per month. But those first 50,000 users turned out to be worth their weight in gold. Earning more than $100,000 a year on average, they were self-rated computer experts, almost entirely between the ages of thirty-five and forty-five, and 95 percent male. "We called them the rich male nerds," Dubinsky said affectionately. "Those 50,000 guys became our sales force. They went out and told all their colleagues and their neighbors and their friends. They bought it for their friends and their colleagues for Christmas, and that was how the Pilot started taking off." (See figure 5–1.)

Figure 5-1:   The Pilot Becomes One of the Fastest-Growing Consumer Devices in History

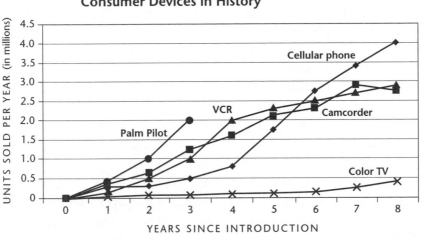

Source: Donna Dubinsky, unpublished document nominating Jeffrey C. Hawkins for the National Medal of Technology, December 1998.

Playing the Puppy Dog

Dubinsky and Hawkins were naturally intent on seeing the Pilot succeed. But at the same time, they realized that a rapid ramp-up could cut two ways. It would drive Palm solidly into the market, creating an entrenched base. But it would also attract unwelcome attention from competitors like Microsoft, who might be tempted to take down the new entrant before it got too strong.

In order to minimize this danger, Palm's leaders carefully positioned the company on the periphery of the PC world. Rather than play up the Pilot's full potential, Dubinsky and Hawkins portrayed it as a product that filled a limited need. "We didn't call it a computer; we didn't call it a PDA," Dubinsky recalled. "We said, 'this is just a little organizer that happens to connect to your PC.'" At one level, the message was aimed at consumers, whose expectations had been raised and then dashed by the Newton and other handheld machines. "There was so much overpromising and underdelivering, we had to swing to the other extreme," Dubinsky explained. But Palm's competitors were another audience the company wanted to reach. By positioning the Pilot as "a companion to the PC, not a substitute," in Hawkins's words,

Palm was saying to potential entrants into the market, "Don't worry about us. This is no big deal."

Fortunately, when Palm began its meteoric rise, the organizer market was a sideline for the PC world's heavy hitters—companies like Microsoft, Compaq, and IBM. "This was really low on the totem pole for them," Dubinsky observed. In the shadow of the Internet, Palm's niche was easy to overlook. The same companies that had poured hundreds of millions of dollars into handheld computing just a few years earlier were now obsessed with the Web. Nowhere was this more true than at Microsoft, which by this time was focusing its fire on Netscape. For Dubinsky, this was a tremendous stroke of luck. "We were just joyous when we realized that the Internet was happening," she recalled. "We said, 'Oh, that's going to distract Gates for a long time.' We always felt that the handheld guys at Microsoft were the B players. It never got strategic attention. It was never anywhere near as critical on Gates's list. The Internet came to really dominate the new direction of the company—and justifiably so."

But Palm didn't take Microsoft's benign neglect for granted. Dubinsky and Hawkins remained cautious when it came to positioning the Pilot, staying away from areas where Microsoft was most sensitive to attack. Netscape had struck for the jugular by positioning Navigator as an alternative platform with the potential to supersede Windows, the foundation of Microsoft's strength. But Palm, by contrast, defined the Pilot not as a platform, but as a device. (In fact, as the company realized from the beginning, it was both.) "We always said, 'Look, if Microsoft had a decent platform we would consider it. We are first and foremost a device company,'" Dubinsky said. "Of course," she added, "they didn't have a decent platform, so it was sort of a moot point."

These moves were not bold or glamorous, but they worked. According to Microsoft's Steve Ballmer, Palm still hadn't grabbed his attention as an important competitor almost two years after the Pilot's debut. "They must have been on my radar screen by early '98," he mused, "but not at the top of my radar screen." In part this was due to the distractions of the Internet, but Microsoft's lack of alarm also owed something to Palm's success in portraying the handheld market as an unthreatening niche. "Let's say the market quadruples," Ballmer observed, recapping Microsoft's calculations.

"Roughly we're talking about $400 million in potential operating profits for all players. Palm's still going to have some share, and then I have to split the rest with my OEMs [original equipment manufacturers]. At the end of the day, the total profit pool in this business doesn't excite most of our OEMs or Microsoft."

By contrast, if Palm had positioned the Pilot as a PC alternative, and the Palm operating system as a direct threat to Windows, Ballmer might have found a great deal more to get excited about. And Palm would have had a great deal more to fear.

MOVEMENT AT PALM: THE PUPPY DOG PLOY

The Challenge: As you build a position in the market, you risk drawing the attention of more powerful competitors.

The Solution: Try to look unthreatening in order to avert a full-scale attack.

- Build an initial position by appealing to thought leaders and early adopters, rather than attacking the mass-market head-on.

- Position alongside your competitors' products by showing how they can coexist.

- Avoid threatening your opponents' core business before you're strong enough to fight.

Staying Ahead: 1996–1997

By the end of 1996, Palm had raced to first place in the handheld computing category, winning 51 percent of the market after shipping 360,000 Pilots in nine months. Former market leader Hewlett-Packard was second, with devices based on the same GeoWorks operating system the Zoomer had used. And with 9 percent of the market, Apple's Newton had been relegated to third place.[5]

But tougher competition lay ahead. After two failed efforts in five years, Microsoft returned to the handheld market in November 1996 with its third pocket-sized operating system, Windows CE. Designed to be used primarily in conjunction with a keyboard, WinCE offered the familiar Windows interface and the ability to run stripped-down versions of standard Microsoft applications like Word and Excel. In addition, Microsoft's latest operating system had a powerful coalition on its side, with major computer manufacturers, including Compaq, Hewlett-Packard, and NEC, lining up to produce WinCE-based devices. The early CE devices were no match for the Pilot in simplicity and elegance, but given Microsoft's track record, Dubinsky and Hawkins knew that they would eventually improve.

Speeding to Market

In order to stay ahead of Microsoft, Palm turned itself into a moving target, bringing new product generations to market at least once a year. The PalmPilot, a more rugged version, with backlighting and new applications, followed the original Pilot by eleven months. Palm engineers then started working on the Palm III, V, and VII, which ran on parallel tracks (see table 5–1). Despite the management challenges involved, the decision to run three projects concurrently grew out of the conviction that this strategy would allow Palm to "leapfrog the competition," Dubinsky explained.

While the Palm III was an evolutionary follow-on product, the V and VII reflected much more ambitious efforts to rethink the product and continuously redefine the competitive space. "The Palm V was all about style, and style was not one of Microsoft's fortes," Hawkins observed. "And with the Palm VII, we created a truly integrated, wireless connectivity solution, which was again rewriting the rules. No one had done anything like that. I said to myself, 'Microsoft can't do this.' And it's true. They can't."

Mike Gallucci, who headed manufacturing logistics at Palm, identified three practices that helped the company keep up with Hawkins's ideas and move to market at a world-class pace. The first was the design philosophy that drove the entire process. "We didn't take technology risks," Hawkins said. Palm's engineers avoided rocket science and lengthy wish lists that could delay a launch by months or even years. "We didn't try to do cutting edge," added Gallucci. "What we did was simplicity in its most elegant form." As a consequence, the company avoided the technology-related delays that slow many ambitious start-ups down.

This feet-on-the-ground approach was also reflected in Palm's reliance on concurrent engineering. The traditional approach to

Table 5-1:   Speeding to Market

Launch Date	Product Generation
April 1996	Pilot
March 1997	PalmPilot Professional and Personal editions
March 1998	Palm III
February 1999	Palm IIIx and Palm V
May 1999	Palm VII

Source: Company press releases.

product development unfolded sequentially, as Gallucci explained: "Engineering goes off and designs the product and then hands it over to manufacturing, and then manufacturing tries to figure out how to manufacture it and finds a lot of problems." By contrast, Palm focused on implementation upfront. "From the minute Jeff woke up in the middle of the night in his pajamas and said, 'Eureka! I've got the next brilliant idea for a product!' we formed cross-functional teams that included manufacturing, and we were in there from day one giving input and being part of that design team to make sure that the product was manufacturable," Gallucci recalled.

Finally, Palm turned to outside partners to handle many non-core tasks, rather than spend scarce time and resources developing these capabilities in-house. "We didn't have many people in the early days—maybe twenty-five or twenty-eight," said Dubinsky. So the company outsourced almost everything it could: electrical engineering, mechanical engineering, industrial design, and manufacturing. While Hawkins's vision guided the development of all the Pilot's components, Palm engineers developed only the basic software (the operating system and the main applications—the calendar, address book, to do list, and memo pad) on their own.

Initially, Palm's strategy was a product as much of necessity as of design. But even after the company had the resources of USR, and later 3Com, at its disposal, Palm executives preferred to rely on partners for many tasks. The company's philosophy, Gallucci explained, was to focus on its core competencies. "We're a company that develops and markets handheld computers," he said. "We're not in the manufacturing business; that's not our expertise." But by working with partners in areas like manufacturing, Palm could tap the expertise of companies that truly excelled in these fields.

This strategy became a bone of contention between Palm and its corporate parents, because both USR and 3Com had manufacturing capacity to spare. While USR and 3Com wanted to put unused capacity to work, Dubinsky believed that outsourced manufacturing would be faster and better meet Palm's needs. In the end, both sides compromised on a strategy that contracted out some of the work and kept the rest in-house.

Speeding to Market Share

Palm's efforts to speed to market served a larger goal: building and maintaining its share of the market in the face of growing competition. By moving first and defining the competitive space, Hawkins and Dubinsky had bought themselves a precious window of opportunity. But they knew that they had to make every minute count. Microsoft had a history of stumbling when the starter's pistol went off. The first and second versions of its products often failed. But in most cases, Microsoft eventually got it right. Consequently, the pressure was on for Palm to lock in a massive installed base before Microsoft could come up with a comparable product and kick its marketing into high gear.

Palm moved aggressively to reach critical mass by starting with low prices ($300 as opposed to $500 for a typical Windows CE device) and lowering them every year. The importance of beginning with the right entry point was a lesson Hawkins had learned in his years at GRiD. After the company priced its first handheld product at more than $8,000, "people always thought of GRiD as the company that makes expensive computers," Hawkins recalled, "no matter what it did to try to shake the image."

Palm executives often found themselves defending their strategy to USR and 3Com higher-ups. "[3Com CEO] Eric Benhamou kept saying, 'Why are you lowering prices? You own this market,'" marketing head Ed Colligan recalled. "And we just kept saying, 'Because we can and we should and we want to be aggressive—and we've got to keep going to market. We're going to keep pushing this so that there's no room for people to enter.'" "There was no doubt at that point that this business was a star," Dubinsky added, remembering the fierce debates. "And my feeling was that when you are in the number one position in a vast new market, you throw everything you possibly can into it, and you take that investment out of other businesses. Instead, what I got every quarter was, 'You have to cut your expenses. You have to deliver more earnings.' Every time I lowered a price on our schedule, I got a nasty e-mail from the powers that be."

As it was, Palm had only modest losses in its first two and a half years, totaling 10 percent of its $122 million in sales, and the company reached profitability in 1998. By the time of its IPO, it had earned $48 million on sales of $563 million.[6] But 3Com always wanted more. Despite the pressure, Dubinsky's response was the same every time: "You know, you're crazy to focus on my profitability today." Palm could deliver profits, if need be, she argued, but becoming a fat cat would hurt Palm further down the road. Palm had won a battle, but it had yet to win the war.

Several calculations drove Dubinsky's decision to put market share before profitability at this stage in the game. By keeping its prices low, Palm took share away from other competitors and drew new buyers into the market. As a result, the company moved quickly down the learning curve, making it more difficult for other entrants to compete. But the most compelling argument behind Palm's strategy stemmed from the fact that the company's product was a platform for third-party applications, as well as a device. "And the idea in the beginning of a platform business," Dubinsky observed, "is to get as much market share and installed base as possible and to draw as many developers as possible. And then the network effects kick in." As Palm's market share grew, other companies would begin to develop and sell applications that would make the Pilot an even more useful device. This would lead more people to buy the Pilot, which would lead developers to create even more applications, and on and on, until Palm had locked in an enormous installed base. At that point, Dubinsky explained, "We can have a product line that supports higher margin products, and we'll be protected against the competition."

Palm could help this process along by reaching out to developers. But it couldn't launch an all-out offensive without violating the puppy dog ploy. Instead, the company quietly released a software development kit, together with the Pilot, in early 1996. In addition, to make it easier for developers to create new software for the Pilot, Hawkins took the unusual step of publishing the source code for Palm's basic applications two years before the open source movement really took off. But the biggest inducement the company could offer other programmers was a proven market for their wares. Consequently, it was only after Palm had reached 1 million users that the company began to court developers aggressively, holding its first developers conference in October 1997.

This strategy gave Palm a critical weapon in the battle with Microsoft to win developers' hearts and minds.[7] Microsoft could offer other software companies resources that Palm could never match. "They'd offer funding for the initial development," Colligan explained. "They held all the development kitchens. They always put on a big dog-and-pony show, and we did our little nothing thing." What's more, Microsoft's fearsome reputation carried a lot of weight. When Windows CE was released, "people did have to say, 'Hmm, is Microsoft just going to kill Palm?'" Colligan recalled. "And for a small point in time, a lot of people started going to the Microsoft product." But Palm was able to win back many of the defectors with a simple argument: Palm had more buyers in its camp. By the end of 1997, Palm held two-thirds of the market, while products based on Windows CE trailed far behind at 20 percent.[8]

MOVEMENT AT PALM: FOLLOW THROUGH FAST

The Challenge: You've built a healthy lead over the competition: what next?

The Solution: Use this window of opportunity to build the strongest position you can.

- Streamline internal processes in order to continue upgrading your products or services at a rapid pace.

- Don't be greedy, especially in industries where network effects play an important role. Price aggressively in order to win market share and build a large installed base.

Staying Focused: 1997–1998

Throughout this period, Palm had many opportunities to extend its brand. "We had people knocking at our door to license this bit or that bit for this thing or the other thing, whether it was for set-top boxes or big-screen phones," Dubinsky recalled. "We were constantly struggling with the tension between trying to take advantage of this opportunity we had created, which seemed limitless and very broad, and trying to remain a small, focused organization that could deliver."

In a few cases, Palm decided to go for the opportunity. In September 1997, Dubinsky negotiated a partnership with IBM to sell the Pilot, relabeled as the IBM WorkPad, in the enterprise market. In addition, IBM agreed to handle marketing and sales for the Pilot in Japan. One month later, Palm and Symbol Technologies announced an alliance to deliver Palm-based products for vertical markets, including retail, parcel delivery, and manufacturing. And in February 1998, Qualcomm signed up to incorporate the Palm operating system into cellular phones.

In most cases, however, Palm turned its suitors down. "We just couldn't execute everything at once," Ed Colligan commented, "so we had to pick our shots." Even as sales exploded, Palm needed to focus its resources on just one goal: building and selling the best handheld device in the world. If the company grew overextended, it might falter and create an opening for the competition. "Consequently," Dubinsky explained, "we declined most of our licensing opportunities because we felt that the fit was not great and therefore the amount of work to force our product into what they had in mind would be a big diversion—a lot of effort for what was not our core business."

In order to make the Palm operating system run on a desktop big-screen phone, for example, Palm's developers would have had to add support for a larger display. Once that was up and running, overlapping windows would have been a natural request. And then from overlapping windows, scaleable fonts would have been the next logical step. "The complexity of it starts growing enormously," Dubinsky observed:

So even though it seemed like a wonderful way to propagate the operating system and the standard everywhere, it was very much a false god. It was going to be for a couple bucks a unit on a very scary proposition of a device. It wasn't clear screen phones were going to make any sense whatsoever. And it meant a hell of a lot of work involving key people who could be doing the next generation of the Palm product.

"It's very hard to say no," she concluded, "but those, I think, were decisions that we were very good at making. I would say we had more discipline than most other companies in terms of saying, 'This is what we will do; this is what we won't do.'"

MOVEMENT AT PALM: FOLLOW THROUGH FAST

The Challenge: As you become more successful, you face constant temptations to extend your products and your brand.

The Solution: Stay focused. Overextending your resources is a fast path to slow growth.

- Initially, choose only complementary projects that don't overtax your core resources.

- Carefully broaden your scope as the company scales and management bandwidth expands.

"Be a Leader and Stay a Leader"

Palm showed similar discipline in responding to its most serious challenge yet. In January 1998, Microsoft stepped up its attack on the handheld market by introducing a new version of its operating system, Windows CE 2.0, and a new device, dubbed the Palm PC. Unlike its predecessors, which weighed in at close to two pounds and incorporated a keyboard, the Palm PC was virtually indistinguishable from Palm's handhelds in size and design, as well as name.[9]

For Dubinsky and Hawkins, the launch of the Palm PC signaled the beginning of an all-out war. Not only had Microsoft copied Palm's look and feel, the company ended its briefing for developers with a slide showing a target with a Pilot at its heart. It was clear that no amount of clever positioning would avert a full-scale assault. In the face of Palm's success, its credibility as a puppy dog had melted away.

Moreover, the Palm PC posed a much greater threat than earlier products based on Windows CE. Microsoft had done more than get the form factor down to an acceptable size. Together with its hardware partners, Microsoft had lowered the average price of its newest device to about $400, roughly equivalent to the Palm III, which was launched around the same time. In addition, the Palm PC had a host of new features, including a voice memo recorder, the ability to vibrate when receiving pages, a LED light that blinked to alert the user to appointments, and a larger screen.

Palm faced considerable pressure to match Microsoft's latest moves. "The press was coming out and saying, 'CE products have more features than Palm; they're going to squash Palm,' and people believed it, even inside the company," Hawkins recalled. But Hawkins and Dubinsky were convinced that getting dragged into responding to Microsoft could be a fatal mistake. Palm had built its success by defining the rules and setting the pace for the industry. By letting itself get thrown on the defensive, Palm would be conceding this role to a powerful opponent. And that could be the first step on the road to ultimate defeat.

As the Zen of Palm warned, Palm's greatest danger lay in copying Microsoft. "Frankly, my bigger worry is that we try to play *their* game," the presentation ran. "It's tempting for eagles to look at gorillas and think, 'Hey, those guys have arms. We should get arms. And opposable thumbs! Think of what we could do with those.' Next thing you know your eagles become fat, slow, and ugly."

Rather than imitate the competition, Palm had to be a leader and stay a leader. "We were the clear leader by every measurement out there," Dubinsky recalled. "My feeling was we had to act like the leader by setting the agenda and driving the industry." Palm, not Microsoft, had to continue to define what mattered in handheld computing. Consequently, Hawkins and Dubinsky made a conscious decision not to get dragged into copying specific Windows CE features unless they proved to be truly compelling. Many within the organization found this approach hard to swallow. Hawkins remembered repeated conversations, always following the same script: "The VP of sales would come in and ask how we were going to respond to some new feature in Windows CE. I would say, 'Trust me, we're going to do something totally different.' But this response made everyone feel uncomfortable."

Nonetheless, Hawkins and Dubinsky stuck to their position, refusing, for example, to copy the voice recorder in Windows CE. In the first place, Dubinsky said, the product was terrible. "Your voice sounded like you were talking into a balloon," she laughed. Moreover, Palm's research showed that most consumers had little interest in this feature. But perhaps more important, Palm's restraint embodied the company's basic approach to competition. "We never allowed ourselves to get on the defensive," Mike Gallucci recalled. "Our attitude was: We have the lead; we know what we're doing. Don't feel like you have to react."

BALANCE AT PALM: AVOID TIT-FOR-TAT

The Challenge: Despite your best efforts to stay out of harm's way, your opponent launches a head-on attack.

The Solution: Avoid getting pushed onto the defensive by trying to counter all of your competitor's moves.

- Stay on the offensive by continuing to define the competitive space.

- Play your game (not theirs) and maintain your status as a leader.

- Carefully assess your competitor's initiatives and match only the most compelling ideas.

Epilogue: From Palm to Handspring

By the end of 1998, the rewards of Palm's strategy were clear. Palm devices accounted for 79 percent of the handheld market, leaving the Windows CE camp far behind at 15 percent.[10] It was even rumored that Microsoft was preparing to throw in the towel by acquiring Palm. But Dubinsky and Hawkins were no longer around to share in Palm's triumphs. After failing to convince 3Com's management to spin off the Palm division, the duo had opted to leave the company and start a new venture in July 1998.

Palm after Hawkins and Dubinsky

Palm initially had a tough time regaining its footing after Dubinsky and Hawkins left. It took the company eighteen months to find a stable CEO in the person of Carl Yankowski, the former president of Sony Electronics. In the meantime, the pace of innovation at Palm slowed. Both of the company's major product launches in 1999—the stylish Palm V and the Palm VII, with integrated wireless capability—had been designed on Hawkins's watch. After his departure, Palm added color screens to its product line, but there were no breakthrough products.

Hawkins and Dubinsky after Palm

By contrast, Handspring, the start-up that Hawkins and Dubinsky formed in November 1998, was actively pushing the Palm platform forward. Like Palm, Handspring had been founded with a simple goal: to become "the leader in handheld computing and the pre-eminent brand," in Dubinsky's words.

In principle, the company could have gone head-to-head with Palm by building an entirely new product, complete with its own operating system, from scratch. Despite its rapid growth, the handheld market was still immature, with hundreds of millions of units expected to be sold over the next ten years. In a market that size, there was room for multiple products and companies to play. But building from the ground up would be expensive and time-consuming. Moreover, it would force Dubinsky and Hawkins to battle against the network effects they had set in motion at Palm. Consequently, they decided to push when pulled. Handspring licensed the Palm operating system in order to take advantage of its momentum and extended it in order to create its own competitive advantage.

Introduced in September 1999, Handspring's first product, the Visor, was a Palm-compatible Palm III look-alike in a colorful translucent case. But it also contained an important innovation: the Springboard expansion slot, which turned the Visor into an infinitely mutable device. The Palm III was essentially a handheld organizer, built around a calendar, an address book, and room for taking notes. By contrast, the Visor could be virtually anything a developer's imagination could conceive. By snapping in an expansion pack— as simply as snapping a cartridge into the back of a GameBoy—users could turn the Visor into anything from a digital camera to an MP3 player to a cellular phone.

The combination of Handspring's innovation and aggressive pricing translated into impressive sales. While the Visor was initially sold only through Handspring's Web site, it became the top-selling PDA once it entered retail distribution in the spring of 2000. In its first week on retailers' shelves, the deluxe version of the Visor grabbed 27 percent of the market, followed by the Palm IIIe at 15 percent.[11] On the strength of its early results, Handspring went public in June 2000, earning a first-day valuation of $3.4 billion, despite a soft market for IPOs.

By then 3Com had reversed course, spinning Palm off in March 2000. (3Com stole some of Handspring's thunder by announcing this decision one day before the Visor's debut.) The new company was moving away from its dependence on hardware sales by aggressively licensing its operating system to companies like Nokia and Sony. But in the short term at least, building and selling devices remained a central part of its business, making Palm Handspring's biggest competitor (and vice versa). This rivalry intensified as Palm brought out lower-priced models to compete directly with the Visor and announced plans to use an alternative expansion slot technology in its devices. Yet despite the fierce competition, Handspring and Palm both saw their sales explode. (See figure 5–2.)

This success bolstered both companies in their struggle against a common rival: Microsoft, which introduced its third revision of Windows CE in April 2000. Renamed Pocket PC, Microsoft's latest entry in the handheld computing market had been rewritten from the ground up in order to simplify the interface and upgrade its e-mail and Web browsing features. In addition, Microsoft's hardware partners, which still included heavy hitters like Compaq, Hewlett-Packard, and Casio, were hard at work on sleeker designs in the spirit of the Palm V.

Microsoft remained determined to win the battle for handheld computing, ensuring that the competition would be intense and prolonged. "We can't afford not to," Ballmer explained. "We can't afford to give up a potential choke point on our core platform." But

Figure 5-2: Revenues at Palm and Handspring Explode, FY 2000

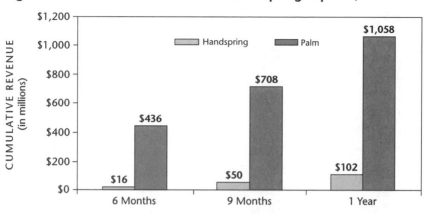

Note: Fiscal year ends June 2, 2000 for Palm; June 30, 2000 for Handspring.

Source: Company reports.

while Microsoft could never be discounted, Hawkins and Dubinsky's two successive ventures had built an impressive lead between 1996 and 2001. By mastering movement as well as balance, the two partners deftly guided Palm to first place. And in Handspring, they created the only company that had succeeded to date in taking meaningful share away from Palm.

6

Rob Glaser

Maintaining Balance at RealNetworks

Keep your friends close and your enemies closer.

—Rob Glaser, CEO, RealNetworks,
quoting from *The Godfather*

THE WEB IN ITS INFANCY was a still, silent place. Click as you might, you were unlikely to stumble on anything other than the occasional picture and endless pages of print. To jazz up their Web pages designers turned to color, clip art, and funky fonts. But the end result was still text—only now it was harder to read. Ironically, while the world's airwaves crackled with music, television, and just plain talk, the Internet—the defining technology of the late twentieth century—was dominated by the written word.

All that changed in 1995. All of a sudden, the Web acquired a voice—a scratchy, cutting in and out voice to be sure, but still a voice that could instruct, entertain, and sometimes annoy. And that wasn't all. Several months later video appeared, and the Web could jump and move. The first online videos were a couple of square inches in size, and the images moved about as smoothly as a flip-action book. But for the first time, convergence—that much-heralded melding of computers, consumer electronics, and entertainment—seemed to be truly on its way.

Rob Glaser and his company, RealNetworks, were as responsible as anyone for bringing sound and motion to the Web. They weren't always the first to market, but they were the most effective by far at getting consumers and content providers to incorporate streaming media—on-demand audio and video—into their businesses and into their lives. In six years, Glaser built a company worth more than $12 billion at the market's height. Real's software continued to deliver more than 85 percent of all streaming media content five years after its debut. And Real's streaming media portal became one of the most popular destinations on the Web.

But numbers alone don't give the true measure of Glaser's success, for RealNetworks didn't take this market unopposed. Beginning in late 1996, Microsoft began to compete with Real head-to-head. And even before that, Glaser—a Microsoft alumnus—had been aware that the Redmond giant posed a potentially lethal long-term threat. This meant that speed and innovation had to be critical elements of Glaser's strategy from day one. "The best way to keep the lead is to keep leading," he later said.

In addition, a combination of balance techniques helped Glaser to stay on his feet and stay ahead. As Real faced off against Microsoft, Glaser gripped his opponent, with the goal of strengthening his position at the stronger company's expense. Glaser also learned to push when pulled and use the momentum of competing technologies to his advantage. Finally, by developing a multifaceted business model, Glaser was able to avoid tit-for-tat. Rather than get dragged into a losing battle over price, Real remained on the offensive against Microsoft, choosing its own weapons and terrain.

The competition between RealNetworks and Microsoft continues as of this writing, and the end of the story is not yet known. But Real's mastery of balance techniques helped it sustain a leading position for more than five years. Few of Microsoft's competitors can make a similar claim.

Getting Real: 1994–1995

"Intense" and "driven" are the first words Rob Glaser brings to mind. Dressed in black from his half-rim glasses to his shoes, he flashes a swift smile before settling back into all-business mode. Asked about

RealNetworks, Glaser doesn't just talk—he *streams*. Words and ideas spill forth in a constant current, forming sentences, paragraphs, and entire pages composed on the go. Intent on what he's explaining, he stares at the table in front of him while his gravelly voice builds momentum, looking up at the last moment to drive the point home. Glaser doesn't shout—although he's reputed to have done his share of yelling in his time. He doesn't fidget or use expansive gestures to help his arguments along. But in keeping with his reputation as a ferocious competitor, he exudes a steely determination to win.

Glaser joined Microsoft fresh out of Yale in 1983. The company's big breakthrough had come two years earlier, with the release of IBM's first personal computer, which ran on Microsoft's Disk Operating System (MS-DOS). By the time Glaser came on board, Microsoft had around 250 employees and $50 million in annual sales. But despite its size, the company still offered the scrappy start-up environment that Glaser craved.

Glaser and Microsoft grew up together over the next ten years. While the company went from $50 million to $3.8 billion in sales, Glaser rose steadily through the ranks. After a stint managing Microsoft Word, he spent two years in Microsoft's networking group before moving into multimedia computing in 1989. Four years later, as Glaser's tenth anniversary with the company approached, he was vice president of multimedia and consumer systems, part owner of baseball's Seattle Mariners, and a multimillionaire, thanks to Microsoft's 1986 initial public offering (IPO). But his job satisfaction, he later recalled, "had gone down from 90 percent to 70 percent."[1] Microsoft had become a corporate giant, and Glaser preferred the underdog role. In addition, he was widely believed to have locked horns with Nathan Myhrvold, a Princeton-trained physicist who had become Bill Gates's confidant.

Glaser left Microsoft in early 1993 and spent a few months traveling through Germany, Greece, and Egypt. He also jumped into the nonprofit arena, becoming a board member for five organizations, including the Electronic Frontier Foundation and the Foundation for National Progress, the group that publishes *Mother Jones*. But this relative inactivity did not come naturally to someone of Glaser's drive. Soon the itch to get back into the swing of things took hold.

"This Great Phenomenon Called the Internet"

By this time, the concept of a 500-channel universe was beginning to generate a lot of buzz. Time Warner was investing tens of millions of dollars in an Orlando, Florida, trial of video-on-demand. TCI, the country's largest cable company, had announced plans to buy as many as 1.8 million digital set-top boxes to deliver interactive programming. And not to be left behind, a number of the regional Bell operating companies were thinking about launching pilot programs of their own.

Glaser was drawn to the vision of a 500-channel world, but he harbored serious doubts about the cable operators' and telephone companies' ability to get this world built. After taking soundings in the industry, Glaser quickly concluded that their approach had two fatal flaws. First, it had "no technical bootstrap"—all of the technologies behind interactive television were being invented from scratch. Second, the economics of the business were horrendous as a result. Since the fixed costs associated with launching interactive television were so high, a company had to earn at least $1,000 in net present value per household in order for its investment to pay off.

"Meanwhile," said Glaser, "there was this great phenomenon called the Internet." Through his work with the Electronic Frontier Foundation, Glaser had come into contact with some of the Internet's pioneers. And through these contacts, he discovered the Mosaic Web browser in July 1993. Mosaic provided the epiphany that Glaser had been waiting for. As soon as he got on the Web, "It became absolutely clear to me, game over, that this was going to be where the future was built," he said. The Web did not have the problems that accompanied interactive television. It had a technical bootstrap in the form of the phone system, which was not great, but "good enough to get the ball rolling." And it had a business bootstrap in the form of the browser, which provided a supportive framework for new technologies and companies like the one Glaser planned to build.

Progressive Networks, as RealNetworks was originally named, was incorporated in February 1994 with the initial goal of developing software for sending audio over the Internet.[2] The wired world was young. Most dial-up connections ran at 14.4 kilobits per second (kbps)—a tiny pipe for text and images, let alone sound and motion. So along with the Internet, RealNetworks would learn to walk before trying to run.

Audio was a significant market in its own right. "Even in this day of television, the average American spends fifteen hours [per week] listening to audio of various kinds as opposed to twenty or twenty-two hours of watching video," Glaser observed. But more important, audio would serve as a bootstrap for other products down the road. As Glaser recounted, "We figured, okay, rather than doing a terrible job of doing everything at once, let's do a decent job of creating video and audio by starting with audio and then getting to video as bandwidth and the processing power of computers improve."

Fat Files, Skinny Pipes

In 1994, when Real's developers set to work, an audio file had to be downloaded in its entirety before it could be played. Early online services, such as Prodigy, CompuServe, and AOL, maintained down-loadable sound clip libraries for subscribers' use. But the enormous amount of data involved—1,378 kilobits for every second of CD-quality sound—meant that with a 14.4 kbps modem, the ratio of download to listening time could be close to 100 to 1. Even at lower standards of fidelity, downloading a five-minute clip could take any-where from twenty-five minutes to more than an hour.

RealNetworks's innovation—streaming audio—did away with the wait, allowing Web surfers to download and listen to audio at the same time. Three pieces made up the original RealAudio system: RealAudio Studio, which allowed content providers to create streaming audio files; RealAudio Server, which served them up; and RealAudio Player, a piece of client software that handled playback. Using the RealAudio Player (since renamed RealPlayer), you could click on a file—say, the day's news on NPR—and listen to it play in real time. Nothing was stored on your hard drive; in order to replay the file, you had to return to the Web and click again.

Codecs—algorithms that *co*mpress and *de*compress data—lay at the heart of streaming media technology. RealNetworks developed its own codecs to format audio, and later video, files. In addition, the company's developers created a number of technologies to over-come problems associated with the Internet, such as latency (delays in transmission) and the possibility of losing information packets along the way.

From Here to Ubiquity

By July 1994, the RealAudio prototype was at what Glaser called the "Watson, come here; I need you" stage—"where we proved to our-selves that it would actually work." Nine months later, Glaser launched RealAudio at the National Association of Broadcasters's Las Vegas convention. RealAudio 1.0 used eight kilobits of data to represent a single second of sound. The resulting streams could squeeze through a 14.4 kbps modem, but sound quality was poor. "Recognizable" was the best that one reporter could find to say about music played through RealAudio, while voice, he said, sounded like "a medium-quality AM radio with unremarkable reception."[3] Yet despite its tinny quality, RealAudio 1.0 quickly took off. Within four months, the company had distributed nearly 230,000 copies of its playback software.

One reason for its fast-growing popularity was simple: RealAudio Player could be downloaded for free from the RealAudio site. (The company received revenues from servers and encoding tools.) As Glaser explained, taking price out of the picture was a central ele-ment of his strategy from the start. "It was clear to me that once we established this idea, there would be a race, and we didn't want any-body to have a stronger or purer strategy towards ubiquity than we did," he recalled. "So that was an important element of the way we set the business up: that we would have free products. We thought that over time we could also have consumer products that we would sell, but we figured that we would take a 'damn the torpedoes view,' get our ubiquitous products out there, and then over time build rev-enue on top of that." (See figure 6–1.)

With so much at stake, RealNetworks didn't just rely on people finding its home on the Web. The company also negotiated distri-bution deals with Microsoft and Netscape, as well as with smaller Internet software companies such as Spyglass and Spry. RealAudio Player was the only product bundled with Microsoft's Internet

Figure 6-1: RealProgress: Installed Base and Quarterly Revenues, 1995–2000

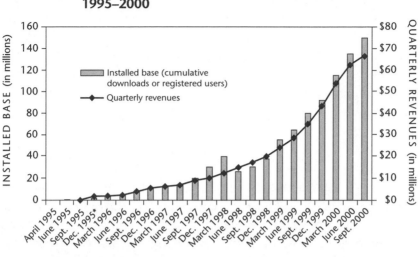

*Represents revenues for the preceding twelve months.

Note: In the spring of 1998, RealNetworks switched from counting cumulative downloads to registered users.

Source: Company press releases, authors' estimates.

Explorer, which launched together with Windows 95 in August 1995, and the Microsoft Network drove traffic to RealAudio by bookmarking its site. Netscape also distributed RealAudio Player, but not for free. In order to get RealAudio Player from the company, consumers had to buy Netscape's Power Pack, a $55 package of add-on applications for Navigator.[4]

In addition to arranging for large-scale distribution, Glaser worked to build an audience for RealAudio by wooing content providers to give the technology a try. There was no point in having a RealAudio Player, after all, if there was nothing out there to play. Exciting content would lead more people to try the player, encouraging content providers to create more RealAudio files, leading in turn to higher rates of adoption for the player, until ubiquity had been achieved. This process, which Real insiders referred to as their "virtuous circle," was a classic example of network effects at work.

National Public Radio and ABC were the first partners Glaser signed. Both companies made news clips available on the RealAudio site in April 1995, while other publishers began to incorporate RealAudio into their own properties on the Web. By the fall, Real had enough users to entice big-name companies into experimenting with RealAudio on a significant scale. ESPNet SportsZone broadcast a Mariners-Yankees game live from New York in September 1995, and several days later, ABC RadioNet inaugurated live news broadcasts, somewhat inauspiciously perhaps, with coverage of the O. J. Simpson trial.

Facing Off: 1995–1997

RealNetworks announced the first upgrade to its software, RealAudio 2.0, in October 1995. By then, customers had downloaded at least 450,000 copies of RealAudio Player, and more than 130 sites offered RealAudio content. But Real was also facing competition for the first time. Xing Technology, a California start-up, released an audio and video streaming system in August 1995. VDOnet, another upstart, unveiled its streaming video technology the same day that RealAudio 2.0 debuted. And in July 1996, Macromedia entered the market with a new version of Shockwave, the popular multimedia plug-in, that featured CD-quality streaming sound.

Glaser's strategy for dealing with relatively small, focused competitors centered on speed. "It seemed to us we were going to face a couple of waves of competitors," he explained:

> One would be the small technological innovators, of which we were one, that didn't have structural advantages in terms of access to huge pools of capital or distribution reach. They would try to out-innovate us, and we certainly didn't want that to happen. So we set in motion to have a very, very rapid pace of innovation. In the five years since we introduced the first version of RealAudio, we've had seven major versions of our system, and we've maintained a pretty consistent pace of innovation, introducing significant new versions probably every six to twelve months.

In addition, Glaser sought to preempt competitors by moving swiftly to lock up a formidable installed base. RealNetworks didn't just spread its net wide; it also went deep, creating direct relationships with its customers. Unlike Netscape, which had pioneered free downloading as a commercial distribution strategy, Real could contact most of the people who downloaded RealAudio Player from its site. Prior to downloading, users were required to provide an e-mail address, a now-standard practice that provoked controversy at the time. The process was easy to subvert. Anybody could supply a fake address, as long as it matched basic e-mail syntax. If users opted not to be contacted, Real honored those requests. But this occurred only 10 percent of the time, allowing the company to stay in touch with most of its customer base. The real payoff to this strategy came a couple of years later, when the company started to build automatic updating into its software. This feature allowed Real to issue updates to customers as new versions of the software were released, making RealPlayer much harder for a competitor to dislodge.

MOVEMENT AT REALNETWORKS: FOLLOW THROUGH FAST

The Challenge: You're first to market, but competitors are already on the move.

The Solution: Make the most of your first-mover advantage by building and, if possible, locking in a massive installed base.

- Make market share, not revenue, your immediate goal—especially in industries where network effects play an important role.

- Invest in processes, such as automatic updating, that tie you closely to your customer base.

- Innovate constantly—don't get blindsided by a competitor with the latest technology.

"We Always Knew We Had a Window"

From the beginning, Glaser recognized that "indigenous competitors," as he termed them, were unlikely to be Real's biggest obstacle. Down the road loomed the prospect of facing off against Microsoft and his old boss, Bill Gates. According to Glaser, as soon as he grasped the promise of the market, the potential for conflict in this quarter—and the need for caution—became clear. As a result, the company lay low at first, adopting a variant of the puppy dog ploy.

"It was likely," Glaser recalled, "that we would cross paths, maybe cross swords—maybe not—with Microsoft. So we were quite careful about who we told what we were doing and who we didn't."

Mitch Kapor, RealNetworks's first outside investor and a member of its board, similarly remembered thinking, "Microsoft hasn't figured this out yet at all, but surely they will."[5] Eventually the software powerhouse would grasp the importance of first the Internet and then streaming media. From there it would be a short step to the decision to integrate streaming media technology into the Windows operating system. "We always knew we had a window of time," Kapor said. The question was, how much? "Perhaps eighteen months to two years," he believed. "That's the absolute max."

Speed was again a key weapon as Real sought to make the most of its first-mover advantage before Microsoft entered the game. But Glaser didn't rely on speed alone. More ambitiously, he aimed to grip Microsoft and use his future opponent's strength to his advantage—a task, he hoped, that might be eased by Microsoft's all-out war with Netscape. As Jim Breyer, one of Mitch Kapor's colleagues at Accel Partners and a fellow Real director, explained, "It was very clear that Microsoft and Netscape were going to fight vigorously for a period of time. Therefore, we felt that there was an opportunity to partner with at least one of the companies and build some long-term advantage." In particular, Breyer believed that the chances for cooperation with Microsoft, in the short term at least, were good. "Streaming media in 1996 and even in 1997 had not been raised to a high level of strategic visibility," he observed. "Part of the bet we were making was that Microsoft would continue to fight very core, strategic battles with companies such as Netscape and Oracle in areas where billions of dollars were at stake. The streaming media market was not going to evolve into a multibillion dollar market overnight. And therefore we felt we had time to continue to work with Microsoft productively in certain areas."

Real's bundling deal with Microsoft was the first example of this strategy at work. Rather than stay out of Bill Gates's way, as the puppy dog ploy might recommend, Glaser harnessed Microsoft's distribution muscle and used it to drive RealAudio deep into the market. Microsoft distributed at least 40 million copies of Internet

Explorer in its first year, and every one of them contained a free copy of RealAudio Player.

Setting Standards

At the same time, RealNetworks made moves to work with both Microsoft and Netscape on defining standards for streaming media technology. "We felt we were in an eighteen- to twenty-four-month period of time where setting standards would be critical," Breyer recalled, "and without one of the major browser companies, we would not be able to influence standards appropriately"—or in a manner that would preserve Real's ability to compete.

In March 1996, RealNetworks pledged to support a new Microsoft file format for streaming media known as ASF (Active Streaming Format). In addition to making future versions of RealAudio compatible with ASF, Real agreed to promote the new technology as an industry standard. In the end, nothing came of this particular agreement. But in the short term, Glaser secured an important tactical goal by keeping Microsoft on his side.

At the same time, Real worked closely with Microsoft arch-rival Netscape. In the fall of 1996, the two companies led a forty-member coalition in announcing support for Real-Time Streaming Protocol (RTSP), a specification that would promote interoperability among products from different vendors. RTSP's backers constituted a virtual *Who's Who* of the emerging Internet economy—Adobe, Apple, IBM, Macromedia, Netscape, RealNetworks, and Sun—with the exception of Microsoft, where officials said they had first heard of the proposed standard shortly before its release.

Real's efforts at cooperation did not eliminate the threat of further competition. Both Microsoft and Netscape released their own streaming media products in late 1996. But Real succeeded in strengthening its competitive position by working with its future rivals rather than keeping out of their way. Distribution deals with Netscape and Microsoft helped Real build a significant lead. And by offering to cooperate on the development of key technologies, Glaser helped ensure that when it came to setting standards, RealNetworks would not be left out in the cold.

BALANCE AT REALNETWORKS:
GRIP YOUR OPPONENT

The Challenge: You've built a strong initial position, but powerful competitors loom on the horizon.

The Solution: Build relationships that weaken your competitors' positions while strengthening your own.

- Grip competitors by tapping them as a distribution channel and turning their customers into your own.

- Grip competitors by working on common technology standards—which will limit their room to maneuver if they decide to attack.

By the summer of 1996, Glaser had sufficient confidence in Real's market position to start charging for a premium version of the player. The basic version of RealAudio Player remained free. But beginning in August 1996, consumers had the option of paying $29.99 for RealAudio Player Plus, a premium version that offered customized broadcasts, quick scanning of Internet radio stations, and buttons that could be preset to favorite sites. Within the company, RealAudio Player Plus was a controversial move. Many doubted that users would be willing to pay for something that they could essentially get for free. But by mid-2000, premium versions of the player had generated $75 million in revenue, proving the skeptics wrong.

Shortly after bringing out RealAudio Player Plus, RealNetworks also introduced a next-generation release, RealAudio 3.0, which offered higher-quality sound. This was followed in February 1997 by the launch of RealVideo, which featured three five-minute films commissioned for the occasion from Spike Lee. At 100 kbps and above, RealVideo streamed close to fifteen frames per second, delivering what the company termed "near TV broadcast quality." Customers with 28.8 kbps modems, however, only received five to ten frames per second, resulting in a picture that reminded at least one viewer of the jerky images of Neil Armstrong beamed down from the moon.[6] Anticipating consumer disappointment, Real executives tried to downshift the hype. At dial-up speeds, streaming video was clearly not a prime-time experience—at least, not yet. But RealNet-works couldn't afford to sit out the market while other companies took the lead. VDOnet, which was partially owned by Microsoft, had already distributed at least 4.5 million copies of its streaming video player, and the next release of Microsoft's NetShow streaming media system was slated for June.[7]

Microsoft Enters the Ring

At that point, Microsoft had not yet become a significant threat. As Len Jordan, who headed Real's media systems division, recalled, "We had started to compete a little bit with Microsoft, but they hadn't taken the streaming market that seriously in terms of making invest-ments. They weren't very broadly used, and there wasn't much con-tent in their formats." By Real's estimates, RealAudio accounted for about 85 percent of the streaming sound files on the Web.

But signs of trouble in Real's relationship with Microsoft were beginning to emerge. Kelly Jo MacArthur, who became Real's gen-eral counsel in 1996, pointed to the bundling agreements as the first area of dispute. After the release of RealAudio 3.0, Microsoft con-tinued to ship older versions of the player, she explained, giving rise to the impression that Real's technology was obsolete.

Then, one day in June 1997, a manager at RealNetworks picked up his phone and heard an unfamiliar voice. "Tell Rob Glaser that Microsoft is about to purchase VXtreme," the anonymous tipster said. VXtreme was a two-year-old startup with a highly regarded video streaming technology. Microsoft's interest revealed that the company was about to get much more serious about streaming media. And it was about to do so in a way that would pit RealNet-works against Microsoft head-to-head.

Streaming media had been moving steadily up Microsoft's list of priorities for several months. In an important step, a company reor-ganization put streaming media under the authority of Anthony Bay, general manager of Internet servers, and Bob Muglia, vice pres-ident of server applications, in April 1997. The streaming media team soon presented Bay and Muglia with an assessment of the state of play. After reviewing the risks of allowing Real's business to go unchecked, they recommended "a radical new strategy" to grab 50 percent of the market by the end of the year.[8] One option they considered was to buy Real and "get rid of their problemsome management"—with Glaser in the lead. In the end, however, the team rejected this alternative in favor of buying several of Real's competitors and creating a new best-of-breed technology.

After rescaling the first-year target down to a more realistic 20 percent, Bay and Muglia presented essentially the same case to Bill Gates. As Bay recounted, "We went to Bill and said, 'You have a couple of choices. . . . Either we decide Rob will continue to be in the driver's seat [in streaming media], and we don't care; or we decide he's going to be in the driver's seat and we will try and have some partnership, essentially recognizing their primacy; or we are going to have to basically go compete. You have to choose.'" Gates, not surprisingly, chose to compete—although he still "held open the door to cooperation with Real," Bay believed.

While Glaser was not privy to Microsoft's deliberations, he had his own suspicions as to the company's plans. Upon being alerted to the talks with VXtreme, he launched an all-out effort to stop Microsoft before it moved irrevocably down a separate path. Real's most urgent priority was to put a spike in Microsoft's plans for VXtreme. As Mitch Kapor explained, the thinking among members of the board was: "Try to get a foot in the door to do something so that they don't have this new armament to use against us." Providing a management perspective, Kelly Jo MacArthur expanded on the same theme:

> One of the things we were hoping they wouldn't do was to take their own emerging technology, combine it with the VXtreme technology, and create a fork in the road—an alternative out there to RealAudio and RealVideo that allowed enough content to get encoded in their formats and content served in their streams and facilitated the distribution of their player in a way that would start to marginalize us.

Within hours of getting the tip about VXtreme, Glaser called Paul Maritz, Microsoft's group vice president for platforms and applications, and talked him into meeting with RealNetworks. "The next day we had a meeting," Glaser recalled, "and four days later we had a deal." In the hastily drawn agreement—"It's ugly," MacArthur said with professional disdain—RealNetworks and Microsoft entered into a marriage of convenience. Microsoft paid $30 million to license RealAudio and RealVideo 4.0, which were released in June. In return, RealNetworks agreed to adopt several Microsoft technologies and to work with Microsoft on promulgating its file format, ASF, as an industry standard. Both companies announced that they would work to ensure interoperability between their products, with Microsoft adding that it would continue to distribute basic versions of RealNetworks's players and servers until compatibility was achieved. And finally, Microsoft acquired a 10 percent nonvoting stake in RealNetworks for an additional $30 million.

The complexity of the agreement reflected the four days of intense negotiation from which it emerged. Over those ninety-six hours, Glaser and his colleagues battled to get a firm grip on Microsoft and gain the most from any future relationship, while their Microsoft counterparts parried and riposted in an attempt to get a secure grip on Real. Both companies were fighting for recognition as the dominant force in streaming media software, with the hope of relegating the loser to a secondary role.

Initially, it was unclear who had succeeded in securing the upper hand. When the deal was announced, many observers scored it as a Microsoft win, focusing on Real's apparent endorsement of ASF. "Microsoft streams triumphant," blared a headline in the *Red Herring*, which went on to advise, "Keeping a close watch on streaming video? Go home, folks; the show's over." With hindsight, however, it is clear that Glaser out-negotiated his former employer. The agreement the two sides finally reached was designed to work to Real's advantage even if the effort to work together broke down. There were those at Microsoft, in fact, who believed that Glaser never intended to make the deal work. "We argued, 'Real is trying to screw us,'" recalled Anthony Bay, who strongly opposed the agreement. But Bill Gates, he said, made the decision to give it a try, while hedging his bets by also moving forward with the acquisition of VXtreme.

Glaser contended that these suspicions were groundless. "The deal was structured so that they could've been pretty sure that our success didn't imperil them if they had chosen to look at it this way," he maintained. Glaser interpreted the agreement as paving the way for RealNetworks to become a long-term technology supplier to Microsoft in the streaming media space. Moreover, he said, Microsoft would have the opportunity to profit financially as RealNetworks grew. "I sincerely believed that we were going to win, and that it would be rational for them to have a 20 percent stake in the victor rather than a zero percent stake," Glaser explained.[9]

This optimism might seem surprising, given Glaser's intimate knowledge of how Microsoft worked—and of Microsoft's traditional insistence on controlling core technologies. But Glaser was also prepared for another scenario. "We set our strategies up so that even if [the relationship] turned adversarial, we would have the ability to compete successfully," he made clear. For one thing, for as long as it held, the June 1997 agreement underwrote RealNetworks's ubiquity play by keeping Microsoft as a distribution partner.

Moreover, the deal offered Glaser a chance to shift the terms of combat to his advantage. Looking back three years later, he invoked a colorful analogy to explain his thinking: "As Don Corleone put it, 'Keep your friends close and your enemies closer.' We knew in the summer of '97 that it was highly likely that Microsoft would want to compete in this space, and we thought, 'Well, would it be better for us if they competed in a way that had nothing to do with our technology? Or would it be better if they competed based on our technology?'"

In his eyes, the answer was obvious. Real would be better positioned to beat Microsoft if its own technology provided the competitive terrain—even though Glaser had given Microsoft an option to purchase two further snapshots of RealNetworks's source code. "We did that because we really did want to preserve an opportunity to stay aligned," Glaser explained. "But," he added, "we figured that if they were going to go to war with us, the snapshots probably wouldn't be hugely valuable because they wouldn't get the people associated with creating them." Moreover, Glaser noted, if the relationship went sour, "we would have flexibility in not necessarily licensing them subsequent versions of our technology." In other words, once Microsoft was hooked on RealNetworks's code, the ability to cut his rival off would ensure that Glaser had the upper hand.

BALANCE AT REALNETWORKS:
GRIP YOUR OPPONENT

The Challenge: Your intelligence tells you that your largest competitor is preparing to go up against you head-to-head.

The Solution: Keep your opponent close in order to reduce his incentive to attack (ideally) and reduce the force he can put behind a blow (minimally).

- Co-opt your opponent, if possible, by giving him a stake in your success.

- Reduce your opponent's room to maneuver by making him dependent upon something only you can supply.

- Keep your options open and maintain your freedom of movement.

Very quickly, it became clear that the rush to agreement had left Real and Microsoft at odds over the meaning of the deal they had signed. While Glaser intended to retain his position in streaming media software, Microsoft executives believed that Real had agreed to give up its position of technology leadership and move up the value chain into streaming media services. The misunderstanding surfaced at a private meeting between Bill Gates and Rob Glaser in early July. "The first thing he said," Glaser recalled, "was, 'So what are you going to do now that you're getting out of the streaming media software business?'"

More bad news followed. The joint effort to create an ASF standard soon broke down, amid recrimination from both sides. And in a move that still provokes violent reactions from Glaser and his team, Microsoft released free versions of the RealAudio and RealVideo servers—without pointing out to potential customers that the free software supported only sixty simultaneous streams.

According to Microsoft's Anthony Bay, RealNetworks had no reason to be surprised by this decision. As he recalled, "We paid $30 million for rights equivalent to ownership, and what we said was, 'We will distribute this on the same basis that we distribute our own [streaming media] software'"—or, in other words, free or bundled with Windows NT. Nonetheless, Glaser maintained that Microsoft's move came as "a shot across the bow"—a direct and unanticipated

---

THE MICROSOFT DEAL IN HINDSIGHT

Let's pick another path. Let's pick the Marc Andreessen, "We're going to turn Windows into a collection of mediocre device drivers approach," declaring ourselves a head-on competitor to Windows. Let's say we take that approach. I don't think it would have done any good. We might have gotten a little more famous as a company because a head-on strategy from a PR standpoint is a sexier story. But all of those natural competitive juice dynamics that are there would have been more volatilely engaged. . . .

At the time, we were doing roughly $7 million a quarter. I thought the right thing for us to do was to build for the long haul. Right now we have 115 million registered users. At the end of '99, we had 95 million. At the end of '98, we had 42 million. At the end of '97, we had 17 million. We have ten times more users than we had at the time. So it was clearly the right thing to do to try to defer the head-on competition until a time when we were at a scale that we were likely to succeed, even in the face of head-on competition.

—ROB GLASER

---

attack on the heart of RealNetworks's revenue model, which licensed servers by the stream. "So basically on that day," he recalled, "I think we had a war room meeting, and we decided, 'Hey, let's get farther out as soon as possible.'"

Moving On: 1997–2000

Real's developers immediately stepped up work on RealSystem 5.0, which was introduced that fall. RealSystem 5.0 featured several innovations, including streaming animation, improved audio and video quality for dial-up connections, and full-screen video at higher speeds. In addition, as Glaser explained, "it had the property of taking what Microsoft had licensed from us and rendering it somewhat obsolete." As was common practice, RealSystem 5.0 played all prior versions of RealAudio and RealVideo files, but older servers and players couldn't handle the new, souped-up streams.

Microsoft had an option to license the new code for $25 million but chose to pass. "That first $30 million was wasted quickly," explained Will Poole, who succeeded Anthony Bay as head of Microsoft's streaming media business in February 2000. "That left a pretty bad taste in our mouths."

At the same time, Glaser and his fellow board members decided to take the company public in order to build a war chest for the forthcoming clash with Microsoft. This was a decision he had long resisted, citing as precedent none other than Microsoft, which had remained private for eleven years. But Glaser estimated that the probability of intense competition had risen from around 60 percent in June to 90 or even 95 percent by the fall, so "getting big and getting to a level of scale and visibility was an important consideration," he explained. Accordingly, in late September the company filed for an initial public offering. Two months later, RealNetworks debuted on NASDAQ, gaining 43 percent on its first day.

Seeking Leverage

In the months that followed, RealNetworks used a mix of judo techniques as the company sought to maintain the upper hand. Leveraging his competitors' competitors, for example, was an area where Glaser showed particular skill. In the early days, this largely meant playing Microsoft and Netscape off against each other, as a former Real project manager recounted: "We were very careful in various meetings at various levels at Microsoft to emphasize that we were 'former *Microsofties*' and with Netscape that we were '*former* Microsofties.'"[10]

Continuing in the spirit of this approach, Real started negotiating with Microsoft competitor Sun Microsystems in late 1997. In January 1998, the two companies unveiled an agreement to port Real's software onto Sun's Solaris, a heavy-duty operating system that competed with Windows NT. This deal highlighted Real's ability to use leverage against Microsoft by developing software for non-Windows platforms.

"We're Really in the Media Delivery Business"

But driving technology forward remained at the heart of Real's strategic plan. In April 1998, the company introduced RealSystem

G2, a "bet the farm" effort to rewrite Real's source code from the ground up. RealSystem G2 introduced two new Real formats, Real-Text and RealPix, which integrated text and still images into multimedia presentations. In addition, it supported several non-Real technologies, like the Microsoft-developed audio file format WAV. But Real wrapped all of these technologies in a layer of innovation that only G2 could provide. Software from a number of vendors might stream and play the same types of files. But RealPlayer had more bells and whistles for consumers, such as built-in channels and streaming media search. RealServer offered content providers unique features such as in-stream ad insertion, which was introduced in May 1999. And both consumers and content providers had to use Real's products in order to get the benefits of features like SureStream, a technology that automatically tuned transmission quality as network conditions changed.

By adding value to the entire streaming process, Glaser hoped to commoditize the level of technology—file formats—where Microsoft had focused its assault. In addition, this strategy was designed to reduce Real's vulnerability to piecemeal attack by ensuring the company offered a complex integrated system, rather than a component—like a browser or a player—that could easily be replaced. "Because our business involves so much visible software, people perceive that we are in the stand-alone consumer software business, whereas we're really in the media delivery business," Glaser explained, adding, "I wouldn't be in the stand-alone client business against Microsoft. There are some games where their financial resources and operating system distribution are highly influential if not dispositive. It's been our strategy not to play those games."

Yet despite Glaser's caution, he could be drawn on occasion into losing plays. In the summer of 1998, for example, Glaser began to hear reports that Windows Media Player was automatically replacing or disabling the latest version of RealPlayer G2—making it impossible to access the latest versions of RealAudio and RealVideo files. In July, in response to an invitation from Senator Orrin Hatch, he made this charge public, declaring in testimony before the Senate Judiciary Committee that Microsoft was "breaking" Real's products. Microsoft counterattacked immediately, arguing that a bug in

Real's software was the cause of the problems Glaser had described. The ensuing controversy, coupled with the painful reminder that Real and Microsoft were not, after all, on the same side, drove Real's stock down 35 percent over the next several days. Moreover, independent analysts ultimately concluded that Real bore most of the responsibility for the problem, although there was blame enough to go around.[11]

The Rise of MP3

While Real's relationship with Microsoft was sinking to new lows, the company faced a challenge on a new front. Glaser had guided his company to unquestioned leadership in the streaming media market. But streaming itself was being forced to make room for a fast-growing alternative by the summer of 1998. Download-and-play was making a comeback, driven by an obscure compression standard known as MP3. MP3 (or MPEG-1 Audio Layer-3) is a technology for reducing a file to one-tenth or even one-twelfth its original size while preserving near-CD quality sound. While MP3 files can also be streamed, their main advantage is that they make it possible to download and store music on computers and portable players and play it back offline.

MP3 had been around since 1992, but for several years limits on bandwidth and computing power prevented it from entering mainstream use. In 1996, only a tiny group of geeks had heard of MP3. In 1997, it became an underground movement, sweeping college campuses from coast to coast. By 1998, MP3 had gained enough momentum to become a legal battleground, as the recording industry fought to shut the budding sector down. Many of the MP3 files available on the Internet were clearly legal—singles, for example, that unsigned bands released through MP3.com. The majority, however, had been "ripped" from commercially issued CDs and e-mailed, posted on the Internet, or traded through new peer-to-peer networks such as Napster and Gnutella.

The music industry was desperate to end this traffic. Bidding for the labels' support, a number of companies entered the market with secure downloading technologies that attacked MP3 head-on.

Between 1997 and 1999, at least four major players—AT&T, IBM, Sony, and Microsoft—developed copyright-friendly digital download formats that were touted as alternatives to MP3—although Microsoft also supported the insurgent standard.

Embracing MP3

In mid-1998, Glaser decided that RealNetworks had to embrace MP3. "That summer, MP3 hit a tipping point and became a phenomenon," recalled Alex Alben, vice president for government affairs. "We knew that MP3 was going to be a leading standard for some time to come, and RealNetworks products had to support MP3 encoding and decoding if we were going to offer consumers what they wanted." At the same time, however, Glaser remained mindful of the music industry's concerns. The major labels, after all, were important customers and content providers for Real.

The result was a dual-track strategy that preserved the company's future options while harnessing the momentum behind MP3. Real supported the recording industry's efforts to develop downloading standards that protected copyright holders' rights. In addition, the company partnered with several of the companies developing digital rights management systems, including AT&T and IBM. But Real's primary focus was on developing RealJukebox 1.0, a digital downloading product that debuted in May 1999. RealJukebox recorded (Real avoided the word "rip") tracks in two formats: RealAudio G2, which was the default option, and MP3. For download and playback, it supported a wider range of competing formats. In addition, Real's latest software enabled consumers to create and manage personal music libraries by organizing tracks in a database and creating playlists that could be transferred to portable listening devices.

RealJukebox was a relative latecomer to the market. Two other products—Winamp, which had recently been acquired by AOL, and MusicMatch Jukebox, which was developed by a San Diego startup—had a one-year lead. Moreover, according to influential technology columnist Walt Mossberg, Real's jukebox was inferior to MusicMatch's, then in version 4.1.[12] But Real quickly pushed ahead, backed by the sixty-million-strong RealPlayer installed base. One million copies of RealJukebox were downloaded in the first ten days. After three months, Media Metrix reported, RealJukebox held more than half the market, with 2.2 million unique users in June 1999.

By spring 2000, when RealJukebox 2 appeared, RealJukebox had more than 34 million unique registered users and supported technology from seven other companies—including Microsoft's Windows Media audio format—in addition to MP3 and its own formats. "We are making RealJukebox a universal product," Glaser explained. His goal was to make RealJukebox the default choice for consumers who didn't care what type of files their music came in, as long as it played. But supporting all popular formats was only one part of Real's bid for ubiquity in digital downloading. Following the model it had set in the streaming market, Real also wrapped all the technologies it embraced in a set of value-added features. Even the difficult-to-please Mossberg praised the interface, visualization graphics, and information-rich features added to RealJukebox 2.

By embedding MP3 into a distinctive, value-added product, Real had both embraced and enhanced the standard. This became even more evident when Real started charging for RealJukebox Plus, which was introduced in August 1999. By contrast, Microsoft, which incorporated jukebox functionality into Windows Media Player in April 2000, continued to offer its software for free.

BALANCE AT REALNETWORKS:
PUSH WHEN PULLED

The Challenge: In addition to attacks from larger competitors, you constantly face challenges from new technologies and start-up companies.

The Solution: Embrace alternative technologies and use their momentum to your advantage.

- Commoditize new technologies and make distinctive value-added features the basis of competition.
- Be inclusive rather than exclusive, making your products the default choice.

Building an Ecosystem

In building an audience for RealJukebox, Real once again sought out partners to help drive demand. The company formed marketing partnerships with Warner Music and Sony, and agreed to incorporate secure downloading formats supported by Sony and Universal Music in order to gain access to their catalogs of songs. On the hardware side, the company lined up more than twenty device manufacturers to announce support for RealJukebox 2.

In forming a broad coalition of partnerships, Real was implementing one of the strategic principles that had guided the company since its debut. Glaser had long believed that creating a prosperous ecosystem—a network of companies engaged in mutually beneficial relationships with Real—would be vital to his long-term success. In addition to underwriting Real's popularity, a strong ecosystem would raise the bar for competitors trying to imitate Real's achievements.

Consequently, Glaser sought to work with a broad spectrum of companies, including content providers and online services like AOL, independent software developers, hardware manufacturers, and other technology companies, such as broadband provider Covad Communications and chipmaker Intel. And while critics might charge that Real gained an unequal advantage from some of these relationships, their importance to the company's strategy remained beyond dispute.

Real's role within its ecosystem was initially confined to that of a technology provider. Over time, however, the company's business model became more complex. Real's first major move outside the technology business came with the launch of the Real Broadcast Network (RBN) in August 1997. Created in partnership with MCI, RBN provided turnkey services to companies that wanted to run Internet or intranet broadcasts but didn't know where to begin. RBN did it all: develop and promote the content, provide the hardware and software, and serve up the streams, live or on demand, from hundreds of locations across the country. ABC Radio, Rolling Stone's video-on-demand service, and the Jerry Lewis telethon were early customers of the service, along with CNN, which used RBN to broadcast President Clinton's testimony in the Lewinsky affair in September 1998.

Services were not the only addition to Real's portfolio. Content delivery was another area of activity that grew in importance over time. Real's content offerings began modestly in April 1995 with a site that pointed to the handful of companies experimenting with RealAudio 1.0. Five years later, Real.com had nearly 13 million unique visitors each month, making it the eleventh most visited property on the Web. RealGuide, the streaming media portal built into Real.com, showcased the latest in film trailers, live music, Internet radio stations, sports, games, and news. In addition, RealGuide channeled users to more than 100 content partners from ABCNews to ZDTV.

Real also delivered content directly through the player, adding programmable destination buttons to RealPlayer 4.0 in 1997. One year and two generations later, RealPlayer G2 incorporated a search engine for RealAudio and RealVideo content, as well as more than seventy preset channels featuring content from partners like the *Wall Street Journal* and ESPN. But Real's most ambitious foray into programming was Take5, a service launched in November 1999. Combining text, audio, video, and links in a slick interface, Take5 delivered daily top picks exclusively to users of RealPlayer 7, which debuted at the same time.

These content offerings served primarily to build and maintain Real's installed base, "evangelizing the platform," as Tom Frank, Real's COO, explained. At the same time, however, they created additional opportunities to monetize the traffic that flowed through RealPlayer, RealJukebox, and Real.com. In addition to advertising and sponsorships, Real began to sell placement in RealPlayer's channels in early 1999. Critical partners continued to be carried for free—"if we really want their content or they send us a lot of people for downloads," explained Shelley Morrison, vice president for media and distribution sales. But a growing number of companies began to pay for the traffic that RealNetworks sent their way. (For a breakdown of revenue by source, see figure 6–2.)

Real's evolving business model had risks. As the company expanded into services and content, the potential for conflict with customers such as Yahoo! Broadcast, a leader in streaming media delivery, increased. But this stategy also offered Real an important short-term advantage: By developing unique assets and maintaining

Figure 6-2:   RealRevenues: Revenues by Source, 1995–1999

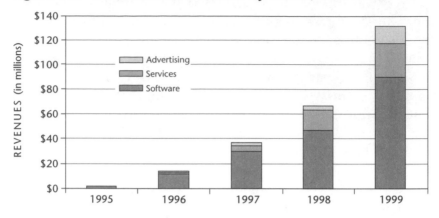

Note: Software license payments by Microsoft accounted for 13 percent of net revenues in 1997, 15 percent in 1998, and 8 percent in 1999.

its technological lead, the company could counter Microsoft's attack on the market without engaging in tit-for-tat.

Real's sales force was out in the trenches every day, competing against Microsoft for streaming media customers. In these battles, price was Microsoft's weapon of choice. Microsoft's streaming media server came bundled with Windows 2000, while Real's pricing started at $1,995 for software that supported sixty simultaneous streams. (The twenty-five-stream RealServer Basic was free.) Moreover, Microsoft offered financial bonuses, such as chits for free hosting, to customers who picked Windows Media over Real.

Real resisted the pressure to cut prices on its bread-and-butter products. "We have never matched them," Kelly Jo MacArthur affirmed. "We've always continued to sell. We've continued to sell servers ranging from the low thousands of dollars to millions of dollars worth of server technology. And to our knowledge they give most of that away for free." But conceding the high ground on price didn't mean that Real was bowing out of the game. Instead, the company typically countered Microsoft's giveaways with a package of services—cross-platform software, hosting, promotion, and distribution—that Microsoft could not yet fully match.

BALANCE AT REALNETWORKS: AVOID TIT-FOR-TAT

The Challenge: Your biggest competitor offers all of the products you sell for free.

The Solution: Rather than respond in kind, shift the terms of competition to play to your strengths.

- Contain your opponent's attack by selectively matching his most compelling and easily neutralized moves—giving away products at the lower end of the market, for example.

- Create and use assets, such as unique content delivery vehicles, that your opponent lacks.

Epilogue

In five years, Rob Glaser accomplished what only a handful of CEOs have achieved: he engaged Microsoft in an intense battle—one that got Bill Gates's attention (and goat)—and came out a winner. Yet the jury on RealNetworks is still out. Multimedia technology continues to evolve rapidly, and Microsoft remains a fierce and dedicated competitor.

What's more, Real faces the danger that the economics of the Internet will eventually overrun its core business. As the streaming media market matures, many customers will resist paying "per stream" license fees—especially if Microsoft succeeds in narrowing the technology gap. As a result, Real's largest source of revenue may stop growing or even decline. Alternative revenue streams from content aggregation, advertising, hosting, and consulting can help make up the shortfall. But as Real moves away from its dependence on software sales, the overlap between its business and that of powerful customers like Yahoo! and AOL is likely to grow. Some of these companies may decide to take their business elsewhere—even if Real is willing to provide its software for free.

However, it would be a mistake to underestimate RealNetworks and its founder. As even one of Glaser's toughest critics, Anthony Bay, admits, "Rob is incredibly smart, and he is a fierce competitor. Frankly, a lot of lesser people would have blown it up by now."

Instead, Rob Glaser has joined Intuit's Scott Cook, Palm Computing's Donna Dubinsky, and a handful of others in a select club: those who successfully challenged the software industry's Goliath and could still claim leadership after more than five years.

7

Halsey Minor and Shelby Bonnie

Maximizing Leverage at CNET Networks

Any company that carries the baggage of their current business tends to think with respect to their old models . . . We had no legacy anything.

—Shelby Bonnie, CEO, CNET Networks

HALSEY MINOR and Shelby Bonnie could easily have sailed through the 1990s as members of Wall Street's elite. Both men were to the manor born: Minor, the great-grandson of an early benefactor of the University of Virginia, and Bonnie a descendant of colonial Boston's Winthrop clan.[1] And as the decade opened, both Minor and Bonnie were on their way to promising financial careers.

But in early 1994 they packed up their belongings and moved out West, following the trail blazed by earlier generations of pioneers. This was before the commercial Internet took off, making the decision to start afresh a bold and risky move. Nonetheless, Minor and Bonnie were convinced that by trading in their bankers' pinstripes for Silicon Valley khakis, they could strike it rich. The partners' plan was to give technology media a platform worthy of its subject by "publishing" on television and online. But in pursuing this vision, they did much more than simply exploit a new channel for information—they largely rewrote the rules of the tech publishing game. CNET Networks, the company Minor started in 1992, democratized the industry by making technology news accessible to everyone, not just geeks and chief information officers (CIOs).[2] In addition, Minor and Bonnie built a new and successful model of e-commerce by challenging the traditional balance of power between advertisers and consumers.

CNET's success was far from preordained. At every stage of its rise, the company had to do battle with the pillars of the $2 billion technology media establishment. But under Minor and Bonnie's leadership, CNET prevailed by finding the weaknesses hidden in its competitors' strengths. Minor and Bonnie forced their opponents— billion dollar companies such as Ziff-Davis Publishing and International Data Group (IDG)—to confront the prospect of cannibalization by skillfully leveraging their assets, partners, and competitors. As a result, CNET was able to forge ahead while keeping the industry's giants at bay. By 2001, the company controlled the largest technology media empire on the Web, and Halsey Minor and Shelby Bonnie could count themselves as fully paid-up members of the new Internet elite.

Halsey and Shelby's Excellent Adventure

CNET began in the summer of 1992 as a flash of inspiration. Halsey Minor had had many bright ideas in his twenty-seven years: a three-dimensional version of checkers when he was nine, a computer-based apartment-finding service launched while he was at the University of Virginia, and Global Publishing, an intranet builder that Minor started at Merrill Lynch.[3] Minor and future Amazon.com founder Jeff Bezos had even collaborated on a business plan to create a personalized news fax for financial professionals. But this was something different, something radical, something really big. For his latest scheme, Minor planned to create the world's largest media company devoted to the world's fastest growing industry: technology.

As Minor began working out the details of his new venture, a former classmate introduced him to Shelby Bonnie, who became the second member of CNET's team. A fellow graduate of UVA, Bonnie was working at Tiger Management, the hedge fund group founded by fabled investor Julian Robertson. Bonnie liked Minor's pitch and helped him develop a business plan. He also became one of CNET's first investors, wiring $25,000 from the Caribbean in response to an urgent appeal for cash.[4] (Eventually, Bonnie invested more than $1.5 million, creating a stake that landed him seven places ahead of Minor on *Fortune's* list of the forty richest Americans under forty in 1999.)

Calm and understated, Bonnie was the yin to Minor's yang. "I'm not as aggressive or as outspoken or as in-your-face as Halsey," Bonnie acknowledged, "so I'm a nice check." Where Minor was brash and ebullient, Bonnie was courteous and reserved. While words spilled in a torrent from Minor, one idea chasing the next, Bonnie marshaled his thoughts and chose his words with care. As Minor dashed across the country, shaking his fists at the enemy and rallying his troops, Bonnie followed in his wake, smoothing any feathers that Minor may have ruffled. "You'd want to invest in a company run by Halsey, and you'd want your daughter to marry Shelby," one admirer of both men said.[5]

From On-Air to Online

The two partners initially saw CNET as "the next step in television."[6] "C|NET's mission is to redefine television in the age of interactive media," the company's original business plan proclaimed. Starting from two hours of programming a week, carried on a sponsor network, C|NET: The Computer Network would be developed into an independent channel offering technology news, reviews, and features twenty-four hours a day.[7] In addition, CNET would create a community of viewers and deliver interactive programming online. "We were dealing with a topic that was very information-rich in a shallow medium," Bonnie recalled, "so the idea was to create a complementary online service that could be the depth to the breadth of television." Online users would be able to drill down into material that could be handled only superficially on TV and, not incidentally, they would have the opportunity to purchase software and other products featured on-air.

With no experience in providing programming either on-air or online, Minor and Bonnie struggled to find investors to back their vision and partners to air their shows. Both searches came up dry for months, and Bonnie had to dig deeper into his pockets to keep CNET afloat. But the hunt finally paid off in the fall of 1994, when

Paul Allen, the cofounder of Microsoft, invested $5 million in the venture, which bought him a 22 percent stake.

Once Allen was on board, a distribution deal quickly fell into place. Two sister networks, the USA Network and the Sci-Fi Channel, agreed to host *c|net central*, CNET's first show, in return for warrants for 5 percent of the company's stock.[8] *c|net central*, which one CNET executive described as a technophile version of *Entertainment Tonight*, debuted on April 1, 1995. Twelve weeks later, CNET launched a companion Web site, which quickly became the true core of the company's business.

A Crowded Field

By then, CNET had to move fast in order to advance to the front of the field. The fledgling venture faced heavy competition both in television and online. On the broadcast side, CNET was squaring off against the Jones Computer Network, a division of the country's eighth-largest cable company, which launched round-the-clock programming in the fall of 1994. Meanwhile, the technology media heavyweights were already staking out their turf on the Web. Three companies dominated the burgeoning field of technology publishing, which raked in nearly $2.2 billion in advertising in 1995.[9] (See table 7–1.) Ziff-Davis Publishing led the list with 29 percent of the U.S. market, followed by CMP Publications and IDG at 18 percent each.

Founded in 1927, Ziff-Davis was a pioneer in the field of special-interest magazines, launching newsstand stalwarts like *Car & Driver*, *Popular Photography*, and *Modern Bride*. In the mid-1980s, the family-run company sold off most of its titles and refocused on computer magazines. The star of its portfolio was *PC Magazine*, which debuted in 1981. *PC Magazine* was not only the top-ranking publication in its field; it took in more advertising pages than any other magazine in the country and ranked sixth in terms of revenue in 1995.[10]

Within the industry, Ziff-Davis was known for its hard-driving management style. "Bill Ziff [Jr.] was a genius," Minor said. "He hired great people and threw money at them—and I mean that in a positive way. It was all about quality. They were the class act of the industry." Ziff retired from an active role in late 1993, and the company twice changed hands, passing from buyout firm Forstmann

Table 7-1:   The Technology Media Market, 1995

Title	Publisher	Ad Pages	Ad Revenues (in millions)
PC Magazine	Ziff-Davis	7,359	$214
Wall Street Journal	Dow Jones	1,473	$129
PC Week	Ziff-Davis	7,049	$118
Computer Shopper	Ziff-Davis	8,159	$103
Computerworld	IDG	4,668	$87
PC World	IDG	2,912	$86
Computer Reseller News	CMP	7,420	$80
InfoWorld	IDG	4,550	$80
Business Week	McGraw-Hill	1,612	$75
PC Computing	Ziff-Davis	3,056	$70

Source: Data from AdScope, Inc., cited in "Biggest Books Are Bullish after Billion-Dollar Banner Year," Media Industry Newsletter, 29 January 1996.

Little to software distributor (and budding Internet powerhouse) Softbank at the end of 1995. But the change of ownership only accelerated Ziff-Davis's growth. Under chairman and CEO Eric Hippeau, the Ziff-Davis empire quickly expanded to encompass nearly 100 titles, a market research unit, an online university, and a trade show business (which managed Comdex), all helping to generate $1 billion in sales by 1997.[11] In addition, many of ZD's titles created their own Web sites, which were later consolidated under ZDNet.com.

With revenues of $1.4 billion by 1996, arch-rival IDG outpaced Ziff-Davis around the world but trailed it in the United States.[12] Since its founding by Pat McGovern in 1964, the IDG lineup had grown to around 275 magazines. Like Ziff-Davis, IDG also owned a market research firm and a trade show group, as well as the highly successful "Dummies" line of books. But when it came to structure and strategy, the two companies stood far apart. Still majority owned by McGovern, IDG was highly decentralized, operating essentially as a federation of independent businesses. This approach was reflected in the company's Internet strategy, which was organized around individual titles and communities. "It makes no more sense for us to have one Web site or one portal than it would for us to have one computer publication," Kelly Conlin, IDG's CEO, explained.

CMP, the third major player in technology publishing, was actually the first of the three to establish a significant Internet presence, launching TechWeb as the Web home for all its magazines in late 1994. The company's dozen titles took in close to $390 million in revenue the following year, keeping it slightly ahead of IDG in the U.S. market. But the company stumbled in the mid-1990s, sinking millions into an unsuccessful Internet directory and falling short of expectations after going public in 1997. As a result, CMP never figured as prominently in CNET's calculations. (See figure 7–1.)

Whatever shortcomings the big three may have had, Minor and Bonnie didn't make the mistake of underestimating the competition. "They had tons and tons of content and information," Bonnie recalled. "They had relationships with advertisers, they had relationships with vendors, and they had lots of money, which we didn't have." But there was also a bright spot amidst all this gloom. Very few companies had been able to transition brands across mediums. Consequently, CNET was willing to bet that by focusing, it could do a better job.

Launching CNET Online

CNET.com debuted in June 1995, offering a wide range of resources, including technology news, product reviews, user forums, and a shareware "library" that directed users to sources for software downloads around the world. With interest in computers and the Internet booming, the service rapidly gained traction. More than 100,000 users registered online in the first ten weeks, and CNET was soon serving up 1.4 million page views per week—twice as many as rival ZDNet. By the fall, CNET's Web site employed sixty-five people, while forty continued to work on *c|net central*.[13]

CNET's television programming played an important role in promoting the company's efforts online. But CNET also relied heavily on the Web to drive traffic to its site. In October 1995, the company announced the most ambitious online ad campaign to date, spending $1 million on Web advertising from December 1995

Figure 7-1:   Sizing Up the Competition, 1995

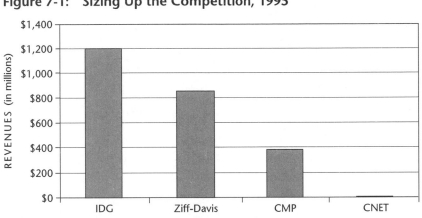

Source: Phyllis Furman, "Ziff's Favorite Son," *Crain's New York Business,* 5 August 1996; authors' estimates; company reports.

through June 1996. "I was bigger than AT&T, Microsoft, IBM, the top five advertisers combined," Minor recalled. "We ran so many ads on Lycos that when they did a survey of their users, the number one dislike was that there were too many CNET ads."

For a company CNET's size, spending on this scale represented a substantial risk. But Minor calculated that by investing early, CNET would get a bigger return on its investment. "A million dollars went a long way then," he recalled. Moreover, online advertising was more effective at the time, as early Web users were less jaded and more receptive to ads. When it started out, CNET got astonishing click rates on its banner ads of 12 percent to 25 percent, compared to less than 1 percent on average in 2000.

High click-through rates weren't all that was different about the online environment in 1995. As part of its advertising campaign, CNET signed a deal with Yahoo! that prevented any of CNET's competitors from advertising on the site for eighteen months. But when Yahoo! wanted to display a link to Ziff-Davis, which had recently bought a small stake in the company, Minor let Chief Yahoo! Jerry Yang out of the deal. "It was a collegial environment in those days," he commented. Would he do the same today? "No, it's a contract. It's a legal contract," Minor dryly observed.

MOVEMENT AT CNET: FOLLOW THROUGH FAST

The Challenge: Your competitors dominate the business—how do you get known?

The Solution: Invest aggressively in newer (and cheaper) channels that your rivals are likely to ignore.

- Bet on distribution channels that are too small or too risky for your competitors.

- Lock in partners with exclusive deals before other companies have a chance to react.

Spotlight on Downloading: 1995–1996

Using the Web as its main marketing channel was only one example of CNET's ability to make the most of the new medium. The company also hit upon a branding and customer-acquisition strategy that was particularly suited to this brave new world. It all started with the Virtual Software Library, CNET's popular download service, which accounted for half of the company's Web traffic by the fall of 1995. At that point, CNET decided to redesign the service and spin it out under a new Web address, Shareware.com. The response was dramatic, as Matthew Barzun, CNET's number four hire and later chief strategy officer, recalled: "We did 150,000 page views within the old site, which is what it was doing before, and Shareware.com did 150,000 pages on its own. We doubled traffic just by having more stuff out there."

That's when the light bulbs went on. Realizing that intuitively obvious domain names could be a critical asset, Barzun made it his mission to hunt down and buy "easy-to-understand, easy-to-spell domain names for what we thought users wanted," including News.com, Search.com, and Computers.com. "Download.com is a really cool name," Barzun continued. "Bought it for $20,000. We got Search.com for $7,000. We got a lot of really good ones early on. And we weren't acting like a big scary company. It was like, 'We're kind of small, so we'll send you some T-shirts and write you a check. We don't have a lot of money; we'll do what we can.'"

This strategy provided CNET with a war chest of high-visibility domain names at a time when the going rates were low.[14] Moreover, using generic domain names to extend its reach played to CNET's strength as a relative unknown. While Ziff-Davis and IDG were reluctant to abandon brands like *PC Magazine* that had cost them millions of dollars to create, CNET could invent itself for the Web economy from scratch. By staking its identity to domain names like Computers.com, CNET was ideally positioned to capture novices surfing the Web.

Ziff-Davis eventually woke up to CNET's strategy and responded with a copycat move. "One day someone in Ziff went and looked up all our names," Minor reported. "One week later, we discovered that Ziff had 'ChatNow,' 'EventsNow,' 'NewsNow,' etc. They just took what we had and added 'Now.'" In the end, nothing came of this effort, as Ziff decided to stick to its well-known brands. CNET, however, got in one last jab of its own: "We started getting names like Community.com and CommunityNow.com, and all the 'Nows' are in a company called ZDNow.com—which is now a subsidiary of our company," Minor said, laughing.

LEVERAGE AT CNET:
LEVERAGE YOUR OPPONENT'S ASSETS

The Challenge: Your competitors have some of the best-known brands in the industry—how do you compete?

The Solution: Create new brands that uniquely leverage the new medium and confront your competitors' with a dilemma: whether to ignore your move or to match and undermine their existing brands.

Puppy Dogs Need Not Apply

CNET's experience with downloading illustrated a broader advantage the company enjoyed. "We had no legacy anything," Bonnie liked to say. Consequently, CNET could exploit sweet spots like downloading that a print-focused organization was likely to ignore. By contrast, Bonnie believed, the technology media leaders were trapped by their own success. "Any company that carries the baggage of their current business tends to think with respect to their old models," he observed.

Minor, CNET's first CEO, was far from shy when it came to trumpeting the advantages of the company's approach. From the very beginning, he opted for an aggressive, in-your-face approach to the competition. "Personal computer magazines are the mainframes of the '90s," he told *Forbes* in mid-1996. "We are going to gut them. . . . By the year 2000, either *PC Week* or *InfoWorld* will be gone."[15]

Looking back, Minor described his bold positioning as a conscious choice. His provocative statements, he explained, were calculated to make CNET's competitors work on his behalf. "I tried to make Ziff-Davis my greatest marketer. I was always very inflammatory so that they would talk about me," he maintained. "I took every weakness that I saw in their business model and started to exploit it publicly." And when critics charged him with behaving like Netscape, Minor had a quick answer at hand: "I said, 'No, when you have 100 percent market share, you don't go out and rile up the competition. When you have zero percent market share, that's when you rile up the competition.'"

Strategy, not arrogance, drove Minor's bravado, he claimed. "Ziff-Davis was as good a company as you're going to find in media," Minor said. "I never ever took them lightly. There was a purpose behind all of my comments, and that was to get these guys on the defensive. They play terrible defense. They're great on offense, so you have to put them on defense." What Ziff-Davis should have done, Minor argued, was ignore its pesky but puny rival. But Minor was determined to force his main competitor to react. "It's like the guy in the football game who taunts the other guy, who then commits the foul and gets thrown out of the game," he explained. "That's what we did to them."

As proof that his strategy had worked, Minor pointed to an ad that Ziff-Davis ran in several publications, claiming that ZDNet was larger than Time Warner, Disney, and CNET online. It was inaccurate, Minor said, but that was just a quibble. The main point was that Ziff-Davis had anointed tiny CNET as a major player. "Time Warner, Disney, CNET.com!" Minor exulted. "I couldn't have written a better ad myself."

But CNET's strategy had a downside as well, as Dan Rosensweig,

---

A NOTE ON THE PUPPY DOG PLOY

There is one exception to the rule that safety lies in the puppy dog ploy. If you have effective leverage *and* little to lose, the advantages of attacking aggressively may outweigh the risks. A bold approach can win you attention and credibility when it matters most, while your leverage makes it difficult for rivals to respond. But remember that taunting your rivals will ultimately provoke them into action, as CNET discovered. So reserve frontal attacks for situations where your leverage is strong enough to give you a one- to two-year lead.

---

who became president of ZDNet in 1997, pointed out. "We were extremely fortunate that they were so focused on us," he observed. "It woke us up. We're a mightily competitive bunch, and this was our turf. We weren't going to give it up, and we didn't, though I think they leapfrogged us by two to three years initially." Without Minor's constant taunting, Rosensweig believed, Ziff-Davis might have continued to downplay the Internet. Moreover, CNET taught ZDNet important lessons about how to compete in the online world. "Had I not been focusing on them, I'd have been stuck in the mud like the other traditional players. Instead, they put the spotlight on every thing they were doing. It made it easier," Rosensweig explained. "We got Ziff so churned up that when we stopped playing a little bit, they really were able to marshal their resources and push their way back in," Bonnie agreed.

But in early 1996, ZDNet's comeback lay in the distant future. The moment belonged to CNET, which was rolling up viewers and advertisers as fast as it could. By April 1996, the company's Web sites were producing more than 1.3 million page views per day, on average, while the television audience for *c|net central* was estimated at 1.1 million viewers per week. In its first year of operations, TV advertising accounted for nearly 90 percent of CNET's $3.5 million in revenue, but by early 1996, the online side of the business was rapidly pulling ahead. In the first quarter of the year, CNET.com and its subsidiary sites generated more than $1 million in advertising revenue, making it the fifth-largest ad-supported property on the Web.[16] Three months later, Minor and Bonnie took the company public, raising nearly $40 million in July 1996.[17]

Spotlight on News: 1996–1997

Much of the money from the initial public offering was quickly invested back into projects such as News.com. CNET had offered news since its launch, but its initial offerings were limited. Lacking the resources of a Ziff-Davis or IDG, CNET pulled together news from other sources and did a relatively small number of product reviews, mostly of CD-ROMs and PCs.

In mid-1996, Jai Singh left IDG's *InfoWorld* to scale up this small operation and, as he put it, "go after the trade guys and eat their lunch." News.com launched in September 1996 with a simple strategy: to offer the most and the freshest technology news available on the Web. While ZDNet might publish four or five stories a day, CNET would post thirty to forty stories in the same time. In large part, this reflected the differences in the resources that the two companies devoted to their sites. Ziff-Davis's resources dwarfed CNET's in the aggregate, but the larger company had only a handful of people writing online news—five or six, by Singh's estimation—while News.com employed twenty to twenty-five.

The extra investment landed CNET a big prize in December 1996, when the *Wall Street Journal*'s Walter Mossberg put News.com on the map by singling out the site as "a must-read for anyone who cares about technology news."[18] In particular, Mossberg praised CNET's ability to publish a package of stories on Apple's acquisition of NeXT Software less than three hours after the deal was announced: at 7:15 in the evening on the Friday before Christmas. In comparison to CNET, online coverage at *PC Week* and *InfoWorld* was "sketchier and slower," the influential technology columnist said.

Publishing on Internet Time

Real-time coverage was an important source of leverage for CNET. A weekly publication like *InfoWorld* might go to press on Thursday and come out Monday. That meant that if a big story emerged, *InfoWorld* would be unable to break it for anywhere from four to ten days. That gave challengers like News.com an important opening. "We don't even have to be better than [our competitors]," said Bonnie. "We can actually be worse because we have four days to catch up at a minimum."

News.com could break stories practically as they happened and then update them as reporters gathered more information throughout the day. While their first cut at a story might lack depth, CNET's journalists would keep at it until their coverage was the most complete and the most up-to-date choice around. This strategy allowed CNET to take full advantage of the Internet's strengths as a medium, eliminating much of the friction from the publishing process and providing readers with news on demand. By contrast, Singh summed up his competitors' online strategy with two words: "warmed-over content." "The crown jewels were still being saved for the print publications," he explained.

In part, CNET's edge was due to differences in culture and training. "What we tried to create was a hybrid unlike any other, with the immediacy of broadcast and the depth of a newspaper," Singh argued. "To train reporters and editors to think that way is very hard." When News.com launched, Singh required reporters to write three stories a day, as opposed to the one or two per issue required at a weekly magazine. Moreover, the News.com team had to learn to write around the clock, rather than aiming for a daily deadline. These changes would have been difficult to swallow in any environment, but the bar to acceptance was particularly high at IDG and Ziff-Davis, where many writers were expected to do double duty by writing for the print and online editions at the same time. "They were asking their staff to serve two masters," Singh observed. "It cannot work."

But more than staffing issues made it difficult for Ziff-Davis and IDG to match CNET when it came to the timeliness of their online content. Both companies were concerned about killing the audience for their magazines if they stopped embargoing items online. Why, after all, would a reader buy *PC World* or *PC Magazine* if he could get the same information more quickly on the Web for free? And why would a publisher cannibalize its print publications, which generated tens of millions of dollars each year, in order to build traffic online, where profits were few and far between? "It was a hell of a business," said Singh, describing traditional technology publishing. "When I was at *InfoWorld*, our profits were about $15 million on revenues of $75 million or $78 million. *PC Week* and *PC Magazine* make over $200 million. How can you just say, 'Well, let's get it out on the Net for free'?"

As it turned out, IDG and Ziff-Davis couldn't—and wouldn't—give away their content until the growing threat from CNET forced their hand. "We never hear any more discussion about the Web site cannibalizing the print product. It's not a factor anymore," IDG's Conlin said in the spring of 2000. "But, depending on the market, it was a transition that lasted from several months to more than a year."

Redefining the Market

CNET also benefited from its lack of a legacy when it came to defining the company's market and brand. Unlike its competitors, CNET started with a clean slate: no preconceptions about who its audience was, no prejudgments about what they wanted online. "We just said, 'Well, what's cool about the Web, and how can it make life better for people who are interested in computers?'" Matthew Barzun explained.

This attitude gave CNET a distinctively consumer-oriented feel. CNET presented technology in a user-friendly, unintimidating way that appealed to Web surfers who were discovering an interest in the subject for the first time. The company's editors and producers worked hard to make the business of technology accessible to executives who were just learning to type, while also providing content tailored toward plugged-in teenagers looking for the latest games. This strategy gave a wonky topic mass appeal and turned CNET into one of the most popular destinations on the Web, with more than 8 million unique users per month by early 1998.

"We wanted to reach a mass readership," Singh explained, "because the information systems and information technology audience, depending on whose word you take, is about a million tops in the U.S." This approach made sense for a start-up, but the established players were reluctant to follow CNET's lead due to the strength of their existing reader base. Both Ziff-Davis and IDG had built their success on carefully controlling circulation and offering advertisers a high-quality, carefully segmented audience. This formula allowed the publishers to charge higher advertising rates. Consequently, if *InfoWorld* or *PC Magazine* adopted a more mass-market approach, it would risk seeing its enviable margins decline. As Kelly Conlin explained, "It can be much more profitable to have a

100,000-circulation magazine with a really qualified audience, high CPMs [cost per thousand impressions], and a robust information franchise, including a conference, event, and online site, than it can be to publish a 1,000,000-circulation magazine that can't sustain its rate base."

The "gadgets and gizmos" approach might work for CNET, he said, but IDG's advertisers were looking for something else. They expected IDG to deliver high-end customers with significant technology buying power: namely, CIOs and technology-oriented CEOs. And these people would, in turn, expect a different experience than the average technology buyer.

Moreover, even if a publisher wanted to broaden his brand, competition from sister titles could make this hard to do. At Ziff-Davis, for example, each magazine maintained a strong identity. "To give you a hypothetical example, if I were on *PC Computing*, and I wanted to do something differently, I would have to make sure that it didn't butt up against or fracture the franchise of a *PC Magazine* or a *Yahoo! Internet Life*," explained Richard Marino, who held senior posts at both Ziff-Davis and IDG before becoming CNET's president in 1999. "So you are strategically boxed in."

This segmentation gave CNET yet another source of leverage. Since each magazine focused on its own niche, no single publisher or editor measured the threat that CNET posed as a whole. "We would all look at just certain segments of CNET," Marino observed. "We never really looked at it as the whole entity because we were all so focused on what we looked at as our competitive set."

Resetting the Bar

Within these constraints, some rival publishers did try to respond vigorously to CNET's moves. But once again, the burden of maintaining profitability tied their hands. This was particularly true at IDG, where each magazine constituted an independent business unit. (At Ziff-Davis, by contrast, responsibility for circulation and back-office operations was centralized, and publishers functioned primarily as senior sales executives.) Each IDG publisher received a profit number and a revenue number every year, and her job was to meet or beat those targets.

In the print world, maintaining profit growth was already a challenge. Factor in the costs of developing an online business, and the hurdle only rose. Online investments, which were typically projected to produce operating losses for the first few years, not only dragged down the bottom line, they also made it more difficult for the print business to hit its numbers by threatening to cannibalize sales. As a result, while all of IDG's titles created Web properties, managers had little incentive to push for growth. Instead, publishers often treated their online operations as an add-on, something else to throw into the pot when selling ads in print. This approach, of course, made it even harder to justify investing additional resources on the Web.

CNET, by contrast, had more room to maneuver than its traditionally offline competitors. "CNET was a pure play," said ZDNet's Dan Rosensweig. "They had tons of cash, they had almost no obligations or responsibilities, and they needed to produce very little revenue to have a currency that could allow them to build and grow." Consequently, it was ZDNet that had all the disadvantages, Rosensweig maintained. "We had the legacy," he said. "We had to deal with the brand issue. We had no money that we could spend. We had to be profitable six months after I got the job. And we had to compete with one of the smartest competitors out in the marketplace."

LEVERAGE AT CNET:
LEVERAGE YOUR OPPONENT'S ASSETS

The Challenge: Your competitors have revenue streams and profits that far outstrip your own.

The Solution: Design a strategy that turns your competitors' desire to maintain their profitability into a brake on their ability to respond.

- Invest in activities that force your competitors to cannibalize their assets or business models in order to counter your moves.

- Redefine the market in a way that requires your competitors to choose between losing their existing (profit-generating) customers and losing overall share.

- More broadly, leverage the expectations created by your competitors' past strength by forcing them to choose between profits and growth.

Pointing to Competitors

A third area in which CNET distinguished itself from the competition was in its willingness to point readers to competitors' stories. To many publishing veterans, promoting the competition was an unthinkable act. When Minor and Bonnie proposed this strategy, Singh's first reaction was, "Over my dead body," he recalled. But the two persevered, and Singh agreed to give it a try. In retrospect, he said, "that was the best damn decision we made because it confounded and confused our competitors at Ziff and IDG. We actually got an e-mail from the editor-in-chief at *InfoWorld* saying, 'Well, gee, thanks, I suppose, for pointing to us.' They didn't know what to make of it."

ZDNet's Dan Rosensweig downplayed the significance of this move. "The story is, they couldn't afford to create their own depth and breadth of content," he argued. "We, on the other hand—where did we need to link to when we had all this information and content? How much more did you need?" But Singh suggested that it was more than belief in their own content that kept ZDNet and IDG from matching CNET in this case. Due to the longstanding rivalry between the two companies, he believed, "Ziff was not going to point to IDG, and IDG was not going to point to Ziff." And this gave CNET a valuable opening to create the leading one-stop shop for technology news on the Web.

LEVERAGE AT CNET:
LEVERAGE YOUR OPPONENT'S COMPETITORS

The Challenge: You face well-entrenched competitors that have been locked in rivalry for many years.

The Solution: Exploit the competition between your competitors by cooperating with one or all—even unilaterally—in ways that enhance your product or service. This is a strategy that rivals of long standing are unlikely to match in kind.

Spotlight on Commerce: 1997–1998

While CNET's executives took great pride in News.com's achievements, they ultimately believed that, "Great editorial is not a goal in and of itself," as Minor wrote in a December 1997 e-mail that troubled some of his staff.[19] The real goal, he repeated two years later, is to "position yourself between buyers and sellers."

Early on, CNET performed essentially the same functions as a print magazine. Readers sought product information in its pages, and manufacturers and retailers chased after the readers' attention by placing ads. However, Minor pushed CNET to do more to exploit the power of the Internet by developing an online marketplace for computer-related products. The new service closely integrated content and e-commerce, allowing users to read product reviews, get real-time price information on identical products from competing vendors, and then connect with sellers at a single click. In addition, CNET pioneered a revenue model based on charging advertisers a fee for each click-through or lead instead of, or in addition to, fixed advertising rates.

The executive responsible for implementing Minor's vision was Kevin McKenzie, who was hired away from the Internet Shopping Network in early 1996. McKenzie partnered with Matthew Barzun to develop CNET's first "catalog of catalogs," Computers.com, which launched in November 1997. "We started really simple and drew a picture of what users do when they buy a computer," he recalled. Consumers, he explained, begin by looking for product information or reviews. Using the information they've gathered, they compare products on several dimensions. Once they've decided which product to buy, they then need to figure out where to buy it. "The neat thing about the Internet," McKenzie said, "is that it can make the whole process seamless, unlike in a magazine or in the physical world."

In addition to overseeing the development of the software that powered Computers.com, McKenzie focused on two pieces of the strategy. The first was ensuring that CNET's marketplace would aggregate the greatest possible amount of information, allowing users to research not just the top ten products, but over 150,000 SKUs. Second, McKenzie spent much of his time evangelizing Computers.com to leading manufacturers, such as Gateway and Dell, by demonstrating how CNET's new service could contribute to their growth.

As Computers.com began to build a following among buyers and sellers, CNET extended the model, rolling out a broader technology shopping service, Shopper.com, in June 1998. By December 1998, three months after the lead-based model kicked in, the company was generating 90,000 leads per day and an estimated $875,000 in daily revenue for seventy participating vendors. Two years later, this business was on track to generate $100 million in revenues for CNET in 2001.[20]

Rethinking "Church and State"

Ziff-Davis and IDG both ran similar comparison shopping service sites. Ziff-Davis launched NetBuyer, the online version of *Computer Shopper*, in the fall of 1996, while IDG's WebShopper debuted at roughly the same time as Computers.com. But CNET's services had several advantages over the competition. A clean, efficient interface made them easier to use. They integrated editorial content more closely with product information, making it easier for buyers to choose from a bewildering array of options. And CNET's sophisticated database made it possible to do pinpoint price comparisons, instead of asking users to compare apples to oranges. As a result, in its first full month of operation, Computers.com had roughly three times as many visitors as NetBuyer or WebShopper, according to market research firm Media Metrix.[21]

There were several reasons why Ziff-Davis and IDG found it difficult to match CNET's latest offering. The simplest was the time and effort required to develop the underlying technology. CNET devoted substantial resources to building expertise in software and database management, first internally and then through acquisitions. (CNET later reaped additional benefits from this investment by licensing its database to other e-commerce companies.) By contrast, neither Ziff-Davis nor IDG—which saw themselves as publishing and not technology companies—developed the same capabilities in-house.

In addition, executives from the publishing world were reluctant to lower the traditional barriers between content and commerce.

"There are a lot of editors who are uncomfortable with CNET's approach," said IDG's Conlin, citing CNET's practice of charging slotting fees as an example. When a user requested a price quote on CNET's site, the order in which the quotes appeared was determined in part by whether or not advertisers had paid these extra charges. "There is no disclosure about this practice," Conlin commented. "We, on the other hand, don't manipulate product listings on the basis of which advertiser paid some promotional fee; we find the practice would undermine our editorial independence and credibility.[22]

But beyond issues of technology and culture, the strength of IDG and Ziff's position also made it difficult for them to respond. Many advertisers were wary of a service that made it easier for consumers to cut through the marketing messages and focus on comparing identical products on the basis of price. Traditional advertising allowed manufacturers and resellers to control which products were presented to the public and how. By contrast, as Richard Marino explained, "With the one product, multiple pricing model, we are taking control of the purchase out of the hands of the advertiser and basically putting it in the hands of the consumer."

CNET found it easier to move in this direction because it started with an essentially clean slate. With few advertisers—and most of those manufacturers, not resellers—it had little to lose. The risks of cannibalization for both CNET and participating vendors were relatively low. But for established companies such as Ziff-Davis and IDG, it was a different story. "They could not afford to cannibalize their existing business or disrupt their existing advertisers," Kevin McKenzie observed. "That was the number one thing that they had going against them, and we had going for us."

LEVERAGE AT CNET:
LEVERAGE YOUR OPPONENT'S PARTNERS

The Challenge: Your competitors have long-standing relationships with important partners—how do you horn in?

The Solution: Challenge the status quo.

- Sharpen the conflict among the interests of the various constituencies that your competitors need to reach.

• Find new ways of working with partners that put your competitors' fundamental values or revenue models at stake.

Snap!

With work on CNET's shopping service under way, Minor turned his attention to a new target: building a Web portal called Snap! Online. "I took a bet that Ziff was so far behind us that I could actually have the luxury of going off and competing against Lycos, Excite, Yahoo!, and the rest of the guys," he recalled.

Developed at a cost of $25 million and with the involvement of 40 percent of CNET's Internet employees, Snap! debuted in September 1997.[23] The service had two components: a Web site with content organized in sixteen channels and a CD-ROM tutorial designed to guide new users onto the Internet. Minor's strategy was to offer customized, cobranded versions of the site to Internet service providers (ISPs), telecommunications companies, and computer manufacturers as a way of adding value to their products. By the end of the year, CNET had signed up more than thirty-five distribution partners, including AT&T WorldNet, EarthLink, MCI, and Sprint.

Snap! netted some positive reviews and grabbed analysts' attention with trash-talking T-shirts announcing, "Good-bye, AOL." But the service failed to take much of a bite out of established portals like Yahoo!. By June 1998, Snap! had lost close to $25 million, dragging CNET's share price down. Finally, NBC came to the rescue with an offer to purchase a controlling interest for $5.9 million. NBC also received an option to triple its holding to 60 percent for $32 million and, at the same time, paid $26 million for a stake of nearly 5 percent in CNET itself.[24] One year later, NBC folded Snap! into its new Internet subsidiary, NBCi.

Lessons Learned

Snap! was a traumatic episode in CNET's history. The novel experience of not winning in a category sapped company morale. "I underestimated the importance of that," Bonnie admitted. "People want to be on a winning team."

Even more important, Snap! was a big drain on the company's

resources. For about a year, developing new products for CNET was put on hold, while many of the best engineers focused on building Snap!. The rest of the team tried to compensate by developing low-cost tools, such as newsletters, to maintain traffic. Nonetheless, CNET.com suffered from the diversion of resources, giving its competitors a chance to catch up. "There was a time in mid-1998 when I went online, and I came out of my office and said, 'You know what? ZDNet is better,'" Minor admitted. Moreover, when it came to audience numbers, ZDNet had jumped ahead.

Minor enumerated the lessons he learned from the two years CNET invested in Snap!: "Know your limits. Only enter markets where you have a strong competitive advantage. Don't ever risk your core business unless you have to. Ideas don't matter, management does, in the end." But as he got to the end of the list, Minor's native enthusiasm resurfaced: "And on the Internet, you can screw up and still make $700 million on a $20 million investment," he laughed. In exchange for its remaining 40 percent interest in Snap!, CNET received a 12.7 percent stake in NBCi—an investment worth over $700 million in February 2000, at its height.[25]

Staying Focused

While selling Snap! was a particularly high-profile event, it wasn't the first time Minor and Bonnie had redeployed assets in order to focus on their core business. Over the previous two years, CNET had spun off a content-publishing software business, sold its stake in a cutting-edge entertainment site, and allowed a management group to take its online software store private.[26]

In one important case, CNET maintained its focus by choosing not to enter a losing game. In May 1998, Ziff-Davis threw down a gauntlet by launching ZDTV, a twenty-four-hour cable channel devoted to technology. Given that this had been their original goal, Minor and Bonnie might have been expected to respond aggressively to this move. But CNET's vision had come a long way. The company studios still produced four half-hour shows, in addition to programming for a variety of shorter slots. But by 1997, Internet revenues were nearly four times as large as TV revenues. CNET's heart was clearly online.

Twenty-four-hour television programming was a market that CNET was willing to let Ziff-Davis have.[27] "I'd run spreadsheet after spreadsheet," Bonnie said, "and we'd pretty well concluded that there wasn't a really good business argument for doing a twenty-four-hour cable network." "A lot of people get caught up in responding," Minor added. "I thought our strategy was right, which was not to spend a whole bunch of money that we didn't have."

BALANCE AT CNET: AVOID TIT-FOR-TAT

The Challenge: Larger opponents broaden their attack by moving into new markets adjacent to your business.

The Solution: Stay focused on your core business in the absence of significant, provable economies of scope.

- Avoid being pushed "off-strategy," especially when competitors are attacking in new terrain.
- Constantly track your activities for strategic fit—and be willing to divest peripheral businesses that don't strongly reinforce the core.

From Judo to Sumo: 1999–2000

In the wake of Snap!, CNET focused on building up its core business—offering information and services to connect technology buyers and sellers online. Minor and Bonnie built the engineering team back up to 100-plus, then went on an acquisition spree, buying nine companies in 1999. (See table 7–2.) CNET also started to expand its definition of technology, moving into categories such as consumer electronics and enterprise computing. Finally, after stabilizing its base, CNET began to move into new markets. In its biggest bet to date, CNET acquired MySimon.com, one of the leading shopping search engines, for nearly $740 million in February 2000. By combining MySimon's product reach with CNET's expertise in bringing consumers, content, and commerce together, Minor and Bonnie hoped to create an e-commerce powerhouse.

But CNET's most eye-catching effort was the company's first all-out marketing campaign. Flush with cash, in February 1999 Minor

Table 7-2: CNET Acquisitions through June 2000

Company	Business	Price (in millions)	Date
U.Vision	Pricing and availability engine for buying computer products on the Internet	$21	May 1998
NetVentures	Online store-creation system	$12.5	February 1999
AuctionGate Interactive	Online auctions of computer products	$6.5	February 1999
WinFiles.com	Software downloading service	$11.5	February 1999
KillerApp	Online comparison shopping service for computer and consumer electronics products	$47	March 1999
Sumo	Internet service directories	$30	April 1999
GDT	Multilanguage, multimarket database of product information	$50	July 1999
Nordby International	Provider of customized financial information	$20	July 1999
SavvySearch	Metasearch services	$22	October 1999
Manageable Software Services	Automated software and hardware updating services	$3	November 1999
Digital Media Services	Tools for product-specific promotions	$18	February 2000
MySimon	Online comparison shopping service	$736	February 2000

Note: In addition, CNET acquired Linux Search in 1999. No further information on this transaction is available.

Source: Company financial reports.

signed a two-and-a-half-year deal that made CNET the exclusive supplier of computer buying guides on AOL at a cost of at least $14.5 million. Five months later, CNET announced plans to spend $100 million—an amount roughly equal to the company's 1999 revenues—on an eighteen-month branding campaign.

CNET's brand clearly needed the help. Company research showed that CNET had only four percent unaided brand awareness within its target audience.[28] "Our competition wasn't really another Internet company," Bonnie concluded. "It was ignorance."[29] But equally important, CNET's leadership saw an opportunity to use their new-found strength to bring the competition down. "We recognized that we had a great business—we'd had five profitable quarters—and we decided that the rest of the players in the category were very vulnerable, and now was the time," Minor explained. "Ziff was losing a ton of money. They were hemorrhaging money on ZDTV, and they had missed their numbers three quarters in a row. So they were not in a position to respond. They had $30 million in cash in the bank. We had roughly $700 million in cash and securities. . . . So we said, 'Well, let's just up the ante.'" The $100 million campaign would push CNET into the red, but Minor and Bonnie were willing to take that risk. "Halsey's attitude was, if you're going to be a bear, be a grizzly bear," Bonnie recalled.

CNET's stock price dropped more than 10 percent once these plans were announced. But from a competitive standpoint, the gamble seemed to have worked. "Two weeks later, Ziff is for sale, and [later that year] IDG pulled plans to put $35 million into an effort to build a Web-based competitor to us," Minor crowed. In addition, according to its own figures, CNET more than doubled its brand awareness within six months.

Epilogue

Five years after CNET's online launch, Minor and Bonnie could point to some telling signs of success. With upward of 9 million unique visitors per month, CNET controlled one of the Web's largest properties. Moreover, the company was one of only a handful of Internet start-ups to have reached profitability.[30] But the ultimate vindication of the founders' vision came in July 2000, when CNET announced that it was acquiring its major rival, ZDNet, for $1.6 billion in stock.[31] While Minor resigned soon thereafter in order to pursue new ventures, Bonnie stayed on as chairman and CEO. Dan Rosensweig became president of the combined company, which immediately became the eighth largest network on the Internet with 16.6 million unique users per month.

ZDNet had flourished since Rosensweig first took the reins, running neck-and-neck with CNET when it came to audience reach. But the same could hardly be said of its once-proud parent, Ziff-Davis, which had been sold off for parts, beginning in 1999. The market research group was the first to go, followed by the information technology-training division, and then Ziff-Davis's magazines.[32] Arrangements were made to spin off the trade show business, and what remained of the company was slated to be merged into ZDNet when the deal with CNET took place.

IDG, by contrast, remained a potent threat, scaling up to $2.5 billion in revenue by the end of the decade. "We grow CNETs inside IDG," Conlin said, citing the success of ventures like *The Industry Standard*, IDG's e-business magazine. The picture for the company was less bright on the Web. Due in part to its strategy of fostering individual magazine-linked communities, rather than one master site, none of IDG's Web properties made it into the top fifty worldwide. But Conlin remained confident that his approach would pay off in the end. Over the long run, he believed, IDG would continue to benefit from its global reach, its broad scope of operations, and its ability to span offline and online platforms.

But CNET didn't need IDG to fail in order to claim the laurels of success. Starting from nothing in 1992, Halsey Minor and Shelby Bonnie had built one of the leading Web sites in the world, and a $400 million company in a market once dominated by billion-dollar competitors. And no matter what the future held, no one could take that distinction away.

PART III

Responding to Judo Strategy

8

How to Beat a Judo Master
From Judo to Sumo Strategy

A 170 kg frame compensates for a multitude of technical and spiritual sins.

—Mark Schilling, *Sumo: A Fan's Guide*

JUDO MASTERS such as Donna Dubinsky, Rob Glaser, and Halsey Minor are tough to beat. They're quick, they're agile, they're strong, and they're smart. But even the most experienced judo master can be brought down by a more skillful competitor. Consequently, your first option when facing a judo challenger is to master judo strategy yourself. When your competitor grips you, find a way to get a better grip; when your competitor finds a source of leverage, look for leverage of your own. Any company can respond effectively to judo with judo as long as managers have the right mind-set and organizational skills.

This strategy can be particularly successful for larger or stronger companies. While strength alone counts for little in judo, it can be decisive in a match between opponents who are equally skilled. Execution is also critical in this kind of battle, since the smallest error by either player can open the door to a decisive move. But all else being equal, in a contest between opponents with similar expertise, the advantage lies with the more powerful of the two.

However, judo strategy is not your only option if the balance of power is on your side. For companies with strong balance sheets, dominant market positions, and healthy stores of cash, sumo may be a more compelling metaphor. By transforming the game from judo to sumo, a sport where strength and size are central, large and powerful companies can increase their chances of scoring a win.

The Sport of Sumo

Sumo immediately evokes an image of huge bodies colliding. In sumo's top division, the average *rikishi*—as sumo wrestlers prefer to be called—weighs in at nearly 350 pounds. Hawaiian-born Akebono, the first foreigner to attain the rank of *yokozuna*, or grand champion, tips the scales at more than 480 pounds.[1] In daily life, this bulk may be a handicap. But in competition, Akebono uses his heft to stunning effect, propelling his opponents out of the ring in seconds with powerful thrusts.

Even in sumo, of course, weight is not all. One of the greatest grand champions of the 1980s, Chiyonofuji, was a relative lightweight about half Akebono's size. Like Chiyonofuji , the ideal *rikishi* should exhibit a perfect balance of strength, spirit, and skill. But as one experienced commentator notes, "a 170-kg [374-pound] frame compensates for a multitude of technical and spiritual sins."[2]

Sumo Competition

Sumo matches start with an announcer calling out the names of the *rikishi* who are about to fight. They mount to their corners and perform a foot-stamping exercise, raising each leg high in the air. After ceremonially rinsing and wiping his mouth, each man tosses salt into the ring, squats, claps to invoke the gods, and extends his hands to show that he is unarmed. After another handful of salt, he advances to his starting line, squats, places both hands on the ground, and tries to stare his opponent down. If both *rikishi* are ready, the initial charge—the *tachi'ai*—takes place. If not, they rise, return to their corners for more salt, and then squat once again in the center of the ring. This warm-up period can last up to four minutes in the top division; then the actual bout must begin.

In the ideal *tachi'ai*, the two opponents breathe in and out together, make eye contact, and simultaneously explode across the starting lines. The aim in this encounter is to seize the initiative and get the grip or angle of attack that will lead to mastery of the bout. *Rikishi* adopt different means to this end, depending on their physique and portfolio of skills. Some charge in low and shove their opponents back. Others use rapid thrusts to the chest, arms pumping like pistons, to push their opponents out or down. Still others go for an opponent's belt, getting a firm grip and then marching the unfortunate victim, belly-to-belly, out of the ring. Alternatively, once a grip has been secured, the attacker may lift his opponent off his feet or throw him with the twist of an arm.

The conditions of victory in sumo are simple. The loser is the first man to touch the ground with any part of his body, other than the soles of his feet, or to touch down outside the ring. Consequently, sumo has no counterpart to judo's *ukemi*—the art of learning to fall and then return to the attack. In sumo, the game is over once you're down.

Winning in Sumo

The role of physical strength is impossible to ignore in sumo, where outsize champions dominate the ring. But mental preparation is at least as important to the game. Matches and tournaments can be won or lost in the minutes of warm-up that lead up to the *tachi'ai*. Knowing that only seconds of physical combat lie ahead, experienced *rikishi* use this time to seek a decisive psychological edge. If one competitor intimidates the other by communicating an air of unmasterable strength, the contest may be over before it has begun.

The moment of truth lies in the *tachi'ai*. It's often said that 75 percent of sumo is contained in the opening clash. The ability to dominate from the outset is what separates top division *rikishi* from those one level below. A champion imposes his brand of sumo in match after match, using the *tachi'ai* to set up his strongest techniques.

The sumo world recognizes seventy winning techniques. The official repertoire includes varieties of pushing, thrusting, throwing, tripping, bending, and twisting, as well as unclassifiable tactics, such as lifting an opponent by the belt and carrying him out of the ring. However, only ten to fifteen of these techniques are in widespread use. The single most popular way of ending a match is *yorikiri*, in which the would-be victor grabs his opponent by the belt and marches him back. Simple and direct in its application of strength, *yorikiri* is a big man's game. A giant can virtually immobilize his opponent, preventing him from bringing any strength to bear. All he has to do then is power forward, drawing on his lower body strength.

In contrast to *yorikiri*, many techniques are much harder to identify in the blur of the typical bout. And in the heat of competition, it may sometimes seem—at least to the uninitiated—that *rikishi* will do anything to win. But many fighting methods are excluded by sumo's rules. Competitors are barred from punching, kicking anywhere other than the legs, choking an opponent, locking him in a bear hug, bending back his fingers, pulling his hair, or grabbing his belt below the waist. Any of these infractions can lead the referee to disqualify a competitor from the match.

Sumo and Competitive Strategy

Sumo offers three key insights for competitors with size and strength on their side. First, sumo strategy should begin with the opposite mind-set of *The Puppy Dog Ploy*. Larger players can win the battle before it even begins, using a technique that we call *Unnerve the Competition*. In business, as in sumo, gaining the psychological upper hand is crucial, and hesitation is the first step to defeat. Consequently, powerful competitors can use what the high-tech industry has labeled FUD—fear, uncertainty, and doubt—to predetermine the outcome of a bout. By sending aggressive signals and mobilizing customers, suppliers, and partners, a dominant incumbent may block a would-be challenger from even setting foot in the ring.

If you can't deter the competition, the next-best response to fleet-footed opponents is to *Lock 'Em Up*, making it impossible for them to move. Power is ultimately a combination of strength and speed. By removing speed from the equation, you can turn any contest into a battle of strength against strength. Encircle the challenger and force him to confront you head-on. Flood the market, buy off customers, lock up suppliers, and do whatever you can to cut off all potential avenues of escape. These techniques will have less bite against other giants. But they can easily rid the ring of smaller players, such as any judo challengers you may face.[3]

However, one critical caveat applies: this doesn't mean that anything goes. For any competitor employing sumo strategy, the third, critical technique is *Master the Rules*. In business, as in sumo, the ultimate authority lies outside the ring, and misused strength can turn near-certain victory into ultimate defeat. Moreover, in business, at least, it's the biggest and strongest competitors that must devote the greatest effort to playing by the rules. So this chapter comes with an important warning: Don't try this at home without running every move past your legal team. The examples that follow are intended to help you think through the broad array of tactics that can make the most of your strength. But whether or not specific actions are permissible will often depend as much on the identity of the doer as on what is done.

Unnerve the Competition

For a market leader, *Unnerving the Competition* can be as straightforward as preannouncing your moves. Simply by providing information about future prices or technology decisions, you can keep customers in the fold and warn potential rivals away. Back in the 1970s, for example, Texas Instruments decided to announce its forecasted prices for random access memories two full years into the future. As Michael Porter told the tale, "One week later, Bowmar [a smaller competitor] announced a lower price. Three weeks later, Motorola announced an even lower price. Finally, two weeks after this, Texas Instruments announced a price of half of Motorola's, and the other firms decided not to produce the product."[4] Texas Instruments won the battle without firing a single shot.

Sometimes words alone will work. Even bluffing may pay off on occasion—although the government tends to take a dim view of such behavior when it involves market-dominating firms. In many cases, however, it takes costly signals to give credibility to a company's commitments. Consequently, in order to take full advantage of what economists Drew Fudenberg and Jean Tirole call the "top dog" approach—"be big or strong to look tough or aggressive"—remember that actions speak more loudly than words.[5] If you invest in the assets you need to back up your threats, your efforts at deterrence are much more likely to succeed.

In a classic example of this strategy, DuPont used capacity expansion to head off competition in the titanium dioxide business. In the early 1970s, DuPont executives believed that the sector could support 537,000 tons of new capacity over the next thirteen years.[6] Based on this calculation, DuPont decided to preempt its rivals by building an additional 500,000-plus tons of capacity. As part of these efforts, the company not only announced its plans to expand existing facilities but also tried to bluff its opponents by falsely claiming that it was about to construct a new 130,000-ton plant. In the end, DuPont did not succeed in deterring all of its competitors, but nonetheless the tough tactics paid off. DuPont became the dominant producer of titanium dioxide, a title that it continued to hold some twenty-five years later.

Sow Fear, Uncertainty, and Doubt

In the two previous cases, Texas Instruments and DuPont used announcements of their plans for the future to deter competition. Another common tactic is to undermine confidence in the opposition. After leaving IBM to start his own company, Gene Amdahl coined a catchy term to sum up this approach. "FUD," he explained, according to *The New Hacker's Dictionary*, "is the fear, uncertainty and doubt that IBM salespeople instill in the minds of potential customers who might be considering [competitors'] products."[7]

FUD is a particularly potent weapon in industries such as high technology, where large fixed costs, long investment cycles, mission-critical systems, and far-reaching network effects cause companies to think long and hard before risking their budgets on a relative unknown. FUD is simple and yet powerful because it plays on a very real fear: the possibility that a smaller vendor will never really gain traction and might even disappear, leaving customers and partners in the lurch. By contrast, as a popular phrase had it in earlier decades, "No one ever got fired for buying IBM."

A sumo strategist's goal is to make his name synonymous with safety and paint his rivals as dangerous risks, even if their technology seems superior or their package of services has more appeal. This tactic can range from efforts to raise questions about competitors' products to combative announcements that the incumbent will soon be offering more of the same.[8]

Scott Kriens, Juniper Networks's CEO, recalled being on the receiving end of the entire gamut—"denial, delay, containment, and then competition," as he called it—as his company faced off against Cisco Systems. Cisco's initial attitude, he said, was, "An interesting idea, a science project, not a real company." Then the defender's focus turned to delay: "Nice product, too bad it doesn't have A, B, and C." Once this effort failed, Cisco tried to contain the threat by persuading customers to deploy Juniper's products on a limited basis while waiting for Cisco to catch up. "And finally," Kriens said, "the last stage is open competition where it becomes size and scale versus technology and speed."

FUD is particularly insidious because it can be very difficult to prove. In the most successful cases, the sumo player doesn't have to do anything at all. Guided by the instinct of self-preservation, customers and partners automatically steer clear of potential challengers to the throne. As Donna Dubinsky described in chapter 5, the fear of a "Bill call" hampered her efforts to raise funding for Palm Computing. Many companies, she reported, were reluctant even to talk with Palm out of fear of what Bill Gates might have to say.

IBM: The Original Master of FUD. During its heyday, IBM had an official policy prohibiting FUD. The company's "Business Conduct Guidelines" read, in part, "It is IBM policy not to disclose, discuss, or sell IBM products before their announcement. . . . [A]n IBM representative may not attempt to delay a customer decision to order competitive equipment by hinting that a new IBM product is under development."[9] But in practice, IBM was prone to slipping over the line. Whether intentionally or not, the company often announced products that did not ship on time.

IBM marketing representatives were also known to write customers long letters urging them to consider the many "serious" issues raised by competitors' products. IBM support might be less forthcoming, for example, or incompatibilities might emerge if customers attached a competitor's "plug-compatible" machine to an IBM mainframe.[10] In addition, IBM was widely suspected of using product and technology decisions in the 1970s to intensify FUD.

By changing and upgrading the processors and operating systems it used, the company fed customers' fears that competitors would be unable to maintain compatibility with IBM.

Microsoft: FUD in the 1990s. If IBM was the inventor of FUD, by the 1990s Microsoft was widely seen as the leading practitioner of the art. Beginning in the 1980s, Microsoft established a reputation for announcing new products well in advance of delivery. "Microsoft Does Windows!" exclaimed *InfoWorld* in 1983—even though Windows 1.0 was not released for two more years. In addition, Microsoft was a master at promising "future bliss," greeting each announcement by a competitor with the assurance that Windows would eventually deliver the same goods.[11]

In some cases, according to customers and competitors, Microsoft went even further, actively promoting doubts about rivals' prospects. According to an AOL executive who attended a January 1996 meeting between Bill Gates and AOL CEO Steve Case, Microsoft unabashedly used FUD in an effort get AOL to abandon Netscape's Navigator in favor of Microsoft's Internet Explorer. After running down a list of Netscape's flaws, the unnamed executive reported, Microsoft got to the heart of its pitch: "[G]o with the team that not only has better technology and products, but has the size and commitment to make them stick."[12]

FUD can be a two-edged weapon. In filing suit against both IBM and Microsoft, the Department of Justice (DOJ) cited examples of FUD to bolster its case. But with this caveat in mind, uncertainty can be a powerful tool in the hands of a market leader. By building a reputation for toughness and stirring up doubt in customers' minds, larger, stronger players can win the war before the battles begin.

SUMO STRATEGY: UNNERVE THE COMPETITION

- Use aggressive pricing signals to deter the faint of heart.
- Use aggressive capacity signals to prevent weaker players from expanding.
- Use fear, uncertainty, and doubt to keep risk-averse customers and partners in the fold.

Lock 'Em Up

In many cases, a concerted effort to unnerve the competition can head off a contest. But if this technique fails, you should be prepared to throw all of your size and strength into the fight. Your basic goal as a sumo strategist is to force opponents to compete head-to-head, forcing your competitors to exhaust their resources and limiting their opportunities to bring judo tactics into play.

Outspend Your Opponent

One way to achieve this goal is simply to outspend your opponent wherever you can. If victory depends on deep pockets, the larger player is almost inevitably bound to win. So if you're in an advertising-intensive business, out-shout your opponent. Out-R&D the competition if your business is technology-intensive; if your industry is asset-heavy, out-build. Companies such as Cisco, Microsoft, and Intel don't rest on their laurels. They continue to invest heavily in technology, sales, and marketing in order to keep their defenses strong. Intel, for example, spends almost as much money on research and development as its closest competitor, AMD, generates in sales. Old economy champion Coca-Cola has mastered the art of outspending its opponents all over the world, typically offering signing bonuses, discounts, rebates, and large co-marketing budgets in order to guarantee shelf space, end-of-aisle displays, and refrigerated space in stores.[13] While Coke often finds it hard to push Pepsi off the shelf, Coke's sumo tactics frequently squeeze the life from smaller competitors.

Another way to outspend your opponent is to give away products or services, a sacrifice of revenue that less established companies can often ill afford. Free works for larger companies because their scale and scope create ample opportunities for cross-subsidization. Coca-Cola, an old hand at this game, can afford to give away signs, coolers, dispensers, and other add-ons because it enjoys more than 40 percent of the global market for soft drink concentrate combined with margins over 85 percent, luxuries that competitors like RC Cola and 7-Up lack. Similarly, AOL has put enormous pressure on smaller competitors in the United States by offering subscribers 500 hours of Internet access for free.

Lock Up Critical Partners

Another sumo alternative is to lock up the partners who are most critical to success in your business. By integrating forward into distribution, for example, you can choke off competitors' sales. Archrivals Coke and Pepsi took this approach in the 1980s by buying back their bottling networks from franchisees. By the end of the 1990s, both companies owned or controlled almost 90 percent of their direct distribution, leaving little room in the market for independents that might be tempted to work with other players. Coke then turned the same strategy against Pepsi overseas. In 1996, the Atlanta-based giant bought Pepsi's bottler in Venezuela, the only Latin American country where Pepsi had had the lead. In return for a $500 million investment, Coke grabbed 72 percent of the market overnight. Now, that's sumo strategy!

Segment the Market and Target Your Attack

A third approach is to segment the market, using different brands to establish a presence in every slice. Newell became the leader in the housewares market in the 1990s by blanketing retailers with product offerings in three categories: good, better, and best. This strategy of segmentation helped Newell achieve significant economies of scale, while making it difficult for new entrants to find a promising point of attack.[14]

   This tactic can also make it easier for large companies facing judo strategists to fight back. Judo challengers often find leverage in a dominant player's fear of cannibalizing its base. But by segmenting the market, a sumo strategist can reduce the threat of cannibalization and target its response. AOL took this approach in countering Freeserve's attack in the United Kingdom. Eleven months after Freeserve began offering free Internet access (as discussed in chapter 4), AOL matched its service by introducing Netscape Online.[15] Launched in a blizzard of ads and free disks, Netscape Online served as a fighting brand, allowing the company to slow Freeserve down without compromising the premium AOL brand. Within months of its launch, Netscape Online had signed up 300,000 users, taking a sizable bite out of Freeserve's market.

AOL then took the battle one step further by combining sumo and judo techniques. In September 2000, AOL began offering unlimited online access via a toll-free number for a fixed monthly fee. This move turned the tables on Freeserve, which had initially found leverage against AOL by forgoing monthly Internet access fees and splitting the toll charges collected by its telecom partner instead. AOL's toll-free service was a much better deal for consumers who used the Internet more than seven hours a month. But if Freeserve matched AOL's move on toll charges, it would lose its major source of revenue; while if it stood fast, it would probably lose share. Freeserve chose to match AOL and even escalated the battle by charging a lower monthly fee. A few months later, AOL was reporting huge growth in membership and a profit on its service (largely due to its superior ability to generate advertising and e-commerce revenues), while Freeserve, facing mounting losses, had agreed to be acquired by Wanadoo, France's largest Internet service provider.

The Ultimate Sumo Player: Microsoft

While AOL showed talent as both a judo and sumo strategist, it is Microsoft that has become best known for its use of both types of techniques, thanks to *United States v. Microsoft*, the antitrust trial that began in 1998. Several factors contributed to Microsoft's victory over Netscape, which provided the focus of the government's case. Netscape made serious technical and strategic blunders, while Microsoft succeeded in producing a browser that was at least as good as Netscape's in less than two years.[16] But Microsoft's ultimate triumph also owed a good deal to the company's mastery of judo, complemented by a relentless sumo strategy attack.

The general outlines of the story are well known: Netscape vaulted onto the scene in December 1994 and quickly conquered the browser market by skillfully implementing a number of judo techniques (as discussed in chapters 2 and 4). By the time Bill Gates fully grasped the threat that Netscape posed, the upstart had nearly 90 percent of the market—in some eyes, an insurmountable lead.

Leading with Judo. But Gates did not give up. He began his attack on Netscape by deciding to push when pulled, embracing the Internet and all the technologies that Netscape had helped promote. In his May 1995 memo, "The Internet Tidal Wave," Gates announced that he was assigning the Internet "the highest level of importance."[17] Should Microsoft fail to meet this latest challenge, he suggested, the software giant could go the way of the minicomputer companies that had been supplanted by the personal computer. Consequently, he wrote, "I want to make it clear that our focus on the Internet is critical to every part of our business."

Initially, the implications for Netscape were unclear. A team of developers was already "on a jihad to build a world-class Web browser" and compete directly with Netscape, as Ben Slivka, who led the effort, recalled.[18] But others at Microsoft feared that Netscape was too far ahead. Instead of fighting Netscape, they proposed, Microsoft should grip its opponent and "love them to death."[19] "We will give them sufficient reason to align with us (primarily they should make enough money) that they will have sufficient incentive *not* to do things with our competitors," one executive wrote.[20] "The concept is that for twenty-four months they agree to do certain things in the client [browser] and we agree to make their server business successful," Gates agreed, adding "I would really like to see something like this happen!"[21]

In June 1995, a group of senior executives from Microsoft made the trip to Netscape's Mountain View headquarters to propose a partnership, but Netscape refused to be embraced. In the face of this rebuff, Microsoft prepared to play hardball by leveraging its opponent's assets. Although Netscape had initially made waves by making Navigator available to Web surfers for free, the company generated a healthy revenue stream by charging corporate customers to use its browser. For Gates, it was clear that Microsoft could exploit this opening by forcing Netscape to choose between profitability and share. "This whole browser fight is going to be interesting," he observed in an e-mail to some of his senior staff. "Their ambition to make money on browsers will hurt them—it's just a case of getting greedy—they are the ones who made the rules that browsers are free."[22]

Nonetheless, Microsoft did not launch a full-scale attack on Netscape for another six months. With senior management distracted by the forthcoming launch of Windows 95 and MSN, it wasn't until late fall that a hard-core strategy emerged to put Netscape in its place. And the delay might have been even longer if Netscape had played the puppy dog and avoided grabbing Microsoft's attention for another six to twelve months. "Without the press and competitive pressure, I'm not sure we would have changed all the things we did, or done it as quickly, or gotten as riveted," Microsoft CEO Steve Ballmer later confessed.[23]

Following Through with Sumo. As it was, by the fall of 1995, Bill Gates was convinced that nothing was more important to Microsoft than winning 30 percent of the browser market as fast as it could.[24] Setting the target at anything less than half the market might initially seem puzzling. But Gates understood that in the short term Microsoft needed to prevent the World Wide Web from standardizing on Navigator. If Microsoft could grab just 30 percent, it would have won a critical beachhead. Total victory, Gates believed, would then be just a matter of time.

In November, a management team presented Gates with an extraordinarily detailed plan for meeting this goal. Entitled "How to Get To 30% Share In 12 Months," the document provided a six-point blueprint for beating Netscape, including recommendations on what messages to communicate, which partnerships to build, and how to outspend Netscape in order to "clone and superset Netscape" and push forward with an aggressive public relations campaign.[25] (See figure 8–1.)

While Gates did not give blanket approval to this proposal, it set the basic parameters of Microsoft's strategy over the next few years. Gates soon authorized managers to invest at least $100 million per year in building Internet Explorer, outspending the development effort for Netscape Navigator three to one.[26] Microsoft continued to offer its browser for free, while Netscape charged corporate customers. And Microsoft sought to boost its share of mind and market by following the plan's recommendation to "write a check, buy sites, or add features—basically do whatever it takes to drive adoption."

The emphasis on exploiting Microsoft's strength and size recurred in a February 1996 presentation by Paul Maritz, one of Bill Gates's direct reports.[27] The problem, he said, was clear and compelling: Netscape had almost 90 percent of the market, while

Figure 8-1:   Microsoft's Plan to Beat Netscape

HOW TO GET TO 30% SHARE IN 12 MONTHS

SUMMARY RECOMMENDATIONS

1. Get Internet Religion. Today Netscape is the Internet friendly company, and Microsoft is the company that doesn't understand the Internet. As a company, we need to have Internet religion. Each group at Microsoft needs to ask how they are making the Internet better for customers, and how they are providing new value to the Internet that other companies can benefit from. We need to be emotionally committed to Internet success just as we were to GUI and Windows. We need to get focused on a single PR campaign which articulates how we're making the Internet better for business, and how we are creating more opportunities, instead of how we are making it different.

2. Clone and Superset Netscape. PSD needs to get serious about cloning Netscape. We must have a plan to clone all the features they have today, plus new ones they will add between now and our next releases. We have to make this our only priority and put our top people on the job. In addition to our planned Win32/OLE work, we have to get serious about extending and owning HTML as a format, and in the process leverage our existing assets to get ahead. We need to ship the Forms³ runtime with the Internet Explorer, and make sure that the Forms³ runtime can handle HTML extended for 2D layout. We also have to take RTF, re-purpose it so it is a natural extension of HTML, and change our Word and other text editors to read and write this new format.

3. Get 80% of Top Web Sites to Target Our Client. Content drives browser adoption, and we need to go to the top sites and ask them "What can we do to get you to adopt IE?" We should be prepared to write a check, buy sites, or add features -- basically do whatever it takes to drive adoption. We need to refocus our existing ICP evangelism (MSN focused today) on this effort. We need to assign aggressive drivers to this problem, perhaps JonL/RSegal.

4. Deliver Microsoft Content and Tools That Target Our Browser. Building the platform alone is not enough; our tools, content, and applications groups must lead the way in targeting that platform. We need to have the Excel of the Internet, great titles that showcase our runtime. Today, we have terrific technology in MSN and the rest of Microsoft which is not Internet focused; it is instead creating an alternative universe. We have to refocus these technologies on our standard runtime and extended HTML format. It must be the *top priority* of our applications groups to execute on this vision.

- For *Web publishers*, we need a single message, where both MediaView and BlackBird use this extended HTML as their native formats. Coupled with this, we must have a site management tool that can be used to manage existing HTML content as well as different document types (Office).

- For *application developers*, we need to deliver versions of VB and Access which target our runtime, and allow authors to develop both streaming and 2D form types. This must include a 1D streaming Forms³ form type that can be used in VB

GOVERNMENT
EXHIBIT
684

MS6 6007113
CONFIDENTIAL

188

- For *end users*, we have to deliver lightweight editor for send note and home page authoring,. We should not be afraid to spend money here to get in the game — we must consider purchasing existing companies for presence and share.
- *All online titles*, from MSN or from Consumer, must target our runtime. We need to re-purpose our existing MSN focused content (like Car Source and Music Central), and also ensure that new titles (like Cityscape) showcase and drive features in our browser.
- Invest in *new, distinguishing content types*. We need to take a leadership role in bringing new content to the Internet. We need lead the way in Internet gaming, with a combination of a new Games SDK plus Consumer games products. We must execute on promoting family content.

5. **Promote Internet Explorer Aggressively.** Microsoft has always won through marketing, yet we are being out-marketed on the Web by Netscape. *This must change.* We have to match Netscape in the online marketing department, as well as leverage our existing channels to win. Key actions:

- Get to *one site*. It is confusing that we have two sites, we should have one site, which has premium and advanced services. It must be a high-end, slick site with great content, and should be focused on establishing Internet Explorer as the platform; all pages should showcase new features that target Internet Explorer. This site should have great services and content that make users want to come back. This includes traditional content (product support, upgrades. etc.) as well as "new" content (Internet Find, White Pages, etc.). We have to have a product team staffed up whose review goals are based on share of Internet Explorer, and whose focus is keeping IExplore users happy.
- Promote the Internet to *new users*. We need to make sure that Windows is seen by users as the best way to get on the Internet. We need to provide end users with more choices, so that Internet Explorer works for them regardless of access. We need to make new Internet features available in a step-up kit, and get every single Windows 95 user to upgrade.
- Win all *corporate sales*. There is no reason for us to lose a corporate sale. We should focus our sales force on getting Internet Explorer installed in sites. We have to push Office and NT integration. We can't lose these battles.

6. **Reposition and Focus MSN and Related Technologies.** This strategy affects many groups, but has the most impact on MSN. The MSN team has great technology that could be used solve Internet problems and is currently planning their migration to the Internet; we must make sure our new MSN strategy is changed where necessary to promote our Internet browser. There are three issues here.

- The first issue is *positioning*; we need to define MSN and make sure we are evangelizing Internet first, with MSN as a great site on the Internet. We have to consider branding new services from the MSN team as "Internet" and not "MSN."
- The second issue is *distribution*; our bundling of MSN is making it impossible to gain key partnerships for browser distribution. We need to open up the Windows box and give equal access to online services and service providers.

(continued on the next page)

(continued from the previous page)

> - The third issue is *technology*; we have to make sure that the great technology from the MSN team is focused on formats that extend the Internet. This means BlackBird and MediaView must target Internet Explorer as the runtime, and we have to merge www.microsoft.com and www.msn.com so that there is one site focused on promoting Internet Explorer.
>
> The remainder of this document is divided into two parts: an analysis of customer segments and the messages we need to have, and a proposed release timeline for PSD over the next 12 months.
>
> MS6 6007115
> CONFIDENTIAL

Source: United States Department of Justice, Antitrust Division, "How to Get to 30% Share in 12 Months," Government Exhibit 684 in United States v. Microsoft, <http://www.usdoj.gov/atr/cases/exhibits/684.pdf> (accessed 19 November 2000).

Microsoft had less than 5 percent. Even more important, Netscape was using its market position to turn the browser into a "virtual operating system" that might one day replace Windows. But Microsoft had the wherewithal to strike back: "deep assets" on the desktop, on the server side, in applications, and in tools, as well as "more $'s even than Netscape."

Microsoft, he argued, should pour its resources into developing a browser that would outperform Navigator. If that browser was then linked tightly through technology and marketing to Windows, which shipped on more than 90 percent of all personal computers, Microsoft could quickly build a powerful installed base. In addition, he recommended that Microsoft pursue consumers by pushing IE aggressively through trade shows and other high-profile events, paying bonuses to vendors that showcased its Internet Starter Kit, building partnerships with Internet access providers, and advertising broadly, both offline and on the Web. Business customers should be targeted through an intensive education campaign, highlighting the message that Microsoft's Web browser and server were free. Microsoft should reach out to Webmasters and other online content providers, giving them tools, marketing opportunities (such as inclusion on a CD bundled with Windows 95), and co-marketing funds in order to promote adoption of IE. Similar incentives should also be offered to ISPs, software vendors, and manufacturers of PCs. (See table 8–1.)

In this way, Microsoft would force Netscape into a head-to-head battle on multiple fronts, creating a situation where Microsoft's superior strength was bound to carry the day. This prospect appeared particularly promising thanks to a flaw that Maritz had fingered in Netscape's strategy. The challenger, he believed, was "obsessed with Microsoft," evoking "shades of Novell." Netscape was "reactive to MS [Microsoft] strategy" and "willing to match MS across the board"—weaknesses that Maritz hoped to exploit by provoking Netscape into a war of tit-for-tat.

"This Is Your Lucky Day." While much of this plan was above reproach, some of Microsoft's aggressive efforts to grab big deals away from Netscape stirred controversy both inside and outside the company. An early example was Microsoft's successful courting of AOL. Reporting on a January 1996 meeting between Bill Gates and Steve Case, an AOL executive wrote, "Gates delivered a characteristically blunt query: how much do we need to pay you to screw netscape?? ("this is your lucky day")."[28] And Gates did indeed pull out all of the stops, eventually agreeing to pay AOL $0.25 for every member AOL converted to Internet Explorer, offering a $600,000 bonus if AOL succeeded in converting "a substantial portion of its installed base" by a certain date, and putting an AOL icon on the Windows desktop—forcing Microsoft's own online service, MSN, to face competition on its home turf for the first time.[29]

Other companies also received enticing deals. A Netscape sales manager complained, for example, that Microsoft was luring away Acer Computer by offering "a killer price on an upgrade to Win95 from Win 3.1 if they use Internet Explorer exclusively and not Netscape Navigator."[30] Pyramid Breweries, a craft brewer based in Washington state, was promised free advertising and software if it optimized its site for Internet Explorer and removed all references to Netscape for a year. "I'd prefer to remain with Netscape," Pyramid's communications director told the company, " . . . [but] Microsoft clearly intends to spend as much money as necessary to secure IE as the browsing standard."[31]

At times, however, Microsoft took a harsher approach. When Compaq removed the Internet Explorer icon from the Windows desktop on the computers it sold, a Microsoft lawyer wrote to the

Table 8-1:   Microsoft Goes Head-to-Head with Netscape

	Deal with Netscape	Deal with Microsoft
Intranet customers		
Chevron	October 1996	March 1997
KPMG	January 1997	August 1997
Internet service providers and online services		
MCI	November 1994	March 1996
AT&T WorldNet	August 1995	July 1996
Prodigy	November 1995	October 1996
America Online	March 1996	March 1996
CompuServe	March 1996	June 1996
Sprint	August 1996	December 1996
PC manufacturers and software companies		
Apple	August 1995	August 1997
Intuit	October 1995	July 1997
Lotus/IBM	November 1996	July 1997

Source: Michael A. Cusumano and David B. Yoffie, *Competing on Internet Time: Lessons from Netscape and Its Battle with Microsoft.* Copyright 1998 Michael A. Cusumano and David B. Yoffie. Adapted with permission of The Free Press, a division of Simon and Schuster, Inc.

company demanding that it reverse course. "Termination [of your Windows license]," he wrote, "will be effective thirty (30) days after this notice unless Compaq cures the above violation within the thirty (30) day period."[32]

By using a combination of sticks and carrots, Microsoft had increased its share of the market to around 20 percent by early 1997. But that was far from enough. As Brad Chase, a senior marketing executive, told his worldwide sales and marketing people, "We have gained ground, but we are still losing. . . . Despite of all of our hard work, our momentum, and all the press reviews we won, we are weak."[33] This perception led Microsoft to step up the pressure on Netscape on all fronts. In particular, senior executives urged that Microsoft do still more to exploit Windows, the company's most powerful weapon. In a highly charged e-mail, which later became a centerpiece of the Department of Justice's case, Jim Allchin, the executive in charge of Windows, expressed his frustration with Microsoft's strategy. "I do not feel we are going to win on our current path," he complained. "I am convinced we have to use Windows—this is the one thing they [Netscape] don't have. . . . We have to be competitive with features, but we need something more: Windows integration."[34]

In addition to seeking to tie Windows and Internet Explorer more closely together, Microsoft also brought its strengths in office applications into play when it came to winning the big deals. In mid-1997, for example, after a year of frustrating discussions with Apple Computer, Bill Gates decided to stop pulling his punches and force Apple to endorse IE. Apple had become deeply dependent upon the continuing availability of Microsoft Office for the Macintosh. In early July, Gates called Apple CEO Gil Amelio to deliver some bad news. As he told his senior staff: "I asked [Amelio] how we should announce the cancellation of Mac Office—did he want to sue for patents first or should we announce with other ISVs [independent software vendors] that we are reducing our Mac support?"[35]

Already under pressure from his board, Amelio found himself out of a job within a month. And on August 6, 1997, Steve Jobs, in his new role as Apple's acting CEO, announced that he had signed a historic agreement with Bill Gates. As part of a deal in which Microsoft invested $150 million in Apple, Apple would make Internet Explorer its default browser, while Microsoft agreed to continue developing Office for the Mac. Following Microsoft's unabashed display of strength, Apple had decided to give Netscape the boot.

Twenty-four hours later, Microsoft did it again, as KPMG, one of the world's largest accounting and consulting firms, announced that it was throwing out Netscape and embracing Microsoft. In classic sumo style, Microsoft had offered KPMG more than $10 million in cash, along with a wide range of services, if KPMG adopted Internet Explorer, Microsoft Exchange, and Windows NT and agreed to rip out 17,000 installations of Netscape Navigator.

Under heavy pressure, Netscape's position began to deteriorate rapidly in the fall of 1997 and in early 1998, the company ceased charging for Navigator in an effort to win back market share. But Netscape's concession was too little too late. In the fall of that year, Netscape gave up the effort to defeat Microsoft on its own, agreeing to be acquired by AOL for $10 billion. Eighteen months later, the browser war was essentially over, with Internet Explorer's market share rising to 86 percent, and Navigator's falling to 14 percent.[36]

By mastering both judo and sumo strategy, Microsoft secured its initial goal, snatching victory from the jaws of defeat. But the company's aggressive stance also triggered the greatest challenge it had ever faced: the U.S. government's decision to bring the company to court. This double-sided moral should give our earlier warning greater force: Learn from Microsoft's experience what judo and sumo strategy can accomplish if you identify your strengths, pinpoint your competitors' weaknesses, and marshal all of your resources in a concerted attack. But at the same time, remember that even the strongest competitors can only succeed, in the bigger picture, by adhering to the rules.

SUMO STRATEGY: LOCK 'EM UP

- Outspend smaller opponents, putting them on a treadmill to defeat.

- Lock up partners, denying competitors access to critical resources.

- Provoke weaker competitors into wars of attrition or tit-for-tat.

Master the Rules

Despite the ferocity of the typical bout, sumo is a game where clear and stringent rules apply, and infringement can mean disqualification and defeat. The aging judges sitting around the ring may look powerless next to the champions who fight in their midst. But their word is law.

The same is true in business competition. The squadrons of lawyers who enforce antitrust policy labor in unglamorous anonymity while titans of industry such as John D. Rockefeller and Bill Gates take the stage. But the most powerful of companies can be laid low if it's judged to have violated the law. In the United States, for example, following a finding of guilt, the federal government has the power to break up a company, to regulate subsequent conduct, to impose large fines, and to put the responsible individuals in jail. Even companies that are victorious still pay a penalty, as court battles can exhaust a firm's resources, sap management's energy, and sully a company's reputation.

As a result, mastering the rules must be a top priority for any sumo strategist. While perhaps self-evident, this is not nearly as easy as it sounds. Achieving true mastery is more than a question of book learning. It means embedding respect for the rules deeply into your organization without stifling the edge you need to compete. When a *rikishi* charges into the ring, there's no time to think about which moves are permitted and which are banned. Instead, an experienced competitor internalizes the rules of the game. Physical memory allows him to attack aggressively without crossing the fatal line. After years of training, the body acts faster than the mind can think.

Learn the Rules

The first step in mastering the rules is obviously to learn what they are. Antitrust law can be arcane, and some may argue that its provisions are out-of-date. But no large or powerful firm can afford to remain ignorant of the law. In the United States, the legal framework for antitrust policy dates back more than 100 years. The Sherman Act of 1890 set the basic parameters by prohibiting attempts "to monopolize, or combine or conspire with any other person or persons, to monopolize any part of the trade or commerce among the several States." Later laws, including the Clayton Antitrust Act (1914), the Robinson-Patman Act (1936) and the Hart-Scott-Rodino Antitrust Improvement Act (1976), built on this foundation. These acts generally prohibit dominant firms from colluding or engaging in a wide range of activities that substantially lessen competition. These include exclusive sales contracts, bid rigging, predatory pricing, under-the-table rebates, tied or bundled sales, interlocking stock holding, and acquisitions that threaten to restrict competition in a market.

Two nuances are essential for understanding these rules. The first is the distinction between having and abusing a monopoly position: The former is legal; the latter is not. The second is the difference in the standards applied to the behavior of potentially monopolistic and nonmonopolistic firms. Defining "dominance" or even something as seemingly simple as "market share" is an inexact science at best. But to put it simply, the small can do many things that the large cannot. As Cisco's fiercely competitive CEO John Chambers once pointed out, "When you are a cute thirty-pound chimpanzee, what people would consider fun or acceptable behavior in your house is not acceptable when you are a couple of hundred-pound gorilla. To underestimate that would be a mistake."[37]

Negotiating this transition can be a difficult task, especially for fast-growing companies such as Microsoft that remain close to their entrepreneurial roots. Few companies rise to prominence without learning to play hardball when circumstances demand. And playing tough to win can become an addictive game, especially since having more resources makes hardball more fun. As a result, years after the garage days are past, many young champions continue to project the combative intensity that initially served them so well. But it's critical to realize that there comes a moment in a company's growth when the rules change. What the law tolerates in an up-and-comer is often off-limits for a market leader. And regulators subject large companies to more intense scrutiny than the small.

Practice Makes Perfect

Cisco Systems has clearly taken this lesson to heart. Despite its dominant position in Internet plumbing, the giant networking company has avoided, at least to date, the legal troubles that have bedeviled companies such as Microsoft and IBM. Cisco has been careful to keep the channels of communication open with lawmakers and regulators, launching a Washington lobbying office in 1997. In addition, in training employees, the company makes extensive use of Microsoft as a cautionary tale. An internal presentation cautions salespeople against using hot-button language like "kill the competition" and presents a particularly controversial Microsoft e-mail message as an object lesson in what to avoid.[38]

Intel: The Best Defense Is a Good Offense. But if there's a champion in this field, it's Intel Corp., which set its sights on having "the world's best antitrust compliance program" under CEO Andy

Grove.[39] As an innovator in memory chips and microprocessors, Intel had always been a market leader. But it was in the mid-1980s that Grove saw Intel "galloping toward an industrywide leading position," thanks largely to the success of Intel's 80386 microprocessor.

As Intel grew, Grove became increasingly focused on avoiding a fate similar to the recent break-up of AT&T. "I had called on AT&T, and I saw their state of shock. The antitrust case paralyzed the organization," he recalled. So Grove decided to go on the offensive. Rather than wait for antitrust problems to develop, Intel would do everything in its power to ensure that the issue would never arise.

After consulting with Intel's general counsel, Tom Dunlap, Grove "got the impression that the conduct line is not crisp," he explained. "So I suggested we put a 'guard band' on the safe side of the conduct line." A guard band, in engineering parlance, is a margin of safety—the difference between a stated specification and the higher level of performance that is actually required. In the antitrust context, it became shorthand for compliance standards that were "more conservative than our reading of the law."

Developing "new specs for sales conduct, business conduct, and

business practices," as Grove put it, was the easy part. The real challenge lay in communicating the senior management's commitment
throughout the ranks. As Grove observed, "We pay marketing, business development, and sales people to be aggressive. How do you
impose this new guard-band behavior on a group of people for
whom antitrust is antithetical?"

Intel began by instituting live training—not relying only on pam-
phlets or videos—for all affected employees. The legal department
trained the entire executive staff, almost all of their direct reports, and
60 percent to 70 percent of the nonmanufacturing workforce, including everyone involved in sales. The curriculum reviewed a number
of basic dos and don'ts: no price fixing, no exclusive contracts where
microprocessors were concerned, and no talking with competitors
about product and pricing strategies. But it also focused on the gray
areas that were most likely to trip people up, such as technical cooperation and tied sales. "We don't want to make antitrust experts out
of everybody," Dunlap explained, "but we want them to know when
they should contact a lawyer trained in antitrust law."

In follow-on training, Dunlap's team designed customized programs for different parts of the company. The sales force, for example, would explore pricing and tied sales in greater depth, while
product groups might get additional training on intellectual property and the conflicting claims of patent and antitrust law.[40] A typical training session lasted about an hour, with each group within
the company offering classes a few times a year. In addition, the
executive staff also had at least one training session annually.

Andy Grove put the full force of his position and personality
behind the compliance program, giving Dunlap "unlimited airtime"
at executive staff meetings—which he amply used—"to bring up
points, examples, errors, wrong judgments, at any time." "Andy
supported us from the very beginning by explaining to the executive staff that training was important and every executive needed to
cooperate with the legal department," Dunlap confirmed. "Over
time, it trickled down from Andy to every person in the company.
After a few years of this training, it became part of the Intel culture."

But the company didn't rely on lectures and workshops alone.
To embed antitrust compliance deep into Intel's "body memory,"
Grove and Dunlap also took a more active approach. Beginning in

the 1990s, Intel's legal department carried out random audits of employees' files. Lawyers would swoop in and seize a manager's papers, disks, and e-mail, taking all the files that might be demanded by the Federal Trade Commission or Department of Justice. The audits began at the top of the organization chart and fanned out throughout the company, continuing year after year. If any irregularities were found, the legal department investigated the source, imposed a remedy, and updated its training to prevent similar problems from emerging again. "This is one of those areas where you can't do it 80 percent right," said Dunlap, laying out the rationale for his perfectionist approach. "You have to catch even the little things." This attention to detail provided a steady flow of work for Intel's antitrust legal force, which numbered fifty strong by 2000 and included specialists for every business division.

The most powerful weapon in the legal team's arsenal was the mock deposition. Following a raid on a senior executive and down several layers into his organization, Dunlap would hire an antitrust litigator to cross-examine the targeted manager in front of the entire executive staff, using confiscated materials to power his attack. After an hour of intensive questioning, the outside attorney would spend additional time discussing key lessons and answering questions from the often shaken audience. As Dunlap explained, the role-playing served as a dramatic wake-up call for any executive who might have been getting a little lax. "You can't really get the concept of what it's like to be a witness in front of a hostile lawyer," he said, "So we give people that experience to help the training sink in. Think about it: If you see a senior executive being grilled in front of his peers, will you write memos that will make you squirm? Will you let your people say things that will come back to haunt you?"

"It's fascinating to see," Andy Grove agreed. "A memo is introduced into evidence and you shrug. You fully understand how that memo could be written. Moreover, you could have written it yourself. And then you see that memo turned into a tool and a weapon against you, in front of your eyes . . . You start shivering, 'There but for the grace of God go I. I could have written that memo.'" That moment of recognition, Grove said, was what made the mock deposition such an effective tool. "We don't use it that often, but we don't have to," he explained.

Despite Grove and Dunlap's best efforts, Intel did not prove immune to investigation. Given that company's size and strength, it was hardly surprising that regulators kept it under close watch. The Federal Trade Commission looked into Intel's activities twice in the 1990s. Both reviews were closed without further action, although Intel signed a narrow consent decree regarding its use of intellectual property in 1999. In addition, the European Commission launched an investigation in 2001. Yet despite this scrutiny, Intel has avoided the long and deep entanglements that have plagued IBM, AT&T, Microsoft, and other powerful companies over the last few decades.

In explaining why Intel had escaped the fate of other sumo strategists, Andy Grove gave full credit to the company's success at instilling respect for antitrust principles deep into the organization. "The power of Intel's program," he explained, "is that every licensing negotiation and every long-term contract is scrutinized and discussed with members of the legal department as to appropriateness and acceptability subject to our principles. The overwhelming majority of what we do involves substance." Yet no matter how cautious you may be, you have to expect extraordinary scrutiny when you are a market leader. Consequently, Intel pays careful attention to form as well. As Grove noted, "it is entirely possible that when your actions and your heart are both in the right place, one document written in annoyance can outweigh mountains of evidence about your actions, principles and practices." Intel's efforts are designed to guard against even the smallest of such slips. "Since antitrust is embedded in everything we do," Grove concluded, "we can control our destiny."

MASTER THE RULES

- Learn the rules—and realize that as you grow, they change.

- Embed antitrust compliance in your organization's "body memory" through repeated training, role-playing, and drills.

- Sweat the small stuff—when it comes to mastering the rules, the 80/20 rule doesn't apply.

9

A User's Guide to Judo Strategy

"Play offense and play to win."

—Scott Cook, Founder, Intuit

AT ITS HEART, judo strategy is about developing a deep understanding of your competition and the moves that will turn your competitors' strength to your advantage. This is no science. There are no easy formulas for victory—judo strategy demands discipline, creativity, and the flexibility to mix and match techniques. But the power and promise of this approach are equal to the investment it demands, for by mastering the principles behind judo strategy, you can use your competitors' weight to bring them down.

Short-term success does not require you to attain complete fluency in judo strategy. Many of the companies we discussed in this book built strong positions by ably applying a single technique. Inktomi and Juniper, for example, defined the competitive space and rapidly captured the lead in the businesses they had pioneered. Drypers pushed when pulled by harnessing Procter & Gamble's momentum to its own ends. And Freeserve skillfully leveraged its opponent's assets, vaulting past AOL Europe to become the leading Internet service provider in the United Kingdom within a matter of months.

At any one time, depending on the stage of competition you've reached, a single judo strategy principle may play a particularly important role. In the early days, before the contours of the competitive landscape have been fully defined, movement is often the concept most critical to success. Balance takes over as competitors start to pay attention and prepare to attack. And finding and applying leverage usually become crucial once you aim to knock a serious competitor down.

Winning over the long run, however, requires you to master a much larger portfolio of judo techniques. In judo, you sometimes find naturally strong competitors who "tend to use one or two techniques which they can force through by their strength," as one observer wrote. "But if they come up against a good technician, who can anticipate and forestall their favorite technique, they fail completely."[1] Consequently, a true judo master must possess a rich repertoire of skills while at the same time being constantly prepared to learn new ways to win.

The masters of judo strategy profiled in this book have shown themselves to be adept at integrating different techniques into a coherent strategic whole. Donna Dubinsky and Jeff Hawkins, the leaders of Palm Computing, mastered the puppy dog ploy, defined a new competitive space, followed through fast, and carefully avoided tit-for-tat in competing with Microsoft. Once they had left Palm to found Handspring, they also learned to push when pulled, using Palm's momentum to their advantage.

Rob Glaser, the founder and CEO of RealNetworks, demonstrated similar skill at movement, following through fast to build a lead of as much as twelve to eighteen months. In addition, he responded to both the prospect and the reality of an attack from Microsoft by gripping his opponent through distribution, licensing, and equity deals. Finally, Glaser added leverage to his arsenal by cooperating with Microsoft's competitors.

Halsey Minor and Shelby Bonnie, the founders of CNET Networks, made leverage the centerpiece of their campaign to defeat the giants of the technology media world. But the two partners also moved successfully beyond this set of techniques. By 2000, CNET had transformed itself from an underdog into a dominant player, leading Minor and Bonnie to turn from judo to sumo strategy. While continuing to use leverage, they also learned to wield a giant's weapons by outspending their opponents on a high-profile branding campaign and using their high-flying stock to acquire one of their most important competitors.

When Bad Things Happen to Good Judo Strategists

All of the judo strategy masters we profiled (as well as most of the other companies we discussed) remain success stories as we write. But in judo strategy, as in judo, success is never guaranteed. Even good judo strategists will sometimes lose—sometimes because they meet a better opponent, sometimes because they violate the principles of judo strategy, and sometimes because when it comes to implementation, they simply fall short.

Meeting a Better Opponent

One of the great ironies of judo strategy is that success breeds danger. The larger you grow, the more vulnerable you become to other judo strategists. As you build a business, you create commitments, assets, and momentum that can potentially be turned against you. The greater your success, the more numerous the opportunities you create for a newer, stronger, or better player to launch a judo strategy attack.

Once Netscape had captured 90 percent of the browser market, for example, it was able to go public on the strength of the resulting revenue streams. But success in turn made Netscape vulnerable to attack. The company's decision to charge for its browsers created a significant point of leverage, as Bill Gates was quick to see. By creating a comparable product and giving it away, Microsoft forced Netscape to make a tough decision: whether to do nothing and lose share or match Microsoft's move and watch its earnings and share price fall. Netscape struggled with this choice for nearly a year and a half while its market share dropped by nearly one and a half percentage points every month. In the end, Microsoft claimed victory in the browser war.

More recently, Inktomi, one of the companies we discussed in chapter 2, has been under attack from a start-up using judo strategy. Akamai burst onto the scene in 1999 and challenged Inktomi's leading position in the Web caching market by redefining the competitive space. While Inktomi had defined the category as a market for software (besting Cisco, which sought to turn it into a market for a device), Akamai turned the tables on Inktomi by creating a business model based on offering services instead of products. While it is too early to forecast which company will prevail in this struggle, it is clear that Inktomi has found that with success comes vulnerability as well.

You have two options when facing a fellow judo strategist. You can return to your judo strategy toolbox to find new avenues of attack. By finding new sources of leverage or new opportunities to embrace and extend your opponent's moves, you may be able to turn the tables on even the most aggressive judo competitor. Alternatively, if you have the advantage in strength over your new opponent, as we discussed in chapter 8, don't shy away from using sumo tactics to force a smaller or weaker competitor to go head-to-head. Neither approach is foolproof, but by crafting a response that corresponds to your strategic advantages, you significantly improve your chances of scoring a win.

Breaking the Rules

While better or stronger opponents can often claim much of the credit when judo strategists fail, the greatest threats don't always come from the outside. Some companies contribute to their own defeat by abandoning judo strategy or breaking the rules. Netscape CEO Jim Barksdale had a deeply intuitive feel for judo strategy, based on years of competing against giants as an executive at Federal Express and McCaw Cellular Communications. But Barksdale couldn't stop other senior executives from "mooning the giant," and he was unable to stop the company from moving so fast that it spun out of control. Similarly, Novell CEO Ray Noorda understood the problems of competing in a market with large players, but nonetheless went off course by pursuing a strategy of tit-for-tat.

Many companies fail to use judo strategy because they lack the discipline to make hard choices such as shunning the spotlight to play the puppy dog and resisting the temptation to engage in tit-for-tat. Corporate and personal egos often lead competitors astray. But even executives set on using judo strategy can unwittingly break the rules. Judo strategy contains built-in tensions that may sometimes appear insurmountable to the untrained eye. In order to achieve long-term success, it is essential to recognize these subtleties and manage the trade-offs that sometimes exist among techniques.

Managing the Subtleties: The Puppy Dog Ploy versus Follow Through Fast. One of the biggest challenges judo strategy poses for aggressive CEOs is managing to look weak and inoffensive without fading out of sight. Growing companies need to win customers and partners, and they face the constant temptation to get attention by making noise. At some point most puppy dogs want to bark.

If you have an unassailable lead or, like Halsey Minor at CNET, powerful sources of leverage at hand, "mooning the giant" may work. Aggressively positioning yourself as the winner can pay off in credibility, as well as in more tangible rewards. For most companies, however, Palm Computing provides a better model. By quietly courting early adopters and positioning alongside its main competition, while maintaining its product focus and designing internal processes for speed, Palm built extraordinary share of mind and market without provoking massive retaliation. The key to Palm's success was the company's ability to frame the competition as a non-zero-sum game. Palm's victory, by its public positioning, didn't require Microsoft's complete and utter defeat.

After two years, this strategy had run its course. Once Microsoft had made the company a target, Palm was free to adopt a bolder approach. And many puppy dogs will ultimately make a similar transition. But timing this move is a critical decision, and the greater danger usually lies in making it too early, rather than too late. Transmeta, for example, may have made a strategic error by abandoning the puppy dog ploy in early 2000. By publicly challenging Intel, Transmeta bolstered a high-profile initial public offering. But it also stimulated an aggressive counteroffensive with the potential to significantly weaken its future prospects.

Managing the Subtleties: Avoid Tit-for-Tat versus Push When Pulled. A second challenge many judo strategists face is reconciling these two techniques. When Drypers decided to accept Procter & Gamble's coupons, was Drypers using *Push When Pulled* or engaging in tit-for-tat? What about when Wal-Mart posted Kmart's circulars in its stores, or when Microsoft decided to license Java from Sun?

The difference between tit-for-tat and *Push When Pulled* is subtle but important. Tit-for-tat battles are sheer trials of strength, in which both sides fight without constraint. By contrast, when you have an opportunity to force your opponent to fight with one hand tied behind his back, that's when *Push When Pulled* can go to work. Once Drypers accepted Procter & Gamble's coupons, for example, P&G could gain little by intensifying its campaign. Instead, it eventually chose to bring it to an end. Similarly, after Microsoft embraced and extended Java, Sun lost most of its leverage against its bigger competitor—and ultimately had no recourse but to take its fight to the courts.

As these examples should make clear, *Push When Pulled* often involves responding directly to a competitor's moves, but when correctly implemented, it is fully compatible with *Avoid Tit-for-Tat*. Rather than drive an escalatory spiral, as in tit-for-tat, *Push When Pulled* is designed to weaken the force of your opponent's attack.

Managing the Subtleties: Grip Your Opponent. A third issue that confronts many judo strategists is the need to find the right mix of cooperation and competition, especially in gripping opponents. When you use this technique, you're trying to reduce the intensity or likelihood of conflict by aligning your incentives. At the same time, however, the ultimate goals of judo strategy remain beating the competition and winning a larger share of the pie.

As a result, there are two ways to err in implementing this technique. On the one hand, you can be too "nice" and end up accepting your opponents' vision of the future rather than securing a grip that preserves your own. Time will tell whether firms like Amazon.com or Toys "R" Us have fallen into this trap. On the other hand, you can be overly aggressive, provoking acrimony and eventually a bellicose response. In his deals with Microsoft, Rob Glaser veered dangerously far in this direction.

By contrast, eBay and AOL appear to have successfully navigated between these extremes. By moving in small steps (out of necessity, not choice, it must be said), the two companies were able to build a relationship that served both sides. While eBay continued to dominate the consumer-to-consumer auction business, AOL got a profitable piece of the action at the same time.

Failing to Execute

Mastering the finer points of judo strategy will help companies compete more effectively, but the best judo strategists may still fail due to shortcomings in execution. These failings come in all shapes and sizes. Despite its leverage, eToys, for example, found itself unable to meet customer expectations when it came to delivery and failed to raise enough capital early in the game. Sega, similarly, succeeded in using leverage against Nintendo, but was unable to sustain its success when Sony entered the game and changed the rules yet again.

Weaknesses like these can bedevil companies of any size. But they pose a particular problem for smaller competitors. Giant firms like Microsoft have the luxury of having years before their stumbles show up on the bottom line. But for those less well-endowed, the fallout from a bad decision can materialize overnight. Consequently, smaller companies, like smaller judo masters, can beat larger opponents with flawless technique and execution. But against a skilled and powerful competitor, even minor mistakes can quickly result in defeat.

There is no fail-safe method for ensuring that mistakes never occur. But starting with the right mind-set can help. At Ariba, this has meant impressing upon employees the importance of "lasercution." As Bobby Lent, one of the company's founders, explained, "The definition of lasercution is to out-think, out-focus, and out-execute the competition. This is something we ingrain into all of our people." It seems obvious, perhaps, but it's an elementary precaution that's all too often ignored.

Becoming a Better Judo Strategist:
Learn from the Best

Finally, several best practices, as explained by past and current masters of judo strategy, can help you reach the top of your game. While there are no substitutes for mastering the concepts of judo strategy and carefully studying your industry and your competition, keeping these five rules in mind will help you become a better judo strategist.

Rule One: Maintain a Deep Focus on Your Core Business

Whether we are talking about Palm Computing, Intuit, or even big companies such as Charles Schwab, the most successful judo strategists have the discipline to maintain their focus. No matter how attractive outside opportunities appear, one lesson should remain to the fore: The more you focus, the easier it becomes to channel and make the most of your resources. Once your business begins to sprawl, it becomes much harder to direct your energies into a concerted attack.

As Halsey Minor learned after nearly sinking CNET by diverting essential resources into Snap!, "Know your limits. Only enter markets where you have a strong competitive advantage. Don't ever risk your core, unless you have to." "Singularity of focus," in the words of eBay CEO Meg Whitman, is often critical to success in judo strategy. "Our strategy," she notes, "is as much the art of exclusion as it is the art of inclusion, or what you are going to do."

Rule Two: Stay on the Offensive but Avoid Frontal Assaults

Successful judo strategists also stay on the offensive. "Be a leader and stay a leader," as Donna Dubinsky says. Once a smaller or weaker firm starts to play defense, the game is usually over. So "play offense and play to win," is the advice of Intuit founder Scott Cook. "If you play defense, you get a defensive mentality, and you start merely following your competitor," Cook points out.

But staying on the offensive does not mean taking on competitors head-to-head. "Life is too short," Cook says. "I really try to avoid a frontal assault against an established competitor." "You don't do frontal assaults against armies that are ten times your size. Those are suicide missions," echoes David Peterschmidt, Inktomi's CEO.

Rule Three: Plan and Be Prepared to Pivot

It is a common fallacy that fast-moving companies like the ones we describe live only by their wits. The most successful judo strategists plan two to three years into the future, looking beyond today's pressures and problems to the challenges that lie ahead. Executives at Inktomi, eBay, and Palm all maintain that long-term planning is necessary, even when competing at Internet speed. No matter how fast you're moving, you need to anticipate competitors' moves and customers' needs and make long-term investments that will not necessarily pay off in a matter of weeks.

While planning for the long term, however, good judo strategists must also be prepared to "pivot," as Rob Glaser says. "When we make trade-offs between short-term gain and long-term sustainability, we make sure that we are focusing on the long term in all the fundamental ways," Glaser explains. "At the same time, we are prepared to pivot dramatically in those select cases where you have to pivot in order to maintain your advantage." In a rare display of agreement between the two companies, Microsoft CEO Steve Ballmer concurs, emphasizing the importance of being prepared to "pulse" or flexibly engage new issues as they arise. By being constantly prepared to make quick adjustments in response to new competitive situations, Ballmer believes that Microsoft, a company with 30,000 employees, has proven on many occasions to be as a nimble as any start-up.

Rule Four: Look for Leverage in the Strangest Places

In order to exploit leverage, you have to critically examine your competitors' greatest strengths and find opportunities to turn them into sources of weakness. Consequently, judo strategy draws much of its power from counterintuitive thinking. As Scott Cook says, "The big asset of younger people and smaller organizations is they can think outside the box. They can see the world in an entirely different way. When you do that, the big competitors often will never respond. They will never get it. They'll never see it. Or by the time they do, it doesn't matter." But older and larger companies need not despair. By asking new questions, challenging conventional wisdom, and encouraging a steady flow of new ideas, established firms like Charles Schwab have demonstrated their ability to think creatively as well.

Rule Five: Face the Music

Finally, many judo strategists begin with good intentions but end up exhausting their resources on losing battles—especially in the Internet era, as new technologies and competitors create better ways to compete. But as David Pottruck, co-CEO of Charles Schwab, says, "If you're going to have to face the music eventually, why wait?" Pottruck and his team made the tough decision to cannibalize their successful discount brokerage business in favor of Internet trading and ultimately integrated their first Internet effort, eSchwab, into the main business at considerable risk to the company's bottom line. "Nothing good comes from waiting," Pottruck believes. "If you're going to change your business model, face the music. Delaying just erodes your position and gives your competitors a chance to spin from their position."

Strategy and Metaphors: A Final Word

Judo strategy is a metaphor, and like all metaphors, it has strengths and weaknesses. In addition to providing a useful shorthand for describing events and prescribing actions, metaphors give us the power to take a fresh look at problems, to make thought-provoking connections, and to uncover unsuspected truths. By framing the familiar in an unfamiliar way, you can slip the bonds of conventional wisdom and start to think anew.

Metaphors are particularly pervasive in business because they help jumpstart thinking—and also, frankly, because they bring a touch of color and drama to the everyday. But relying on metaphors as a guide to business strategy has risks as well. The power of a metaphor lies in the ability to uncover the common element in dissimilar things. Metaphors abstract away from differences; in the real world, however, the differences remain. In the case of judo strategy, for example, it's important to remember that judo is ultimately a zero-sum game, and business, often times, is not. Moreover, in judo, you can focus solely on a single opponent, while in business, other groups, especially customers, also require your attention.

It would be foolish to confuse a metaphor with a proof, as the French poet Paul Valéry once wrote. But by picking your metaphor wisely, carefully tracing its implications, and observing where it fits and where it fails, you can turn this rhetorical device into a valuable tool. Throughout this book, we have tried to do just that, going beyond the point where more common business metaphors like war, chess, and football often stop. In our hands, judo strategy has been a device for observing, analyzing, and learning about how companies compete; in yours, we hope it will become a tool for building a great business and defeating the competition.

Appendix

List of Interviews

Name	Company	Most Recent Position	Date
Tom Adams*	eBay	N/A	3 August 2000
Sam Addoms	Frontier Airlines	President	13 January 2000
Alex Alben	RealNetworks	VP, Government Affairs	18 July 2000
Ted Augustine	eToys	SVP and Chief Logistics Officer	18 May 2000
Steve Ballmer	Microsoft	CEO	24 August 2000
Matthew Barzun	CNET Networks	Chief Strategy Officer	12 January 2000
Anthony Bay*	Microsoft	General Manager, Internet Servers	14 September 2000
Paul Bialek	RealNetworks	SVP, Finance and Operations, CFO	18 July 2000
Shelby Bonnie	CNET Networks	Chairman and CEO	30 March 2000
Janine Bousquette	eToys	EVP and Chief Marketing Officer	18 October 1999
Jim Breyer	RealNetworks	Director	14 August 2000
John Cassidy	Klutz	CEO	11 January 2000
Ed Colligan	Handspring	VP, Development and Marketing	20 July 1999
Kelly Conlin	IDG	President and CEO	10 May 2000
Scott Cook	Intuit	Chairman of the Executive Committee	10 July 2000
Donna Dubinsky	Handspring	President and CEO	20 July 1999; 11 January 2000; 19 July 2000
Tom Dunlap	Intel	VP, General Counsel, and Secretary	11 August 2000
Chris Dupree	Bowman Capital	Partner	5 May 2000
Clark Edson	Tohoku Judo Club	Head Instructor, 5th Dan	26 January 2000

Name	Company	Most Recent Position	Date
Tom Frank*	RealNetworks	COO	18 July 2000
Mike Gallucci	Handspring	VP, Manufacturing and Logistics	20 July 1999
Frank Gill	Inktomi	Director	10 July 2000
Rob Glaser	RealNetworks	Chairman and CEO	2 May 2000; 21 July 2000
Andy Grove	Intel	Chairman	16 August 2000
Mark Hall	RealNetworks	VP, Media Publishing	18 July 2000
Frank Han	eToys	SVP, Product Development	18 May 2000
Jeffrey Hawkins	Handspring	Chairman and Chief Product Officer	11 January 2000
Len Jordan	RealNetworks	SVP, Consumer Appliances	18 July 2000
George Kalima	N/A	Former *rikishi*	25 April 2000
Mitchell Kapor	RealNetworks	Director	5 May 2000
Percy Kipapa	N/A	Former *rikishi*	25 April 2000
Scott Kriens	Juniper Networks	CEO	9 August 2000
Dan Leemon	Charles Schwab	EVP and Chief Strategy Officer	4 December 2000
Toby Lenk	eToys	President, CEO, and Chairman	9 May 2000
Bobby Lent	Ariba	SVP, Strategic Development	14 August 2000
Kelly Jo MacArthur	RealNetworks	General Counsel and Corporate Secretary	21 July 2000
Richard Marino*	CNET Networks	President and COO	12 January 2000
David Matsumoto	United States Judo	Program Director of Development, 5th Dan	12 July 1999
Kevin McKenzie	CNET Networks	VP, New Market Development	29 March 2000
Harrison Miller	Amazon.com	General Manager, Amazon Toys	21 September 2000
Halsey Minor	CNET Networks	Chairman Emeritus	11 January 2000
Shelley Morrison	RealNetworks	VP, Media and Distribution Sales	21 July 2000

Name	Company	Most Recent Position	Date
Naoki Murata	Kodokan Judo Museum	Curator and Professor, 7th Dan	24 April 2000
Paul Otellini	Intel	EVP and General Manager, Intel Architecture Business Group	13 January 2000
Jimmy Pedro	N/A	1999 World Champion in Judo, 73 kg category	28 June 1999
David Peterschmidt	Inktomi	CEO	8 September 2000
Dick Pierce	Inktomi	COO	20 July 2000; 11 August 2000
Will Poole	Microsoft	VP, Windows Digital Media Division	19 September 2000
David Pottruck	Charles Schwab	President and co-CEO	19 May 2000
Dave Richards	RealNetworks	VP, Consumer	21 July 2000
Dan Rosensweig	CNET Networks	President	24 May 2000
Ben Rotholtz	RealNetworks	General Manager, Products and Systems	18 July 2000; 19 July 2000
Jane Saltzman	eToys	VP, Merchandising	18 October 1999; 18 May 2000
Steve Schoch	eToys	SVP and CFO	18 October 1999
David Shapiro	*Inside Sumo*	Editor-in-Chief	24 April 2000
Jai Singh	CNET Networks	Editor, CNET News.com	30 March 2000
Perry Thorndyke	BroadVision	VP, Business Development	19 July 2000
Jorrit Van der Meulen	Amazon.com	Divisional Merchandise Manager, Amazon Toys	20 July 2000
Meg Whitman	eBay	President and CEO	20 July 2000
Albert Yu	Intel	SVP and General Manager, Microprocessor Products Group	13 January 2000
Lou Zambello*	eToys	SVP, Operations	18 October 1999

Note: In addition, we interviewed executives at Capital One and Fidelity Investments who asked not to be named.

*No longer with the company.

Notes

Preface

1. Scott McNealy, "It's Like . . . " *Forbes ASAP*, 2 October 2000.
2. Michael A. Cusumano and David B. Yoffie, *Competing on Internet Time: Lessons from Netscape and Its Battle with Microsoft* (New York: Free Press, 1998).
3. Gary Hamel and C. K. Prahalad, "Strategic Intent," *Harvard Business Review* 67, no. 3 (May–June 1989): 63–76.

Chapter 1

1. Judith R. Gelman and Steven C. Salop, "Judo Economics: Capacity Limitation and Coupon Competition," *Rand Journal of Economics* 14, no. 2 (1983): 315–325.
2. Peter F. Drucker, *Innovation and Entrepreneurship: Practice and Principles* (New York: Harper & Row, 1985), 230.
3. Inoue Shun, "The Invention of the Martial Arts: Kano Jigoro and Kodokan Judo," in *Mirror of Modernity: Invented Traditions of Modern Japan*, ed. Stephen Vlastos (Berkeley: University of California Press, 1998), 163–173.
4. Jigoro Kano, *Kodokan Judo* (Tokyo: Kodansha International, 1986), 16.
5. Robert W. Smith, "The Development of Judo in America," in *A Complete Guide to Judo: Its Story and Practice*, ed. Robert W. Smith (Rutland, VT: Charles E. Tuttle Co., 1959), 131.
6. Jigoro Kano, *Judo (Jujutsu)* (Tokyo: Maruzen Co. Ltd., 1937), 11.
7. Kano, *Kodokan Judo*, 16–17.
8. Charles Yerkow, *Modern Judo: The Complete Ju-Jutsu Library* (Harrisburg, PA: The Military Service Publishing Co., 1942), 44; original emphasis removed.

Chapter 2

1. Jimmy Pedro, telephone interview with author, 28 June 1999.

2. Network effects exist when the value of a product (such as the telephone) increases as the number of users grows.

3. Drew Fudenberg and Jean Tirole, "The Fat-Cat Effect, the Puppy-Dog Ploy and the Lean and Hungry Look," *American Economic Review* 74, no. 2 (1984): 361–366.

4. George Anders, "Pssst: Wanna See a Great Business Plan?" *Fast Company*, July 2000.

5. Paul Otellini, e-mail to author, 17 December 2000.

6. Mickey Meece, "Products Secret; Edge Is No Mystery," *American Banker*, 25 September 1996.

7. Of all the examples we describe, this one is probably closest in spirit to judo *economics*, as distinct from judo *strategy*.

8. Jeffrey Leib, "New Airline's Bumpy Takeoff," *Denver Post*, 20 November 1994.

9. Scott McCartney, "Upstart's Tactics Allow It to Fly in Friendly Skies of a Big Rival," *Wall Street Journal*, 23 June 1999.

10. Richard Williamson, "The Competitor: After Five Years in Frontier's Cockpit, Addoms Likes What He Sees on the Horizon," *Denver Rocky Mountain News*, 7 February 1999.

11. McCartney, "Upstart's Tactics Allow It To Fly in Friendly Skies Of a Big Rival."

12. Lucien Rhodes, "That Daring Young Man and His Flying Machines," Inc., January 1984.

13. Donald Burr, "Bitter Victories," interview by George Gendron, *Inc.*, August 1985.

14. Michael A. Cusumano and David B. Yoffie, *Competing on Internet Time: Lessons from Netscape and Its Battle with Microsoft* (New York: Free Press, 1998), 316.

15. Bob Metcalfe, "Without Case of Vapors, Netscape's Tools Will Give Blackbird Reason to Squawk," *InfoWorld*, 18 September 1995.

16. Adam M. Brandenburger and Barry J. Nalebuff, *Co-opetition* (New York: Doubleday, 1996), 69.

17. Eric Lundquist, "Netscape's Battle on the Corporate Terrain," *PC Week*, 2 June 1997.

18. Clayton M. Christensen analyzes this strategy from the incumbent's perspective in *The Innovator's Dilemma: When New Technologies Cause Great Firms to Fail* (Boston: Harvard Business School Press, 1997). Judo strategy flips it around to take the challenger's point of view. By

capitalizing on what Christensen terms "disruptive technologies," a judo strategist can define the competitive space in ways that make it more difficult for the reigning champion to compete. In some cases, this approach may even provide leverage as well—if, for example, your opponent's customers feel threatened by the new technology.

19. Dan Moreau, "Hey, Cisco Systems: Your Stock Rose 10,000%. Now What?" *Kiplinger's Personal Finance Magazine*, November 1996.

20. Scott Moritz, "Juniper Snatching Router Share from Cisco," *TheStreet.com*, 22 November 2000, <http://www.thestreet.com/tech/networking/1184179.html> (accessed 16 December 2000); John Shinal, "The Upstart That's Eating Cisco's Lunch," *Business Week*, 11 September 2000.

21. Jason Krause, "Upstart Comes out of the Shadows," *The Industry Standard*, 17 April 2000.

22. Inktomi executive, e-mail to author, 20 October 2000.

23. Cusumano and Yoffie, *Competing on Internet Time*, 93.

24. Robert H. Reid, *Architects of the Web: 1,000 Days that Built the Future of Business* (New York: John Wiley & Sons, 1997), 38.

25. Original equipment manufacturers (OEMs) are computer manufacturers, such as Compaq and Dell, that distribute software by preloading it onto the machines they sell.

26. Cusumano and Yoffie, *Competing on Internet Time*, 102.

27. Ibid., 186.

Chapter 3

1. Kenji Tomiki, *Judo* (Tokyo: Japan Travel Bureau, 1959), 28.

2. We are grateful to an anonymous reviewer for suggesting this example.

3. We are grateful to Barry Nalebuff for suggesting this example.

4. Adam M. Brandenburger and Barry J. Nalebuff, *Co-opetition* (New York: Doubleday, 1996).

5. Tim Albright and Bruce van Raalte, "Amazon.com," Salomon Smith Barney report, 17 August 2000.

6. Stephen P. Bradley and Kelley Porter, "eBay, Inc.," Case 9-700-007 (Boston: Harvard Business School, 1999).

7. Ibid.

8. Game strategists often take a more positive view of tit-for-tat strategies on the grounds that they can deliver benefits by promoting cooperation. The intuition behind this idea is simple: If you can credibly commit to "punish" the other player whenever he makes a hostile move, such as cutting prices, he is less likely to indulge in such behavior. The problem with this argument is that many judo strategists

cannot credibly make commitments of this nature, precisely because they are relatively small and weak. As a result, in the language of game theory, tit-for-tat does not support a subgame-perfect equilibrium (even in a repeated game).

9. Bradley and Porter, "eBay, Inc."

10. Yahoo! ultimately reached the same conclusion, announcing in January 2001 that it planned to begin charging auction-listing fees.

11. Stewart Alsop, "Contemplating eBay's Funeral," *Fortune*, 7 June 1999.

12. Bradley and Porter, "eBay, Inc."

13. Mark J. Rowen and Susan P. Hawkins, "eBay, Inc.," Prudential Securities report, 26 January 2000; Eliot Walsh, "eBay: Crushing the Competition," <http://www.investorlinks.com/commentaries/sectorwatch/00-01/000124-iionline-indus.html> (accessed 21 January 2001).

14. Bruce Posner, "Targeting the Giant," *Inc.*, October 1993.

15. Wal-Mart continues to use this tactic today, as confirmed in an interview with an executive from H.E. Butt, one of Wal-Mart's biggest competitors in the grocery market in Texas, 28 September 2000.

16. Transcript of Bill Gates's remarks at Microsoft's 7 December 1995 Internet strategy briefing.

17. Microsoft initially invested in a proprietary X.25 network to connect users to MSN. After deciding to embrace the Internet, Microsoft abandoned this network and converted to TCP/IP.

18. Luck also helped Schwab in this process. The head of eSchwab, Beth Sawi, had previously arranged for a two-year sabbatical, and the head of the call center was already planning to retire. As a result, the decision to integrate eSchwab did not entail any demotions or significant reassignments. Information from Dan Leemon, EVP and Chief Strategy Officer, Charles Schwab, telephone interview with author, 4 December 2000.

19. Jan W. Rivkin, "Dogfight over Europe: Ryanair (A)," Case 9-700-115 (Boston: Harvard Business School, 2000); Jan W. Rivkin, "Dogfight over Europe: Ryanair (B)," Case 9-700-116 (Boston: Harvard Business School, 2000).

20. Jan W. Rivkin, "Dogfight over Europe: Ryanair (C)," Case N9-700-117 (Boston Harvard Business School, 2000).

Chapter 4

1. Kenji Tomiki, *Judo* (Tokyo: Japan Travel Bureau, 1959), 28.

2. These quotes blend elements of two different translations: Jigoro Kano, *Judo (Jujutsu)* (Tokyo: Maruzen Co. Ltd., 1937), 17–19, and Jigoro Kano, *Kodokan Judo* (Tokyo: Kodansha International, 1986), 18.

3. Kano, *Judo (Jujutsu)*, 10.

4. Joan Magretta, "The Power of Virtual Integration: An Interview with Dell Computer's Michael Dell," *Harvard Business Review* 76, no. 2 (March–April 1998): 72–84.

5. Pankaj Ghemawat, *Commitment: The Dynamic of Strategy* (New York: Free Press, 1991).

6. We are grateful to Barry Nalebuff for suggesting this example.

7. "New IRA Accounts Surge at Schwab and Fidelity," *Wall Street Letter*, 13 April 1992.

8. David Pottruck, President and co-CEO, Charles Schwab, interview with author, Boston, MA 19 May 2000.

9. Joseph Pereira, "For Video Games, Now It's a Battle of Bits," *Wall Street Journal*, 9 January 1990.

10. Ibid.; Anthony Ramirez, "The Strategy Behind Nintendo's Success," *Dallas Morning News*, 26 December 1989.

11. Nikhil Hutheesing, "Games Companies Play," *Forbes*, 25 October 1993.

12. John Burgess, "Sega's Sonic Boom," *Washington Post*, 19 December 1993.

13. Adam M. Brandenburger and Barry J. Nalebuff, *Co-opetition* (New York: Doubleday, 1996), 237–242.

14. Marc Silver and John Simon, "The Rating Game," *U.S. News & World Report*, 21 November 1994.

15. O. Casey Corr, "Nintendo Is Trying to Get Back in the Game," *Seattle Times*, 26 August 1994.

16. Kevin O'Toole, "The King of Low-Cost," *Airline Business*, June 1999.

17. Bertelsmann sold its stake in AOL Europe in 2000, following AOL's decision to merge with Bertelsmann competitor Time Warner.

18. Catherine Yang, Kerry Capell, Jack Ewing, and Marsha Johnston, "'I Claim This Land . . . Whoops!' AOL Is Meeting Stiff—and Free—Resistance As It Heads Abroad," *Business Week*, 14 June 1999.

19. Saul Hansell, "Christmas Is Coming! Time for Another Fight to the Death!" *New York Times*, 25 October 2000.

20. Jonathan Rabinovitz, "Building Stores Online: New 'E-Tailers' Learning It Takes More Than Web Site," *Sacramento Bee*, 9 December 1998.

21. Brandenburger and Nalebuff, *Co-opetition*, 11–16.

22. Nintendo press release, 30 October 1995; Laura Evenson, "Sega Gains on Nintendo," *San Francisco Chronicle*, 4 June 1993.

23. Steven V. Bull and Neil Gross, "Sony's New World," *Business Week*, 27 May 1996.

24. Benjamin Fulford, "Leisure Killer Sequel," *Forbes*, 5 April 1999.

25. The Delaware Chancery Court, quoted in Richard S. Tedlow, *New and Improved: The Story of Mass Marketing in America* (Boston: Harvard Business School Press, 1996), 75.

26. Ibid., 88–89.

27. Note that Pepsi would not have been able to leverage these assets if it had simply cut its price in half.

28. Michael Dell with Catherine Fredman, *Direct from Dell: Strategies That Revolutionized an Industry* (New York: Harper Business, 1999), 201–202; emphasis added.

29. Ibid., 80.

30. Jan W. Rivkin and Michael E. Porter, "Matching Dell," Case 9-799-158 (Boston: Harvard Business School, 1999).

31. Dell, *Direct From Dell*, 78.

32. Ibid., 77.

33. United States Department of Justice, Antitrust Division, e-mail from Paul Maritz, 20 June 1996, Government Exhibit 653 in *United States v. Microsoft*, <http://www.usdoj.gov/atr/cases/exhibits/653.pdf> (accessed 2 January 2001).

34. Michael A. Cusumano and David B. Yoffie, *Competing on Internet Time: Lessons from Netscape and Its Battle with Microsoft* (New York: Free Press, 1998), 127.

35. This section is based on David B. Yoffie, "The World VCR Industry," in *International Trade and Competition: Cases and Notes in Strategy and Management* (New York: McGraw Hill, 1990), 68–86.

36. "Fidelity Offers Competitors' Funds," *Wall Street Letter*, 17 July 1989.

37. Leslie Helm, "Fidelity Fights Back," *Business Week*, 17 April 1989.

38. Dean Calbreath, "Schwab, Fidelity Battle Over 'No Fee' Market," *San Francisco Business Times*, 30 July 1993.

39. Leslie Wayne, "The Next Giant in Mutual Funds?" *New York Times*, March 20, 1994; Steven T. Goldberg, "Hello Discount Broker, Goodbye Fund Paperwork," *Kiplinger's Personal Finance Magazine*, November 1994.

40. Goldberg, "Hello Discount Broker, Goodbye Fund Paperwork."

41. Leslie Wayne, "The Next Giant in Mutual Funds?" *New York Times*, 20 March 1994.

Chapter 5

1. Date from Dataquest cited in Bradley Johnson, "The Marketing 100: U.S. Robotics Pilot: Ed Colligan," *Advertising Age*, 30 June 1997; and Roger C. Lanctot, "Palm-to-Palm Combat Begins—Microsoft Takes on 3Com," *Computer Retail Week*, 19 January 1998; data from International

Data Corp., cited in Deborah Claymon, "Knocking Off PDA Leader," *Sacramento Bee*, 26 May 1999.

2. Anita McGahan, Leslie Vasdasz, and David B. Yoffie, "Creating Value and Setting Standards: The Lessons of Consumer Electronics for Personal Digital Assistants," in *Competing in the Age of Digital Convergence*, ed. David B. Yoffie (Boston: Harvard Business School Press, 1996), 232.

3. Charles McCoy, "Gadfly or Guru? Andy Seybold—Newsletter Writer, Consultant, Evangelist—Is Helping to Shape the Wireless Industry; Who Is This Guy, Anyway?" *Wall Street Journal*, 11 February 1994.

4. Rob Haitani, "The Zen of Palm," PowerPoint presentation, undated.

5. David Einstein, "Shirt-Pocket Computing Revival," *San Francisco Chronicle*, 17 June 1997.

6. Dubinsky and Hawkins maintain that Palm was actually more profitable than the numbers from Palm's S-1 suggested, arguing that 3Com's corporate allocations and tax allocations depressed Palm's net income in the early years.

7. By 2000, Palm would claim 100,000 developers were writing applications that ran on the Palm operating system.

8. Lanctot, "Palm-to-Palm Combat: Microsoft Takes on 3Com."

9. After Palm sued Microsoft for trademark violation in Europe, Microsoft agreed to stop using the Palm PC name.

10. Claymon, "Knocking Off PDA Leader."

11. Stephanie Miles, "Handspring Beats Palm During First Week in Stores," *CNET News.com*, 1 May 2000, <http://news.cnet.com/news/0-1006-200-1795508.html> (accessed 17 January 2001).

Chapter 6

1. Robert H. Reid, *Architects of the Web: 1,000 Days That Built the Future of Business* (New York: John Wiley & Sons, 1997), 76.

2. For the sake of simplicity, we refer to the company as RealNetworks or Real throughout this chapter.

3. Lee Gomes, "Sound Off on the World Wide Web," *Newsday*, 1 October 1995.

4. In 1998, Netscape began to bundle RealPlayer with free downloads of Navigator.

5. While Microsoft had made significant investments in developing streaming media technology by this time, the company's focus was on broadband networks, making projects such as the "Tiger" streaming media server ill-suited to the low-bandwidth conditions of the Internet.

6. Robert Hertzberg, "RealVideo Streams In, and So Do the Doubts," *Internet World*, 17 February 1997.
7. Brett Atwood, "RealVideo Rounds Up Majors' Support," *Billboard*, 22 February 1997.
8. United States Department of Justice, Antitrust Division, "Agenda: Opportunities, Threats, Product 'Holes' Today, 5 Options, Recommendations," Government Exhibit 946 in *United States v. Microsoft*, <http://www.usdoj.gov/atr/cases/exhibits/946.pdf> (accessed 21 January 2001).
9. In conjunction with its initial investment, Microsoft also received warrants for an additional 10 percent of the company.
10. E-mail message to author from a former RealNetworks product manager, 17 November 2000.
11. "Our evidence indicates that the Windows Media Player tries not to disable any RealPlayer client later than 4.x—and that, were RealNetworks simply to make minor changes to the RealSystem G2 installation process, the problem would largely go away. On the other hand . . . [i]f you are running the RealAudio Player 3.0 or earlier, or RealPlayer 4.0.x (including the "Plus" versions that are registered for a fee), installing Media Player will take over the playback of any Real content—without bothering to ask if this is acceptable." "RealNetworks vs. Microsoft," *PC Magazine Online*, 27 July 1998, <http://www.zdnet.com/pcmag/pclabs/inside/in980727a.htm> (accessed 1 December 2000).
12. Walter S. Mossberg, "The Best 'Jukebox' for Playing MP3 Tunes May Surprise You," *Wall Street Journal*, 19 August 1999.

Chapter 7

1. Andrew Serwer, "CNET: Revenge of the Preppies," *Fortune*, 21 June 1999.
2. Initially named CNET, the company was renamed CNET Networks after its acquisition of MySimon in early 2000.
3. Linda Himelstein, "Halsey Minor's Major Plans," *Business Week*, 26 July 1999.
4. Serwer, "CNET: Revenge of the Preppies."
5. Ibid.
6. The company later dropped the slash in C|NET from everything but its logo.
7. "C|NET Business Plan," mimeo, November 1993.
8. Richard Rapaport, "C|NET's Paper Chase," *Forbes ASAP*, 3 June 1996.
9. Keith J. Kelly, "Internet Ignites New Magazines," *Business Marketing*, 1 May 1996.

10. Laurence Zuckerman, "Is Time Right for Purchase of Ziff-Davis?" *New York Times*, 2 October 1995.

11. Jeanne Dugan, "I Live, Breathe, Sleep Computers," *Business Week*, 1 December 1997.

12. Paul C. Judge, "And in This Corner, Pat McGovern," *Business Week*, 12 August 1996.

13. Harley Jebens, "Let TV Be Your Guide," *Austin American-Statesman*, 12 October 1995.

14. On the down side, like many other Internet companies, CNET later had to take a substantial write-off after deciding not to use some of the domain names it had bought.

15. Rapaport, "C|NET's Paper Chase."

16. Mark Evans, "Web Sites Have Content, Need Investors," *Financial Post*, 25 July 1996.

17. In addition to the public offering of 2 million shares at $16 per share, CNET sold 600,000 shares to Intel at the same time. CNET's share subsequently split twice, two-for-one each time, in 1999.

18. Walter S. Mossberg, "The Web Produces a Home-Grown Source for Breaking News," *Wall Street Journal*, 26 December 1996.

19. Serwer, "CNET: Revenge of the Preppies."

20. Eleanor Laise, "One Good Internet Stock, *SmartMoney*, January 2001.

21. CNET press release, 26 February 1998.

22. Shelby Bonnie, who came out of the investment world, had little patience for this type of argument. "The real issue is whether or not your editorial is biased," he maintained, addressing the related question of whether or not ads should be placed next to product reviews. "It has nothing to do with placement. Yet a lot of magazines would bring issues like that to bear, which made it hard for them to accept new ways of thinking."

23. Saul Hansell, "Validation: Even if Halsey Minor's NBC Deal Doesn't Insure Success, It Does Give Big-Media Cachet to His New-Media Strategy," *New York Times*, 15 June 1998.

24. Saul Hansell, "NBC Buying a Portal to the Internet," *New York Times*, 10 June 1998.

25. CNET recovered its investment in Snap! in early February 2000, when it sold less than 10 percent of its stock in NBCi for more than $50 million. However, it had to take a write-off of roughly $380 million in the fourth quarter of 2000 when NBCi's value collapsed with that of other Internet stocks.

26. The companies involved were Vignette, Mediadome, and BuyDirect.com. In at least two of these cases, CNET reaped a substantial

return on its investment, including a gain of nearly $180 million on its stake in Vignette.

27. CNET did, however, enter into a joint venture to launch CNET Radio, an all-technology format, in January 2000.

28. Thomas Eisenmann and Pauline Fischer, "CNET 2000," Case 9-800-302 (Boston: Harvard Business School, 2000).

29. Ibid.

30. CNET reported a profit on its operations in 1998. However, in 1999, marketing expenses drove an operating loss of $61 million. By 2000, the company was profitable once again, excluding taxes, investment gains, and amortization of goodwill.

31. Along with ZDNet, CNET also acquired the *Computer Shopper* magazine and Web site and Smart Planet, an online educational service.

32. ZDNet retained access to the magazines' content through a licensing agreement. Initially, the agreement was for five years, but CNET later renegotiated the terms and shortened the license to two years.

Chapter 8

1. David Shapiro, *Sumo: A Pocket Guide* (Rutland, VT and Tokyo: Charles E. Tuttle Co., 1995), 26; Clyde Newton, *Dynamic Sumo* (Tokyo: Kodansha International, 1994), 77.

2. Mark Schilling, *Sumo: A Fan's Guide* (Tokyo: The Japan Times, 1994), 72.

3. We are grateful to Barry Nalebuff for making this point.

4. Michael Porter, *Competitive Strategy* (New York: Free Press, 1981), 78–79.

5. Drew Fudenberg and Jean Tirole, "The Fat-Cat Effect, the Puppy-Dog Ploy, and the Lean and Hungry Look," *American Economic Review* 74, no. 2 (1984), 361–66.

6. Pankaj Ghemawat, "Capacity Expansion in the Titanium Dioxide Industry," *Journal of Industrial Economics* 33, no. 2 (1984), 156.

7. Eric S. Raymond, *The New Hacker's Dictionary*, 3rd ed. (Cambridge, MA: MIT Press, 1996), 208.

8. For an interesting discussion of FUD, see Eric Lee Green, "FUD 101," 15 November 1999, <http://www.badtux.org/eric/editorial/fud101-1.0.0.html> (accessed 19 November 2000).

9. IBM's Business Conduct Guidelines, quoted in Richard Thomas DeLamarter, *Big Blue: IBM's Use and Abuse of Power* (New York: Dodd, Mead & Co., 1986), 219.

10. Robert Sobel, *IBM: Colossus in Transition* (New York: Bantam Books, 1981), 315; DeLamarter, *Big Blue*, 355–356.

11. Green, "FUD 101."
12. United States Department of Justice, Antitrust Division, e-mail from "Navisoft" at AOL, 21 January 1996, Government Exhibit 38 in *United States v. Microsoft*, <http://www.usdoj.gov/atr/cases/exhibits/38.pdf> (accessed 19 November 2000).
13. Constance L. Hays, "How Coke Pushed Rivals off the Shelf," *New York Times*, 6 August 2000.
14. Cynthia A. Montgomery and Elizabeth J. Gordon, "Newell Company: Corporate Strategy," Case 9-799-139 (Boston: Harvard Business School, 1999).
15. In both cases, subscribers continued to pay toll charges to their telephone company for the time spent online.
16. Michael A. Cusumano and David B. Yoffie, *Competing on Internet Time: Lessons from Netscape and Its Battle with Microsoft* (New York: Free Press, 1998).
17. United States Department of Justice, Antitrust Division, "The Internet Tidal Wave," Government Exhibit 20 in *United States v. Microsoft*, <http://www.usdoj.gov/atr/cases/exhibits/20.pdf> (accessed 19 November 2000).
18. Ben Slivka, e-mail to author, 17 August 2000.
19. United States Department of Justice, Antitrust Division, e-mail from Dan Rosen, 14 June 1995, Government Exhibit 530 in *United States v. Microsoft*, <http://www.usdoj.gov/atr/cases/exhibits/530.pdf> (accessed 19 November 2000).
20. Ibid.
21. United States Department of Justice, Antitrust Division, e-mail from Bill Gates, 31 May 1995, Government Exhibit 22 in *United States v. Microsoft*, <http://www.usdoj.gov/atr/cases/exhibits/22.pdf> (accessed 19 November 2000).
22. United States Department of Justice, Antitrust Division, e-mail from Bill Gates, 24 June 1995, Government Exhibit 537 in *United States v. Microsoft*, <http://www.usdoj.gov/atr/cases/exhibits/537.pdf> (accessed 22 January 2001).
23. Steve Ballmer, CEO, Microsoft, telephone interview with author, 23 March 1998.
24. Cumumano and Yoffie, *Competing on Internet Time*, 111.
25. United States Department of Justice, Antitrust Division, "How To Get To 30% Share in 12 Months," Government Exhibit 334 in *United States v. Microsoft*, <http://www.usdoj.gov/atr/cases/exhibits/334.pdf> (accessed 19 November 2000).
26. United States Department of Justice, Antitrust Division, quoted from

Microsoft's Answers to Interrogatories, Civil Investigative Demand No. 18140, Interrogatory 4, in Direct Testimony of Franklin M. Fisher, Witness for the Department of Justice, 54, in *United States v. Microsoft*, <http://www.usdoj.gov/atr/cases/f2000/2057.htm> (accessed 20 January 2001).

27. United States Department of Justice, Antitrust Division, "Internet Browsers," Government Exhibit 503 in *United States v. Microsoft*, <http://www.usdoj.gov/atr/cases/exhibits/503.pdf> (accessed 21 November 2000).

28. United States Department of Justice, Antitrust Division, e-mail from "Navisoft."

29. United States Department of Justice, Antitrust Division, direct testimony of David Colburn, Senior Vice President for Business Affairs, America Online, in *United States v. Microsoft*, <http://www.usdoj.gov /atr/cases/f2000/2045.pdf> (accessed 21 November 2000).

30. United States Department of Justice, Antitrust Division, e-mail from Mark Tyler, Channel Sales Manager, Asia Pacific, Netscape, 19 June 1996, Government Exhibit 78 in *United States v. Microsoft*, <http:// www.usdoj.gov/atr/cases/exhibits/78.pdf> (accessed 21 November 2000).

31. United States Department of Justice, Antitrust Division, e-mail from Benjamin Myers, Communications Director, Pyramid Breweries, 21 June 1996, Government Exhibit 79 in *United States v. Microsoft*, <http://www.usdoj.gov/atr/cases/exhibits/79.pdf> (accessed 21 November 2000).

32. United States Department of Justice, Antitrust Division, letter from Peter Miller to David Cabello regarding "Notice of Intent to Terminate License Agreement #1107-3053," 1 October 1992, Government Exhibit 647 in *United States v. Microsoft*, <http://www.usdoj.gov/atr /cases/exhibits/647.pdf> (accessed 21 November 2000).

33. United States Department of Justice, Antitrust Division, Brad Chase, memo to FY98 WWSMM Attendees, 4 April 1997, Government Exhibit 510 in *United States v. Microsoft*, <http://www.usdoj.gov/ atr/cases/exhibits/510.pdf> (accessed 21 November 2000).

34. United States Department of Justice, Antitrust Division, e-mail from Jim Allchin, 2 January 1997, Government Exhibit 48 in *United States v. Microsoft*, <http://www.usdoj.gov/atr/cases/exhibits/48.pdf> (accessed 21 January 2001).

35. United States Department of Justice, Antitrust Division, e-mail from Bill Gates, 1 July 1997, Government Exhibit 579 in *United States v. Microsoft*, <http://www.usdoj.gov/atr/cases/exhibits/579.pdf> (accessed 21 January 2001).

36. "Microsoft Browser Share at an All-Time High," 26 June 2000, Stat-market.com, <http://statmarket.com/SM?c=stat062600> (accessed 21 November 2000).

37. Scott Thurm, "Safe Conduct: Microsoft's Behavior Is Helping Cisco Learn How to Avoid Trouble—Lesson No. 1: Seek to Charm Antitrust Regulators, Don't Try to Bully Them—There Isn't 'a Secret Sauce,'" *Wall Street Journal*, 1 June 2000.

38. Ibid.

39. Tom Dunlap, General Counsel, Intel, telephone interview with author, 11 August 2000.

40. This is a particularly complicated issue for Intel and many other technology companies. While patent laws protect monopolies, antitrust laws are designed to prevent companies from exploiting their monopoly power in ways that injure competition. "If you have an intellectual property right, you are allowed to use that right," Dunlap explained, "but you can't tie your patents or trade secrets to another product."

Chapter 9

1. Trevor Leggett, *The Dragon Mask and Other Judo Stories in the Zen Tradition* (London: Ippon Books, no date), 50.

Index

About the Authors

DAVID B. YOFFIE is the Max and Doris Starr Professor of International Business Administration at the Harvard Business School, where he also chairs the Strategy Department and the Advanced Management Program. A leading authority on competitive strategy and international competition, Professor Yoffie is a member of the board of directors of Intel Corporation and several other high-tech companies. He is the editor of *Competing in the Age of Digital Convergence* and the coauthor, with Michael Cusumano, of *Competing on Internet Time: Lessons from Netscape and Its Battle with Microsoft.*

MARY KWAK is a Research Associate at the Harvard Business School and a contributor to *Sloan Management Review.*